THEMES
OUT OF SCHOOL
Effects and Causes

♦

STANLEY CAVELL

NORTH POINT PRESS
San Francisco
1984

The author and publisher wish to thank the University of California Press for permission to reprint "*Coriolanus* and Interpretations of Politics" (© 1983 by the Regents of the University of California; reprinted from *Representations*, vol. 3 (Spring 1983), pp. 1–20, by permission of the Regents).

In memory of my mother and father.

You need only sit still long enough in some attractive spot in the woods that all its inhabitants may exhibit themselves to you by turns.

My epigraph is from Walden *(paragraph eleven of "Brute Neighbors"), whose sun is a generation later in the inhabitation of America, or discovery of it, I mean the imagination of it, than Washington Allston's moon; hence perhaps different in our chances for encounter and exchange. We are almost surprised that we can see Allston's tiny figures under that unknown sky, surprised that they exist, that they seem to find their way of one another, that they cast such clear shadows. It is perhaps in this surprise that this moon and the later sun seem to me steps in the posing of the question, in the hope and in the despair of the question, it may be in the farce and the melodrama of the question, whether there is to be a shareable high culture native to these shores, and whether we should want one, making our own claim to verge on that pitch of the life of the mind.*

CONTENTS

PREFACE

Of the various pleasures I thought to provide in my title and subtitle, I mention one that may not readily dig out, the sense of *causeries* in causes, the idea of conversational topics or topical conversations. I do not mean by this that I am looking for the sound of chat; I am glad to sacrifice that (supposing it were mine to sacrifice) in favor of a chat's sense of the provisional, the sense of passing, not away, and not exactly over, but by: words and their thoughts on their ways. I think of this as a manner of letting these causes affirm their origins, those contacts one might otherwise like to deny, those to which others might otherwise like to reduce one's efforts. So I am reminded that where I grew up the word for what I mean by a chat was *shmooz*.

Noting even this little, concerning the limited bearing on what I do of a standing mode of exchange, calls for a further word of warning. The Yiddish *shmooz* is taken up in German as *Schmus*. My German dictionary, after giving the derivation of *Schmus* from the Hebrew word for things heard, adduces the word *Gerede*. Now *Gerede* is the word Heidegger uses in *Being and Time* to name Dasein's everyday (hence, for Heidegger, our average, inauthentic) modes of Being and understanding, and first our everyday possession of speech; it is translated as "idle talk." (From here a path leads to one of Wittgenstein's diagnoses, or terms of criticism, in his *Philosophical Investigations*, of a certain failure of philosophy, namely that in it language is idling, something he also seems to identify, most

prejudicially, with language's going on holiday. Idlers do not idle.
Can engines loaf? Something Wittgenstein means by philosophical
failure I find better expressed in saying that language is racing.) I
gather *shmooz* relates to *Shema*, meaning "hear," the first word and
the name of a Hebrew daily prayer. This suggests to me why a
shmooz, taken unprejudicially, is as far from a debased public language (say from what we are generally handed as political discourse,
or as talk on talk shows) as philosophical dialogue would be, and
roughly as therapeutic. I am not unaware of the existence of mislead-
ing cognates, the sort grammar books used to call false friends.
These cost, but perhaps no more than failing to train oneself to spot
false enemies.

One of the sayings that would lace my father's conversation was,
"You can learn from anyone." I did not, in the years he was saying it
to me, take him to be singling out my capacities on this score, but to
be rebuking me for some common, desperate effort at snobbery. I
have since come to take the saying as naming a tremendous aspiration. Between the snobbery and the aspiration there is the daily field
on which we do learn from anyone and everyone—sometimes, maybe most often, circulating the discreditable things we already know;
but sometimes circling the better thing, possibly achieving Henry
James's hopes for us not to lose what there is for us to profit from, in
turn something I relate to Thoreau's hopes for reading "out of what
wisdom and valor and generosity we have." I am taking it that there
is such a listening as well. I do not conceive that anyone has had
occasion to learn the better thing from his or her students more than
I—from those I have known, so far, in no more than a stand-up
exchange after a lecture, which maybe I took as encouragement,
maybe as correction for some lazy try; sometimes, so far, from the
lucky continuing of a conversation, it may be quite intermittent, into
the present, when the earlier offices have been outworn.

Why really, come to think of it (I mean of the subject of learning
from the casual or a discontinuous exchange), I ought—as Clark
Gable forever puts it in *It Happened One Night*, concerning, among
other matters, doughnut-dunking—I ought to write a book about it.

To which Claudette Colbert forever replies—after the man has delivered himself of a lecture on the subject—Thanks, Professor.

With one exception the essays lined up here were written in the five or six years since I completed *The Claim of Reason*, which means during the time in which I was also expanding *The Senses of Walden* with a pair of essays on Emerson, and writing out the bulk of *Pursuits of Happiness*. While I want the essays here, in their freer, or more various, formats, to join in and to bear the effects of that further body of work, I have at the same time meant to give them the autonomy of their separate causes. The exception is "Existentialism and Analytical Philosophy," published almost twenty years ago. In introducing it, in its place, I give the reasons I have for allowing its exception and collecting it here. The facts of the first delivery or publication of the essays are given in introductory notes to each, together with other information to make them handier. For permission to reprint I am grateful to the editors and publishers of *Critical Inquiry, Dædalus*, The Johns Hopkins Press, *Representations*, and *The Yale Review*.

It goes without saying, but I'm glad it needn't, that Cathleen, and Rachel, and Benjamin go on contributing, as in the past, to what is good in this book. So does Eugene Smith. In the headnotes and footnotes throughout this collection, I mention a number of students and colleagues and friends (not exclusive classes) to whose intellects and to whose encouragement I am happy and honored to be in debt. In this way I think also of essays by Stanley Bates, by Timothy Gould, and by Karen Hanson, taking off from things I have said, especially concerning Thoreau in *The Senses of Walden*; of a conversation with Charles Bernstein about an early version of my Preface; of a conversation with John McNees about a certain paradox in our characteristically admiring writers who have things to say that it is hard for them to say, and whose hardness is part of what they have to say, and yet our harboring some surmise that, in the next paragraph or the next class, we will discover how to make it all unbullyingly clear—a certain paradox, but a certain innocence, I hope a certain virtue as well; of, among other poems by Vicki Hearne, one that begins, "Must we mean what we say? Stick to it";

of Cary Nelson's and William Schroeder's thoughtful and useful comments, respectively, on "The Politics of Interpretation" and on thoughts after *Pursuits of Happiness*, when I presented this material at Urbana early in 1982; of Michael Fried's mighty account of my work in introducing me the night I delivered "The Thought of Movies" in Washington; and of Kurt Fischer and his colleagues and students at the Philosophical Institute of the University of Vienna, where versions of several of these and of other essays have been given over the past four years and discussed at length in, for me, permanently productive ways. A special word of thanks goes to Gus Blaisdell for his sound advice and good offices in seeing this collection into print.

September 1, 1983

THEMES
OUT OF SCHOOL

◆

THE THOUGHT OF MOVIES

◆

What follows appeared in the Winter 1983 issue of the Yale Review. *It was delivered on May 20, 1982, at the Kennedy Center in Washington, D.C., under the sponsorship of the American Film Institute, as the Second Annual Patricia Wise Lecture. I was told, in my invitation to prepare the lecture, that the idea of the series was to provide an occasion for writers and scholars not centered within the film community to describe the importance to their work, or to contemporary culture, of the existence of movies. I found I wanted to use the occasion to respond with fair consecutiveness to the repeated quizzing I have been subjected to over the years about my interest in film, especially on the publications of my books about film,* The World Viewed *(1971) and* Pursuits of Happiness: The Hollywood Comedy of Remarriage *(1981), the publications which, I assumed, had produced the invitation to me to give the Wise Lecture. So I am glad for the opportunity to have the lecture printed essentially as it was delivered, with no effort to remove what I had been careful to include within it—my sense of its occasion.*

◇

It must be the nature of American academic philosophy (or of its reputation), together with the nature of American movies (or of their notoriety), that makes someone who writes about both, in the same breath, subject to questions, not to say suspicions. The invita-

3

tion to deliver this year's Patricia Wise Lecture is the first time I have been questioned about this combination of concerns, or obsessions, by a group of people committed to sitting quietly for the better part of an hour while I search for an answer.

The question has, I think without fail, come my way with philosophy put first: How is it that a professor of philosophy gets to thinking about Hollywood films?—as though becoming a professor of philosophy were easier to accept than thinking and writing about movies. So defensive have I grown that it took me a while to recognize that for most of my life the opposite direction of the question would have been more natural: How is it that someone whose education was as formed by going to the movies as by reading books, gets to thinking about philosophy professionally?

For a long time I believed the connection to be a private crossroads of my own. It became explicit for me during that period in my life I learned later, in a calmer time, to call my identity crisis. After college, in the late 1940s, I was accepted by the extension program of the Julliard Conservatory as a composition major, following some two years of increasing doubts that music was my life. Almost as soon as I arrived in New York and established myself in school, I began avoiding my composition lessons. I spent my days reading and my nights in a theater, typically standing for the opera or a play, and then afterwards going to a film revival on 42nd Street, which in the late forties was a rich arena within which to learn the range and randomness of the American talkie. What I was reading all day I privately called philosophy, though I knew no more about what other people meant by the word than I knew why it was in philosophy that I was looking for the answer to the question my life had become.

Since I had spent my undergraduate years torn between the wish to be a writer and the fact of composing music for the student theater—for anything ranging from numbers for our annual musical revues to incidental music for nothing less than *King Lear*—what I learned in college would scarcely, I mean by European standards, have added up to an education at all. But I was encouraged to go on learning from the odd places, and the odd people, that it pleased my immigrant, unlettered father and my accomplished mother to take me to—he who was in love with the learning he never would have, and she who while I was growing up made a living playing the piano for silent movies and for vaudeville. The commonest place we went together was to movies. So while before I entered college I would not have heard a performance of, say, the Beethoven Ninth, and lacked any obvious preparation for it in the history of music and of German culture, I had known enough to attend carefully, for example, to the moves of Fred Astaire and Ginger Rogers and Jerome Kern, so that when the chorus in the last movement of the Ninth sings the two principal themes in counterpoint, the ecstasy this caused me had been prepared by my response to the closing of *Swingtime*, in which one of the pair is singing again "A Fine Romance" while the other is singing again "The Way You Look Tonight." This would not have constituted the preparation I claim for high art unless it had gone beyond cleverness. It is essential that each of the Kern songs is as good individually as it is, so that when the pair modify and cast them together in the reprise, each can be seen capable, so to speak, of meaning the separate song he and she have on their minds.

In the same way the lyrics of such songs were preparation for the high poetry I had yet to discover. In my early adolescence lines such as

Heaven, I'm in heaven
And the cares that hung around me through the week
Seem to vanish like a gambler's lucky streak
When we're out together dancing cheek to cheek.

a stanza such as this *was* what I thought of as poetry—nothing else will be poetry for me that cannot compete with the experience of concentration and lift in such words. It seems to me that I knew this then to be an experience not alone of the behavior and the intelligence of the words with one another, nor only, in addition, of the wit and beauty of invoking the gambler's run of luck, but that it was an experience of these (though I would have lacked as yet words of my own in which to say so) together with the drama of using the vanishing of the streak, which is a bad thing, as a simile for the vanishing of cares and the access to heaven, which is a good thing—as if beyond bad and good there were a region of chance and risk within which alone the intimacy emblematized or mythologized in the dancing of Astaire and Rogers is realizable. Eventually I would be able to note that happiness and happenstance spring from the same root, that the pursuit of happiness—whether this is an occasion for a step into selfhood or into nationhood—requires the bravery to recognize and seize the occasion, or as Emerson had put it, "the courage to be what you are." I am not claiming that I, then, on 42nd Street, had already planned my book on the Hollywood comedy of remarriage; but rather that that book is in part written in loyalty to younger versions of myself, some of whom were, or are, there. Certainly I can sympathize with Steve Martin's half-crazed hero in the recent *Pennies from Heaven* when he says, crying from the heart about the songs he peddles and believes, "Listen to the words!" And I am, I guess, claiming that that younger version of myself, playing hooky from Julliard and in the poverty of his formal education reading all day and spending half the night in theaters, was already taking to heart Henry James's most memorable advice to aspiring writers. In "The Art of Fiction" James says:

> The power to guess the unseen from the seen, to trace the implications of things, to judge the whole piece by the pattern, the condition of feeling life in general so completely that you are well on your way to knowing any particular corner of it—this cluster of gifts may almost be said to constitute experience. . . . Therefore, if I should certainly say to a novice "Write from experience and experience only," I should feel that this was rather a tantalizing monition if I were not careful immediately to add, "Try to be one of the people on whom nothing is lost."

By the time the time came for me to write my book about a set of Hollywood romances (*Pursuits of Happiness*), I had come to count on myself as one of the people willing not to be lost to his or to her experience, hence to count on being able to survive the indignities of sometimes guessing unconvincingly and of sometimes tracing things in thin air. So, for instance, in my book I build a sense of the shared structure of the comedies of remarriage out of an understanding of Shakespearean romance; and I discuss the blanket in *It Hap-*

pened One Night in terms of the censoring of human knowledge and aspiration in the philosophy of Kant; and I see the speculation of Heidegger exemplified or explained in the countenance of Buster Keaton; and I find in *The Awful Truth* that when the camera moves away from an imminent embrace between Cary Grant and Irene Dunne to discover a pair of human figurines marking the passage of time by skipping together into a clock that has the form of a house, that in that image something metaphysical is being said about what marriage is, that it is a new way of inhabiting time, and moreover that that is a way of summarizing the philosophy, among others, of Thoreau and of Nietzsche.

So I suppose I should not be surprised that this book of mine has met with some resistance from its reviewers. More than once it has been called pretentious. Put aside for the present the possibility that its ideas are poorly executed or voiced in the writing—there is nothing I can do about that now. If that is not the whole story, then the charge of pretension must have to do with the connections I make between film and philosophy; at any rate, the charge levelled against either separately would hardly be worth responding to. But what in the connections may strike one as pretentious? It is important to me to bring out what I find to be a harmless way of issuing the charge, and a harmful way.

The harmless way takes the connections as a matter of preference, and on this basis I can see that one who is not familiar with the texts I mention may prefer that I not drop their names. I have two excuses for doing so. First, since I find in movies food for thought, I go for help in thinking about what I understand them to be thinking about where I go for help in thinking about anything, to the thinkers I know best and trust most. Second, as is typical of a certain kind of American, I find what I do to be pertinent to any and all of my fellow citizens, and I secretly believe that if they saw it as I do, they would all immediately devote themselves to doing it too. This accounts in part for an American's readiness to lecture his fellows, a practice that made an impression on de Tocqueville during his visit to us in the 1830s, the decade before Thoreau moved out to Walden to prepare his kind of lecturing, or dressing down. It is a practice some will find insufferable and others generous. The practice raises for me the issue whether Americans have anything to their name to call a common cultural inheritance, whether you can name three works of high culture that you can be sure all the people you care about have read or seen or heard. This lack of assured commonality would be another part of the cause for our tendency to lecture rather than to converse with one another.

The harmful way of charging my book with pretension takes it for granted that philosophy and Hollywood movies occupy separate cultural intentions, with nothing to say across their border, indeed with not so much as a border between them. The immediate harm in this view lies in its closing off an exploration of what those Americans to whom it matters may be said to have instead of a common inheritance of high culture, namely an ability to move between high and low, caring about each also from the vantage of the other. This has its liabilities, naturally; for example, of indiscriminateness and of moments of incomprehensibility to the outside learned world. But it also, to my mind, accounts for what is best, or special, in our work; for example, for the reach in Thoreau's prose from the highest sublimity to the lowest pun. I am reminded that de Tocqueville also remarked a liveliness among the populace of our democracy that he missed in his populace at home and which he attributed to the fact that in America there is genuinely public business which requires learning and intelligence to take part in. This seems to me the condition for the kind of mutual respect called upon in putting together the high and the low.

For someone, or most people, to take for granted that there is no border between philosophy and movies, for this to carry its apparent conviction, there must be available fairly definite, if unconscious, interpretations both of what philosophy is and of what the Hollywood movie is. Philosophy would have to be thought of as a more or less technical discipline reserved for specialists. But this would just interpret what it is that makes philosophy professional; and however internal that state is to philosophy and indeed to the growing professionalization of the world, it does not say what makes philosophy philosophy.

I understand it as a willingness to think not about something other than what ordinary human beings think about, but rather to learn to think undistractedly about things that ordinary human beings cannot help thinking about, or anyway cannot help having occur to them, sometimes in fantasy, sometimes as a flash across a landscape; such things, for example, as whether we can know the world as it is in itself, or whether others really know the nature of one's own experiences, or whether good and bad are relative, or whether we might not now be dreaming that we are awake, or whether modern tyrannies and weapons and spaces and speeds and art are continuous with the past of the human race or discontinuous, and hence whether the learning of the human race is not irrelevant to the problems it has brought before itself. Such thoughts are instances of that characteristic human willingness to allow questions for itself which it cannot answer with satisfaction. Cynics about philosophy, and perhaps about humanity, will find that questions without answers are empty; dogmatists will claim to have arrived at answers; philosophers after my heart will rather wish to convey the thought that while there may be no satisfying answers to such questions *in certain forms*, there are, so to speak, directions to answers, *ways to think*, that are worth the time of your life to discover. (It is a further question for me whether directions of this kind are teachable, in ways suited to what we think of as schools.)

It would not become me to proceed, in speaking on this occasion of my interest in movies, other than by way of faithfulness to the impulse to philosophy as I conceive it. Apart from the best I can do in this attempt, I would not have approached the question whether the same sensibility that is drawn to and perplexed about philosophy is drawn to and perplexed about movies.

There is, I suggested, an interpretation of Hollywood movies that is the companion of the interpretation of philosophy as a specialized profession. This interpretation takes movies as specialized commodities manufactured by an industry designed to satisfy the tastes of a mass audience. Conventional capitalists as well as conventional Marxists can equally take such a view. It is no more false than is the interpretation of philosophy as a profession, but it is no less partial, or prejudicial. Just as it would be possible to select films carefully with an idea of proving that film can attain to art (people interested in such selections will on the whole not include Hollywood talkies in this selection), so one could heap together abysses of bad and meretricious movies with an idea of proving one's bleakest view of Hollywood. These are not my interests, and have nothing special to do with assessing the life of movies.

What interests me much more in these terms about Hollywood is that for around fifteen years, say from the middle thirties to the early fifties, it provided an environment in which a group of people, as a matter of its routine practice, turned out work as good, say, as that represented by the seven movies forming the basis of my book on remarriage comedies—work, that is to say, as good, or something like as good, as *It Happened One Night* (1934), *The Awful Truth* (1937), *Bringing Up Baby* (1938), *His Girl Friday* (1940), *The Philadelphia Story* (1940), *The Lady Eve* (1941), and *Adam's Rib* (1949)—work that must participate in any history of film as an art that I would find credible. I am not, perhaps I should say, claiming that this work is the best work in the history of world cinema, nor that these films are better than the experimental or nonfiction films contemporary with them. I am, I guess, claiming that they are good, worthy companions of the best; and also that we have as yet no way of knowing, no sufficient terms in which to say, how good they are. So it is no part of my argument to insist that major work can only come from such an environment or to deny that significant movies continue to be made in Hollywood. But I expect that no one still finds that they come almost exclusively from there, and routinely, say every other week, something like twenty or twenty-five times a year. Over a period of fifteen golden years, that comes to between three hundred and four hundred works, which is a larger body of first-rate or nearly first-rate work than the entire corpus of Elizabethan and Jacobean drama can show.

How could we show that it is equally, or anyway, sufficiently, *worth* studying? Now we are at the heart of the aesthetic matter. Nothing can show this value to you unless it is discovered in your own experience, in the persistent exercise of your own taste, and hence the willingness to challenge your taste as it stands, to form your own artistic conscience, hence nowhere but in the details of your encounter with specific works.

It is time for some more extended examples. I choose two principally, one beginning from a question I have about a moment in *The Philadelphia Story*, the second from a question I have about the mood of *Pennies from Heaven*.

The Philadelphia Story is in some ways the central member of the remarriage comedies brought together in *Pursuits of Happiness*, but beyond allowing me the pleasure of saying something consecutive about my commitment to these comedies, the example here is meant to isolate for attention one of those apparently insignificant moments in whose power a part of the power of film rests. If it is part of the grain of film to magnify the feeling and meaning of a moment, it is equally part of it to counter this tendency, and instead to acknowledge the fateful fact of a human life that the significance of its moments is ordinarily not given with the moments as they are lived, so that to determine the significant crossroads of a life may be the work of a lifetime. It is as if an inherent *concealment* of significance, as much as its revelation, were part of the governing force of what we mean by film acting and film directing and film viewing.

We need always to be returning to the fact of how mysterious these objects called movies are, unlike anything else on earth. They have the evanescence of performances and the permanence of recordings, but they are not recordings (because there is nothing independent of them to which they owe fidelity); and they are not performances (because they are perfectly repeatable).

If what I might call the *historical* evanescence of film will be overcome when the new technologies of video cassettes and discs complete the work of late-night-television and revival theaters, and the history of movies becomes part of the experience of viewing new movies—a relation to history that we take for granted in the rest of the arts—this should serve to steady our awareness of the *natural* evanescence of film, the fact that its events exist only in motion, in passing.[1] This natural fact makes all the more extraordinary the historical fact that films are still on the whole viewed just once and reviewed on the basis of just one viewing, hence that the bulk of the prose even dedicated moviegoers read about movies is the prose of reviewing, not the demanding criticism and the readings and appreciations one takes for granted as being devoted to other arts. It will compensate my having to choose examples that I cannot be assured we have in common if doing so serves to bring this contingency of film viewing and reading into question.

The moment in *The Philadelphia Story* occurs late, when Katharine Hepburn, hearing from Jimmy Stewart that he did not take advantage of her drunken state the previous night, turns from the assembled audience and says, in a sudden, quiet access of admiration, "I think men are wonderful." Nothing further comes of the line; its moment passes with its saying, like a shadow passing. Struck with the strangeness of this moment, I found in composing *Pursuits of Happiness*—and it is something that one of my reviewers, and on the whole a sympathetic and learned one, found more hysterically inappropriate than any other of my perceptions—that to my ear this line alludes to the moment in *The Tempest* at which Miranda exclaims, "How beauteous mankind is!" Evidently I had not, for that reader, made sufficiently clear my general need for the Shakespearean connection in relation to remarriage comedy; nor had I gained sufficient credit with him to get him to put his sense of appropriateness in abeyance for the moment and specifically to try out what I called an allusion amounting almost to an echo. This is something I am going to ask you to consider doing. Let me go over what I am basing myself on in such cases.

The point of the title "remarriage" is to register the grouping of a set of comedies which differ from classical comedy in various respects, but most notably in this, that in classical comedy the narrative shows a young pair overcoming obstacles to their love and at the end achieving marriage, whereas comedies of remarriage begin or

---

[1]Norton Batkin took me back to this idea. His work, represented by *Photography and Philosophy*, the doctoral dissertation he submitted to the Department of Philosophy at Harvard in May 1981, goes far with it, into the nature of photography's stillness.

climax with a pair less young, getting or threatening their divorce, so that the drive of the narrative is to get them *back* together, together *again*. The central idea I follow out along various paths, but *roughly* the idea is that the validity or bond of marriage is assured, even legitimized, not by church or state or sexual compatibility (these bonds, it is implied, are no deeper than those of marriage), but by something I call the willingness for remarriage, a way of continuing to affirm the happiness of one's initial leap. As if the chance of happiness exists only when it seconds itself. In classical comedy people made for one another find one another; in remarriage comedy people who *have* found one another find that they *are* made for each other. The greatest of the structures of remarriage is *The Winter's Tale*, which is, together with *The Tempest*, the greatest of the Shakespearean romances.

But I want the Shakespearean connection with remarriage comedy also for less stupendous structural reasons. Shakespearean romantic comedy lost out, so a way of telling the history goes, to the newer Jonsonian comedy of manners as setting the standard for the future of the English stage. Now I claim that the emergence of film, especially of the talkie, discovered another theater, several centuries later, for that older, Shakespearean structure. Some features of the older comedy that found new life on film are, for example, that it is the woman rather than the man who holds the key to the plot and who undergoes something like death and transformation; that there is some special understanding she has with her father, who does not oppose (as in conventional comedy) but endorses the object of her desire; that the central pair are not young, so that the issue of chastity or innocence, while present, cannot be settled by determinations of literal virginity; that the plot begins and complicates itself in a city but gets resolved in a move to a world of nature—in Shakespeare this is called the green world or the golden world; in four of the seven major Hollywood comedies of remarriage this world is called Connecticut.

But such structural connections are in service of a further reason for the Shakespearean connection, namely to locate the mode of perception called upon in movies, anyway in movies of this kind. The connection in effect implies that what allows film to rediscover, for its own purposes, Shakespearean romance, is that unlike the prose of comic theatrical dialogue after Shakespeare, film has a natural equivalent for the medium of Shakespeare's dramatic poetry. I think of it as the poetry of film itself, what it is that happens to figures and objects and places as they are variously molded and displaced by a motion-picture camera and then projected and screened. Every art, every worthwhile human enterprise, has its poetry, ways of doing things that perfect the possibilities of the enterprise itself, make it the one it is; each of the arts has its own poetry, of course, so has each sport, and so I am sure have banking and baking and surgery and government. You may think of it as the unteachable point in any worthwhile enterprise.

I understand it to be, let me say, a natural vision of film that every motion and station, in particular every human posture and gesture, however glancing, has its poetry, or you may say its lucidity. Charlie Chaplin and Buster Keaton live on this knowledge, and perhaps bring it to its purest expression; it is my claim in *Pursuits of Happiness* that the Hollywood talkie finds an equivalent for this expressiveness, this expression of lucidity, in the way certain pairs of human beings are in conversation. (An implied threat to their happiness is that they are, somehow because of this fortune, incomprehensible to everyone *else* in the world they inhabit.) Any of the arts will be drawn to this knowledge, this perception of the poetry of the ordinary, but film, I would like to say, democratizes the knowledge, hence at once blesses and curses us with it. It says that the perception of poetry is as open to all, regardless as it were of birth or talent, as the ability is to hold a camera on a subject, so that a failure so to perceive, to persist in missing the subject, which may amount to missing the evanescence of the subject, is ascribable only to ourselves, to failures of our character; as if to fail to guess the unseen from the seen, to fail to trace the implications of things—that is, to fail the perception that there *is* something to be guessed and traced, right or wrong—requires that we persistently coarsen and stupefy ourselves.

Business people would not run a business this way; this was something Emerson admired about American business; it is why Thoreau asks for what he calls "a little more Yankee shrewdness" in our lives. And Emerson and Thoreau are the writers I know best who most incessantly express this sense of life as missed possibility, of its passing as in a dream, hence the sense of our leading lives of what they call quiet desperation. The movies I name comedies of remarriage find happiness in proposing that there is relief from just that Emersonian loss, that there are conditions under which opportunities may be discovered again and retaken, that somewhere there is a locale in which a second chance is something one may give oneself. (It is my argument about *The Philadelphia Story* in *Pursuits of Happiness*—which I won't try to go into here—that the Philadelphia in its title is the site of the signing of the Declaration of Independence and of the Constitution of the United States, so that America is the name of the locale of the second chance, or it was meant to be. Remarriage is the central of the second chances.)

Now I'm taking that apparently insignificant moment of *The Philadelphia Story*, the evanescence of the seven syllables "I think men are wonderful," as one in which a character is taking such an opportunity, and the movie proposing one to us. It may help to note that the companion line from *The Tempest*—"How beauteous mankind is!"—is also seven syllables long and that both lines occur at the late moment in their dramas at which the principal female is about to undergo a metaphysical transformation. The Hepburn character is to move from the state of chaste Goddess (a state each of the four men in her life either accuses her of or praises her for) into what she calls feeling like a human being; and in *The Tempest*, in response to Miranda's exclamation, Ferdinand's father asks whether she is a goddess, to which Ferdinand replies

> Sir she is mortal,
> But by immortal providence she's mine.

By the way, while the line of Miranda's I am measuring Hepburn's with does not contain the word "wonderful," its more familiar, wider context runs this way:

> O wonder!
> How many goodly creatures are there here!
> How beauteous mankind is! O brave new world
> That has such people in it!

Remember that *we* are what has become of the new world, the idea
and the fact of which so fascinated Shakespeare and his age.

If one is interested enough to go this far with the conjunction of
Hollywood comedy and Shakespearean romance, one will be bound
to ask what the point of such a moment is, I mean why this crossroads
of wonder is marked so carefully in these dramatic structures. My
answer for the comedies of remarriage would run in something like
the following way. I think of them, as a group, to be dedicated to the
pursuit of what you might call equality between men and women
(and of this as emblematic of the search for human community as
such—but I am letting this pass for the present), the pursuit of their
correct independence of, and dependence upon, one another. What
the comedies of remarriage show is that, as the world goes, there is
an unfairness or asymmetry in this pursuit, because women require
an education for their assumption of equality, and this must be managed with the help of men. The first task for her, accordingly, is to
choose the best man for this work. Because of the history between
them—both their private history and the history of their culture—
they are struggling with one another, they have justified grievances
against one another; hence I sometimes characterize these movies as
revenge comedies. If their relationship is to go forward the pair must
get around to forgiving one another, and, continuing the asymmetry, it must primarily be the woman who forgives the man, not just
because she has more to forgive but because she has more power to
forgive. And yet in these movies it may be hard to see what the particular man in question needs such radical forgiveness for. He has done
nothing obvious to harm the woman, and the specific charges the
women bring against the men—Clark Gable's disdainfulness in *It
Happened One Night*; Cary Grant's craziness in *The Awful Truth*,
and his deviousness in *His Girl Friday*, and his gorgeous thirst in
The Philadelphia Story; Henry Fonda's sappiness in *The Lady Eve*;

Spencer Tracy's forcefulness, even brutishness, in *Adam's Rib*—
these are features the woman honors as well as hates the man for,
which is doubtless why she can forgive him. It is not fully explicit
until the last of the definitive remarriage comedies, *Adam's Rib* in
1949, that what the woman has against the man is fundamentally the
simple villainy of his *being* a man; hence that is what her happiness
with him depends on her getting around to forgiving him for. The
form this takes in the line from *The Philadelphia Story* about men
being wonderful, I take, accordingly, as an expression of admiration
at the sheer fact of their separateness, wonder as it were that there
should be two sexes, and that the opposite one is *as such* admirable.
This is hardly the end of anger between them; there are always their
differences. But it is a kind of promise to spend as long as it takes—
say till death them do part—to work out what those differences are,
what they come to.

At some point—always supposing that one can believe that a conjunction of Shakespeare and Hollywood comedies is not hysterically
inappropriate—a more sympathetic doubt about the conjunction
may seem called for, prompting one to want to know how *serious* I
am about it, whether when I say, for example, that film has a natural
power of poetry equivalent to the power of Shakespeare's dramatic
poetry, I really mean poetry in the same sense. Here I might just
respond by saying that that is not a question to which I have an
answer apart from the thinking and the writing I do and have done,
about movies among other matters. But I want to pause, before turning to my concluding example, to sketch an answer more openly
philosophical, in particular one that accounts more openly for the
periodic appearance of Emerson and Thoreau in my thoughts, those
here tonight and those in *Pursuits of Happiness*. Because while my
insistence on writing about philosophy and movies in the same
breath, insisting on both of them, but especially on their conjunction, as part of my American intellectual and cultural inheritance—
while this has caused me a certain amount of professional tension, it
has caused no more than my insistence on inheriting Emerson and
Thoreau as philosophers.

Do I really mean philosophers? In the same sense that Plato and

Descartes and Kant are philosophers? While this is not a moment to argue the point, I take the moment to ask you to conceive the following possibility: that Emerson and Thoreau are the central founding thinkers of American culture but that this knowledge, though possessed by shifting bands of individuals, is not culturally possessed. It would be an expression of this possibility that no profession is responsible for them as thinkers. Mostly they do not exist for the American profession of philosophy; and the literary professions are mostly not in a position to preserve them in these terms. They are unknown to the culture they express in a way it would not be thinkable for Kant and Schiller and Goethe to be unknown to the culture of Germany, or Descartes and Rousseau to France, or Locke and Hume and John Stuart Mill to England. I do not think it is clear how we are to understand and assess this fact about our cultural lives, but you can see that someone with my interests might wish not to miss the occasion for noting the fact out loud in the nation's capital.

(Here I am seeing our reception of our best writers, like our reception of the best Hollywood movies, as part of America's tendency to overpraise and undervalue its best work, as though the circus ballyhoo advertising of Hollywood movies were covering doubts we have that they are really any good at all. I guess this is a preachy thing to say; and maybe that is what's meant sometimes when I'm called pretentious. But preachiness is equally part of the American grain in me, a risk you run in hanging around Emerson and Thoreau as much as I have lately. It is a tone associated in remarriage comedies especially with Katharine Hepburn's high-mindedness. She gets lectured about it by the men in her life, repeatedly dressed down. And once, in *Adam's Rib*, Spencer Tracy allows himself to say to her, "You get cute when you get causey." Of course this makes her sore. And I think I know just how she feels.)

But now if our central thinkers are unpossessed, unshared by us, it will not be expected that we can readily come to intellectual terms on the issues that matter most to us, as say the fundamental issues of art and of philosophy can matter to us. Emerson and Thoreau fully knew this difficulty in getting themselves understood. I have taken as a parable of Emerson's dedication of himself as a writer the following sentences from one of his early, most famous essays, "Self-Reliance":

> I shun father and mother and wife and brother when my genius calls
> me. I would write on the lintels of the door-post, *Whim*. I hope it is
> somewhat better than whim at last, but we cannot spend the day in
> explanation.

Two remarks about this. First, shunning father and mother and wife and brother is, according to the New Testament, required of you when the Lord calls you and you seek the kingdom of heaven. And according to the Old Testament, writing on the lintels of the door is something you do on Passover, to avoid the angel of death, and it is also where writings from Deuteronomy are placed, in mezuzahs, to signify that Jews live within and that they are obedient to the injunction of the Lord to bear his words and at all times to acknowledge them. So Emerson is putting the *calling* and the *act* of his writing in the public place reserved in both of the founding testaments of our culture for the word of God. Is he being serious?

My second remark about Emerson's passage is that it acknowledges his writing to be posing exactly the question of its own seriousness. In the parable I just cited, he both declares his writing to be a matter of life and death, the path of his faith and redemption, and also declares that *everything* he writes is Whim. I understand this to mean that it is his mission to create the language in which to explain himself, and accordingly to imply both that there is no such standing discourse between him and his culture, and that he is to that extent without justification before himself. The course open to him is to stake the seriousness of his life, his conviction, on what, before his life's work, we will have no words for: call it whim. So if I answer that my insistence on, for example, aligning movies and Shakespeare and philosophy is based on whim, you will know how to take me.

Now I'm ready to offer as my concluding example, to challenge our convictions in the worth of movies as subjects of thought, *Pennies from Heaven*, a much less lucky movie than, say, the seven thirties comedies I listed in the original genre of remarriage. Those movies are likeable and comprehensible enough to be worth taking and treasuring as light comedies, without working to consciousness any more of the material in *Pursuits of Happiness* than occurs to you casually. Whereas if the brilliance of *Pennies from Heaven* doesn't strike you right off, if you don't become convinced at any rate fairly swiftly that the shocking juxtaposition of attitudes it presents is part of a study, among other things, of the unsettling power of movies, it is likely to seem too unpleasant and confused to think about at all. It is bound to be somewhat hard to think about since it is a Hollywood musical that apparently seeks to undermine the conventions that made possible the Hollywood musical. The subsequent paradox is that its success depends on its undermining itself. If it absorbs the power of conviction of the Hollywood musical then it has not undermined that power. If on the other hand it does not absorb the power of the Hollywood musical then it lacks the power of conviction altogether. It would answer this paradox to say: This movie has the conviction of a work that undermines the conventional sources of conviction in its medium, precisely by reconceiving the sources of that conviction. This sounds like something that might be said of the course of modernism in the other major arts; it is a reason I have sometimes said that art now exists in the condition of philosophy, since it has always been the condition of philosophy to attempt to escape itself, which for several centuries has taken the form of each new major philosopher wishing to repudiate the past of the subject—I mean repudiate it philosophically. As famous, and successful, as any such effort in the arts is Bertolt Brecht's repudiation of theatricality by means of theater itself; theater, hence, reconceived. But in thinking about movies this is so far merely words; it is an idea that has no commonly appreciated and acknowledged realization in film itself. It tells us nothing about whether, for example, *Pennies from Heaven* succeeds or fails in the new terms we allow for it. The moral remains that nothing but the details of the individual work can tell.

Take the two most obvious details in which this film calls into question the conventions of classical Hollywood musicals, the fact that they employ the dubbing of voices, and the fact that they go to any fictional lengths in order to motivate realistically their fantastic songs and dances. When the small-time hero, refused financing by the banker, breaks into a happy duet with him, his voice dubbed by a woman's; or when the crippled, mumbling beggar takes on an athletic, dazzlingly mounted performance of the title song; the violence of emotion I felt as I stared at the conventions of the Hollywood musical brought to trial was only increased by the fact that I found the numbers expert and gripping. So if *Pennies from Heaven* is parody, it is at the same time tribute, homage: it acknowledges that the reputedly naive musicals on which it lives were as artful and as mysterious as anything it can claim for itself. It shows that conventions of the Hollywood musical are deeper than we may have thought, that their discovery of human desires and satisfactions cannot be undone or outpaced merely by exaggerating them, and indeed in no obvious way at all. And if this is true of the Hollywood musical, where in successful film, or in art generally, is it not true?

Yet this film fails its own knowledge at the end and strikes, to my ear, so false a note as to help ensure its lack of consideration. What happens is this. The hero is arrested for a terrible crime we know has been committed by the crippled beggar, and the film's examination of the human voice and the sentiments of popular song climaxes with the hero's finding his own voice not in song but in plain speech as, on the gallows, he speaks the words of what may be recognized as the verse to the song "Pennies from Heaven." To ask a writer's words to be so sound that they can be said on the gallows is an ambitious test of writing; I find that these words, said by Steve Martin, passed well enough. If so, then nothing should stand in the way of the fiction's happy ending. The Governor might have driven up in a limousine, his way cleared by screaming motorcycles, and sung a song of pardon to our hero. Instead the movie slinks to a conclusion by having the hero reappear to his sweetheart for no reason within the fiction, mouthing something like, "We've worked too hard not to get a happy ending." This is roughly to suppose that the conventions that lend the movie its power are disposable at will.

How wrong this is is reinforced if we notice that the climax of the movie alludes to a more famous dramatic work with pennies in its title, the Brecht-Weill *Threepenny Opera*, which concludes with its bourgeois criminal hero singing on the gallows and being brought a reprieve by a messenger on horseback. So in failing to find out how to say that its hero deserves a pardon, perhaps in the form of an ironic consolation, *Pennies from Heaven* is faithless at once to its Hollywood medium and to its source in the Brechtian theater of estrangement.[2]

Let us end on this movie's other and most dangerous moment of imitation and homage, the reenactment by Steve Martin and Bernadette Peters of the Astaire-Rogers routine on Irving Berlin's "Let's Face the Music and Dance." What the movie is studying here most extravagantly is the nature of what is called our identification with the figures of drama. This reenactment, along with the voices that take over the characters as they go into song, reveals the identification with figures on film not as a process of imitating them but as a product of being possessed by them. Now of all the impersonations one might have tried of the distinctive stars in the history of Hollywood, from Chaplin to Gable and Hepburn, the one no normal person in his right mind would have tried to translate from the realm of fantasy into the public realm is the sense of himself in an Astaire routine: no one else could perfectly enough lend his body to the demands of that spirit. So one must ask how good the Martin-Peters enactment is of this impossible possession. And I find the answer to be that it is convincing enough to make me ask how convincing the original is, whether *it* fulfills its own dramatic invitation to face the music and dance.

I note that it is perhaps the most weirdly motivated of all the memorable Astaire productions. He prefaces the dance with a little drama in which he loses his money at a casino and then, wandering outside with a pistol to use on himself, sees a woman in an evening gown mount a parapet; he grabs her before she can leap, throws away the pistol, and begins the song and dance. Described in this way, apart from its experience, it may be wondered how they get through all this without laughing.[3] But within the experience, or in remember-

[2]I have added a postscript that amplifies this claim.
[3]Arlene Croce testifies to such a feeling in her elegant and useful *The Fred Astaire and Ginger Rogers Book* (New York, 1972), p. 88.

ing such experiences, we know that Astaire has thought about what motivates dancing, about what provides its occasions, as well as anyone who ever lived; so we had perhaps better think further about it in the present case.

The little opening drama, in which the actions set in music are neither spoken nor sung nor danced, invokes the condition of mime, of what the Elizabethans called a dumb show, of the sort used in *Hamlet* by the players of the play-within-the-play who act out their drama silently before they speak their parts. If you take this undanced prelude or invitation to dance in this way, as a kind of prophecy or parable of Astaire's understanding of his dancing, then he can be taken to be declaring that it is meant as a removal not from life but from death. Though the idea of escaping life is a more common view of dance and of comedy, and I guess of art in general, than Astaire's idea of redeeming death, it is no less metaphysical. Astaire's view of dancing as facing the music, as a *response* to the life of inexorable consequences, which turn out to be the consequences of desperate pleasures, would then be a concrete translation of what such a thinker as Nietzsche meant by dancing (as when Zarathustra speaks, urging: "Raise up your hearts, my brothers, high, higher! And don't forget your legs! Raise up your legs, too, good dancers . . . !")— something I guess he would have learned, among other things, from Emerson, from such a passage in another of Emerson's early essays as this: "All that we reckoned settled shakes and rattles; and literatures, cities, climates, religions, leave their foundations and dance before our eyes." Can an Astaire-Rogers dance, projected on a screen, be this good? How good would this good have to be?—This is serious business.

POSTSCRIPT

It was pointed out to me by a student at Yale, on my return for other matters some months after I had given a version of this lecture there, that the ending of *Pennies from Heaven*, which I criticize as faithless to its sources in the Hollywood musical and in Brechtian theater in its avoidance of a stance toward the hero's threatened execution, is readable as a further reflection of the hero's fantasy life, hence as his last moments on the gallows. We hadn't more than a few minutes in which to pursue the idea, so I may have misunderstood what he said. My response is this.

Dennis Potter's novelized version of the material for *Pennies from Heaven* fairly obviously does not know what its own end should be, whether part of the hero's fantasy life, or a further appeal on its behalf, or some final regret that there is no use in such an appeal, or a complaint against society for not listening more carefully, or a complaint against the songs for being dismissable. Regarded as the prospectus for a movie, these alternatives may well have seemed undecidable, for the movie must work its own way into such matters. The possibility that the movie takes the option of adopting the hero's fantasy is one that crossed my mind, but it makes matters worse, I think, than I said, worse than making some cheap fun of itself.

The hero's prior bursts into song and dance have the effect of authenticating his inner life, convincing us not only of its existence but of the justice, however mad in imagery (in, some might say, the Utopianism), of its demands. An accomplishment worthy of any art. After these outbursts, it followed (as a kind of price of their elations) that the film's return to grim reality was a return to something no less indebted to the Hollywood past than its treatment of the musical is. A way to tell the structure of *Pennies from Heaven* is as one that alternates musical absorptions of Hollywood (of the thirties and early forties) with counter-absorptions of that same Hollywood; the counter-absorptions work as a kind of negative Utopianism to match the mad positive Utopianism of its music and its music's words. An obvious source for the returns, the counter-absorptions, is such a "woman's film" or "tearjerker" (as if we knew what these are) as George Stevens's *Penny Serenade* of 1941, with Irene Dunne and Cary Grant. I suppose this is deliberate, not only because of the connection in name, but because one of the married pair in the earlier film (in this case the woman) is a hawker of popular music (of records, not sheet music), and a spinning record recurrently punctuates the narration as the film works its way through the death of an innocent and the death of innocence. A less specific source of the counter attitude to reality, to reality as consisting of a planet without music, seems to me something like a Fritz Lang *film noir* early in his American career, for example, *You Only Live Once* of 1937, also about a loser condemned to die for a crime of which he is innocent, which also ends (almost) in a prison yard, with a succeeding ironic fantasy of freedom.

The sources of negative or dashed Utopianism will be harder to recognize than those of the musical numbers, but the alternation of genres provides at once an interpretation of the hero's sensibility, of the commonness of his craziness, and an insight of significance into the Hollywood of its golden age, namely that it depicted a unified world, a universe. The "fugitive couple" of certain of its melodramas are negations of just those pairs in certain Hollywood comedies who are hardly less isolated from society, hardly less incomprehensible to it, but whose isolation and incomprehensibility work themselves out with fortune more willing to smile. (The happier pairs have easier access to money. It remains to be determined how far this is the difference that matters, and how far it is the symbol of the difference.)

It is up to each of us to find our participation in these high-hat highs and low-down lows. Now if the conclusion of *Pennies from Heaven* is to be identified as the hero's fantasy, and it is to be taken on the model of his earlier bursts into song, then, since it has no follow-up, it forces us to read his fantasy as merely some apparently well-understood, ironic escape from some well-understood reality.

And this seems to me faithless at once to the hero's inner life, refusing the just appeal in its tawdriness; and to the freedom it seemed to assign us in determining our relation to these events; and to the power of film itself, whose dangers and values of seduction it had honored, if feared, in its own production, but now seems, in an act of self-disrespect, to claim to transcend—to claim some privileged position from which to assess the value of movies, of fantasy, of art, of such freedom as we can find the means to express and hence to claim. Far be it from me to deny the connection between high and low tawdriness, or escape; but to discount them is not something we need art for, high or low.

I take this moment to avert a related ambiguity in what I was saying in my lecture. When I note the extraordinary persistence of the conventions in viewing movies just once (interspersed with the odd cult-object viewed countless times), and reviewing them on the basis of one viewing, I am objecting not to the practices in themselves but to their dominance, and lack of assessment, in general movie culture. Certainly I am not recommending repetitive viewing to no particular point, as the better alternative. On the contrary, the casual, or surprised, appeal to memorable passages has a value that studiedness may sacrifice, a value not merely of spontaneity (whatever that is), but of a depth that only a certain immediacy will capture, as by surprise. The sacrifice of literary immediacy to studiedness is more familiar ground, and I can imagine that the practical difficulties in the way of checking one's reactions to the events of film (for all the technology of casettes, etc.), or one's recall of them, may at some time have a leavening effect on our literary culture, remembering the value there was (however practically necessitated by its own economy) in citing common literary works from memory, a time when a smaller literary world had works in common, a time (except for such things) not to be envied. It resulted in some misquotation (of a particular kind), but its outcome was of contexts in which one recognized the point of having a memory, a public memory. This is something I want from an eventual film culture as much as I want film's rigorous, orderly study. Such is my justification for continuing to explore *Pennies from Heaven* on the basis of one viewing. My excuse is not having had it available since needing to see it again. (*How* hard did I look for it? A new question for one's intellectual conscience.)

◆

THE POLITICS
OF INTERPRETATION
(Politics as Opposed to What?)

◆

A version of this essay was read at Critical Inquiry*'s symposium
called The Politics of Interpretation, held at the University of Chicago's Center for Continuing Education, October 30, 31 and November
1, 1981. It and the contributions of the other eight lecturers, together
with Critical Responses prepared by panelists after the symposium,
constitute the September 1982 issue of* Critical Inquiry. *Professor
Spivak's Critical Response to the symposium, entitled "The Politics
of Interpretations," first appear there. My reaction in turn to those
passages of her paper that concern themselves with what I had said
in my lecture first appeared in a paperback book,* The Politics of
Interpretation, *edited by W. J. T. Mitchell (University of Chicago
Press, 1983) which contains the colloquium issue of* Critical Inquiry
*together with pertinent additional papers. My reaction to Professor
Spivak is reprinted here as a postscript to this item.*

◇

If the politics of interpretation studies the public conditions of one's
discourse, the forces it musters against the forces against it, where
the victory of discourse consists in bringing those conditions to
light, an early essay of mine on the philosophy of J. L. Austin, "Austin at Criticism," is meant as such a study.[1] This is worth my saying

[1] First published in *The Philosophical Review* 74 (April 1965): 204–19; rpt. in my
Must We Mean What We Say? (Cambridge, England, 1976).

for two reasons. First, since I am still not ready to try a systematic account of what I understand either politics or interpretation to be, what profit I can be here, to myself and others, will come from a certain willingness for the autobiographical, both by way of meditating on some themes and instances that I would wish a systematic study to treat and by way of specifying some of the conditions of my discourse that I can recognize as political. These conditions will mostly, or at first, be institutional or professional forces. Second, in the early sixties, when I wrote my essay on Austin and for the dozen years before that, during which I went through graduate studies and began teaching for a living, about the only political questions I heard voiced in professional philosophical circles were about whether Hegel and Nietzsche were proto-Nazis and whether ordinary language philosophy was politically conservative. It will serve to orient these autobiographical notes if I spend my opening comments tracing my course from that essay to this.

No one in my earlier years would have thought that ordinary language philosophy had done the kind of public harm attributed to German philosophy, but on an institutional basis ordinary language philosophy was received as, and took itself to represent, a revolution in philosophy. Certainly it caused changes in the look and the sound of the subject and differences in who was attracted to the subject and who fled from it, who was rewarded by it and who deprived. Austin's claim against past philosophy, what we allowed ourselves to call the tradition, was not that it was wrong in this or that respect but that it was radically insufficient, childishly oversimple, as a mode of discourse altogether. Which is to say that ordinary language philosophy is a mode of interpretation and inherently involved in the politics of interpretation. The way I put this in my early essay on Austin was to say that it is an unmasking philosophy, as analytical philosophy generally is bound to be. (More so than Plato or Kant or Hume or Rousseau or Bentham—i.e., more than any philosophy? Well, let us just say this is its claim to philosophy.) Diagnosis of one's enemies calls forth counterdiagnosis as surely as anger calls forth anger. The counterdiagnosis or unmasking of Austin as politically conservative was shaped, it seemed to me, by a sense of him as socially and intellectually conservative, an impression I attributed in turn to his apparent indifference to speculation and his cultivation, in his prose, of common room wit and superficiality. My defense in turn against this unmasking of him was that it was itself taken in by Austin's use of his mask, that what looked like social manner was internal to what I would like now to call a politics of superficiality, directed accordingly against what Austin would have seen as a politics of profundity and mystification (associated primarily, I suppose, with a perception of German philosophy). (The profundity he was combatting was, I claim, also something he felt tempted to by the depth of his own thoughts—but I won't press that further here.)

Austin's favorite gesture in preparing or justifying his philosophical attacks is to appeal to the idea that the best way to stop a bad thing from happening is to prevent it from starting to happen. If I do not share Austin's confidence that self-mystification can always so be prevented, confident instead that it requires a perpetual undoing, and an undoing of the one who does it, I nevertheless value the gesture and am glad to accept it as an element of what I understand the ordinary to be in ordinary language philosophy.

In speaking of Austin's critical practice here as a gesture, I would studiously avoid letting the political and the psychological possibilities of interpreting the gesture preempt one another. I think of it as a matter of character, of what you might call a writer's worldly character. Austin was committed to the manners, even the mannerisms, of an English professor the way a French intellectual is committed to seeming brilliant. It is the level at which an American thinker or artist is likely to play dumb, I mean undertake to seem like a hick, uncultivated. These are all characters in which authority is assumed, variations I suppose of the thinker's use—as unmasked by Nietzsche—of the character of the sage.

Wittgenstein is always prepared for the undoing that self-mystification calls for, and if I still find him insufficiently clear and explicit on the subject, I am guided by the uncanny beauty of some of his observations concerning it.

> Where does our investigation get its importance from, since it seems only to destroy everything interesting, that is, all that is great and important? . . . What we are destroying is nothing but houses of cards [literally: structures of air] and we are clearing up the ground of language on which they stand.[2]

What I mean by uncanniness in these words is their Zen master–ish assurance that every theoretical attachment to words (structures of air) is an attachment to illusion and the assurance that we have some mode of inhabitation outside such structures, or else that we can live without inhabitation. Wittgenstein is painting his quest for the ordinary and the everyday as a profound thing—a Romantic gesture that Austin must disapprove of. (Wittgenstein's name appears once in the posthumously published lectures, *Sense and Sensibilia*; in private I once heard Austin speak the name, after having for a moment expressed difficulty in remembering it.) So that when Austin voices his similar view of the interest and the importance of his investigation of the ordinary, he reaches for no further power, apparently, than his ordinary character of sociable wit. In the last two paragraphs of the last of the twelve lectures that constitute *How to Do Things with Words*, he announces, hailing us in farewell: "I have as usual failed to leave enough time in which to say why what I have said is interesting." And in the next sentence he instances a topic he says philosophers have been interested in. It is sufficiently obvious that he takes it as unarguable that the philosophers' interest, set beside the twelve hours of fascinating detail he has offered, is boredom itself. Austin says the lectures were bound to be a little dry and boring; but he was saying it mostly to the wrong parties. His first lecture had attracted several hundred people; by the last half-dozen we were down to a core of some twelve to fifteen souls, and not all of these few were happy. But this only means that not everyone is interested in the need for revolution. Put his appeals to interest and boredom together with his having begun his lectures by locating his work on the line of those philosophers who have shown many traditional phil-

²Ludwig Wittgenstein, *Philosophical Investigations*, trans. G. E. M. Anscombe (London, 1958), par. 118, p. 48e.

osophical perplexities to have arisen through mistaking the form of
one's language, which is the thing he claims as without doubt producing a revolution in philosophy. Since the only event in Austin's
lectures that could satisfy the concept of a revolution is the shift of
interest with respect to traditional philosophical problems, I find
that a double implication is to be drawn: first, that the challenge of
philosophy is the challenge of our interests as they stand, including
our interests in philosophy itself, specifically in the present case a
challenge to show that what is called a philosophical problem is in
fact humanly interesting; second, that philosophy has no special or
privileged discourse in which to level its challenge. I take these implications as two further specifications of the claims recorded in the
title "ordinary language philosophy."

In my essay on Austin I did not specify what I took the politics of
my own discourse to be, but the institutional pressures on it, in particular the pressures of the professionalization of American philosophy, were in outline clear enough. I was more and more galled by the
mutual shunning of the continental and the Anglo-American traditions of philosophizing, and I was finding more and more oppressive
the mutual indifference of philosophy and literature to one another,
especially, I suppose, of American philosophy and American literature, and especially philosophy's indifference to the literary conditions of its own existence. (I understand this to imply not an interdis-
ciplinary wish but rather a wish for philosophy to take a further step
toward itself.) I was still near the beginning of what is turning out to
be a lifelong quarrel with the profession of philosophy. One of its
recent manifestations has been the question put to me by certain
professional colleagues whether I do not take satisfaction from the
newer literary theory and criticism, especially as that has been inspired by developments over the past fifteen or so years in French
intellectual life. This would seem to answer my plea at one stroke for
both continental philosophy and for an understanding with literary
matters. The fact is that my ambivalence toward these developments
has been so strong, or anyway periodic, that I have found it difficult
to study in any very orderly way.

The reason for my difficulty is contained in what I mean by my quarrel with the profession of philosophy. That this is a quarrel means that I recognize the profession to be the genuine present of the impulse and the history of philosophy, so far as that present takes its place in our (English-speaking) public intellectual life. This is what makes my quarrel with it a part of what I take my intellectual adventure to be. My point in the quarrel is that I can recognize no expression of mine to be philosophical which simply thinks to escape my profession's paradigms of comprehensibility; so that the invocations of the name of philosophy in current literary debate are frequently not comprehensible to me as calls upon philosophy. It may be that I should care less about this than I do, even less than my ambivalence asks. I mean to bear this in mind as I go on to spend the bulk of my time here considering in a practical way some passages from the writing of two literary theorists who have recourse to the work of Austin. In the case of the passages from Stanley Fish, it may be that my efforts will just amount to clearing up some unnecessarily confusing terminology; some passages from Paul de Man I find more troubling.

As one further preparation for considering these passages I might indicate how hard it has become for me to conduct my quarrel with the profession, to find common ground for it. This difficulty is epitomized by my growing insistence on receiving Emerson and Thoreau as philosophers, figures who from the beginning of the professionalization of American philosophy have been regarded as philosophical amateurs. (Bruce Kuklick's book *American Philosophy* in effect tells the story of the establishment of academic philosophy proper in America, at Harvard, in such a way that it begins, achieves its first accreditation, so to speak, by declaring Emerson an amateur thinker, quite as if repressing Emerson's thought were an essential responsibility of professional philosophy; and if essential then, then still. Kuklick tells the story as a proud one for American philosophy.) The cause of my growing insistence is the work I have been doing that convinces me that Emerson and Thoreau underwrite the emphasis I have placed over the years on ordinary language philosophy. I felt from the beginning of my absorption in its confrontation with skepticism that the ordinariness in question spoke of an intimacy with existence, or an intimacy lost, that matched skepticism's despair of the world. After publishing *The Claim of Reason* several years ago, much of which revolves around this confrontation, I was prepared to see that something I have meant by the ordinary is something Emerson and Thoreau mean in their devotion to the thing they call the common, the familiar, the everyday, the low, the near. Making this connection explicit felt to me like bringing pieces of my mind together, yet I know that to most of my colleagues the underwriting of ordinary language philosophy by transcendentalism would be about as promising as enlivening the passé by the extinct.[3]

This suggests, by the way, the right level of philosophical response to the old charge against Austin as politically conservative. The charge is fed by the idea that ordinary language philosophy is meant to be a defense of ordinary beliefs—say the belief that there are material objects. It may be that certain philosophers are so characterized fairly: G. E. Moore, for example. But for Austin and Wittgenstein, this description is itself an instance of the philosophical prejudices their work is made to bring to light, because it is a departure from ordinary language to say either that I do or that I do not believe there are material objects; so to that extent, it would be incoherent to provide a "defense" of such a "belief." Of course a story can be given that will take up the slack of this departure and realign the idea of belief here—the skeptical story according to which I might come to think of myself as doubting that there are material objects. It is true that Austin was intent on preventing such a story from getting off the ground, but while I regard this as a grave limitation in his philosophizing—a refusal, in effect, to consider why it looked as if he were defending common beliefs—it is something else again to charge that he was in fact defending those beliefs.

Wittgenstein speaks of philosophical procedures as bringing

---

[3]In suggesting that these colleagues cannot be certain that they are right in this prediction, no more certain, at any rate, than they can be that philosophy is a science, I am appealing to this difference between the sciences and the humanities, that with the latter the past may at any time come to life, not merely as the recovery of certain neglected problems within the field but as a recovery of the field's originating, or preserving, authority. Along such lines the authority of philosophy is a guiding preoccupation of the essays in *Must We Mean What We Say?* as a whole, most explicitly, or consecutively, in the foreword to the volume, "An Audience for Philosophy."

words back from their metaphysical to their everyday use—as if our words are *away*, not at home, and as if it takes the best efforts of philosophy to recognize when and where our words have strayed into metaphysics. I have interpreted this task many ways over the years, but it was not until I was able to emerge from *The Claim of Reason* that I felt I had said something consecutive and of a reasonable depth about how words get away and lost, about the intuition I had taken away from my first useful encounter with the *Philosophical Investigations* that the repudiation of the world is as internal to what ordinary language is as its revelation of the world; or put otherwise, that skepticism would not be possible unless ordinary language is such that it can, sometimes must, repudiate itself, put its own naturalness into question. But to care about this, one must, I suppose, have sometimes found in oneself the burden of its revelation, that we had been away in our words, a burden within which Austin and Wittgenstein may be received with the power of a conversion of interest. This is still worth mentioning because those of us who have claimed responsibility for ordinary language procedures, or profit from them, have not to my mind satisfactorily described their performance. I do not mean, it goes without saying, that someone cannot perform them without being able to describe their performance. But to the extent that these procedures are philosophically undescribed, or underdescribed, ordinary language philosophy remains an esoteric practice.

This is not the aspect of ordinary language philosophy that is taken up in what I have been reading of the work of Fish and of de Man. The work of Austin's they cite primarily is *How to Do Things with Words*, that is, roughly, his doctrine of performative utterances, which I might call his most exoteric work. Or I might say it is his most traditionally political work. I mean: here there is comparatively little effort to work out structures within the ordinariness of language, which I regard as his best power; his goal is less to illuminate a system of what you might call natural—or naturally interesting—concepts (which may then have untold consequences for traditional so-called philosophical problems) than to undermine two philosophical theories or tendencies among his competitors within analytical philosophy (which will then allow his more genuine questions to find their own consequences). One tendency was the over-attention to the statement of fact among the speech acts studied by philosophers (most recently associated with the work of the logical positivists); the other tendency was the recent emphasis on the uses, instead of the meanings, of words (an emphasis associated with the later Wittgenstein). Useful and surprising things emerge as Austin works through his tests for distinguishing kinds of speech acts, but the philosophical yield should not be exaggerated. Perhaps most important, it does not for Austin yield a theory of language; on the contrary, he takes this work to show how far we are from anything he would regard as a serious theory of language. This is cause enough for me to applaud Fish's deploring the efforts of "literary people . . . using speech-act theory to arrive at definitions of literature and/or fiction."[4] But Fish's case rests on a view of the question of the ordinary that is at odds with my understanding of it and which I believe may mislead further efforts to use Austin in thinking about language and literature.

For all his approval of certain ideas of ordinary language philosophy, Fish objects to its distinguishing so-called ordinary discourse from some other kind, say literary, and doing so on grounds that it itself, in the view of language taken in its theory of performative utterances, repudiates. Fish summarizes this repudiation by saying: "What philosophical semantics and the philosophy of speech acts are telling us is that ordinary language is extraordinary because at its heart is precisely that realm of values, intentions, and purposes which is often assumed to be the exclusive property of literature."[5] The wit in making ordinary language philosophy say that ordinary language is extraordinary may, I believe, cover up a series of misunderstandings, ironic, sometimes for me disheartening, misunderstandings.

To begin with, Fish does not mean by "ordinary" what Austin

[4]Stanley E. Fish, "How to Do Things with Austin and Searle," in *Is There a Text in This Class? The Authority of Interpretive Communities* (Cambridge, Mass., 1980), p. 231; all further references to this essay, abbreviated "Austin and Searle," will be included in the text.
[5]Fish, "How Ordinary Is Ordinary Language?," in *Is There a Text?*, p. 108.

means. He assimilates Austin's term to a long chain of more or less established distinctions, including that of I. A. Richards between emotive and scientific meaning. Philosophers generally spoke of essentially this distinction as one between emotive and cognitive meaning, a distinction one of whose initial ironies is that it reversed Richards's efforts to give to poetry some function of communication that was intellectually viable even if not scientific and instead ground aesthetic, moral, and religious discourses together as something whose essential character was that they were noncognitive. This distinction, together with its companion distinction between descriptive and normative utterance or discourse, is fundamental to two of the most influential books, or most often cited, in analytical philosophy throughout the years of my graduate studies: A. J. Ayer's *Language, Truth, and Logic* and Charles Stevenson's *Ethics and Language*. It would take considerable novelistic skill to recapture the mood of philosophical debate on such issues in those years, in which these distinctions struck some as being as unassailable as the difference between science and religion and struck others as jeopardizing everything they prized.

Now I think it is correct to say that the single most telling blow *against* the tyranny of this distinction between cognitive and emotive meaning came with Austin's counterdistinction between constative and performative utterances, one major effect of which was to defeat the credibility of the crude distinction between one form of discourse (call it cognitive) as responsible to facts or to reality and another form (call it noncognitive) as not in the same way responsible. I do not say Austin refuted this positivist theory, only that his theory (along with certain other major developments, critically that which attacked the distinction between analytic and synthetic judgments) removed or replaced interest in it. It is possible, of course, that he suffers from the disease he cured, but that is not exactly what Fish accuses him of. If in literary studies people have fastened on the rubric "ordinary language" as something they take as opposed to literary language, that may or may not be unfortunate depending on what distinction they have in mind; but it must certainly be unfortunate to add to their problems by supposing this distinction either to be enforced or debarred by Austin's work.

What Austin did mean by "ordinary" is not, I hope I have begun to suggest, and cannot be, easy to say. Consider that it has no standing, or obvious, contrast. Ordinary as opposed to what—if not to scientific or religious or ethical or literary? In my reading of Austin's practice, the contrast is with the philosophical (what Wittgenstein calls the metaphysical). (Reasonably direct evidence for this is provided by assessing what I call the terms of criticism in Austin's diagnosis of his antagonists.) The errors or discrepancies or follies his appeals to ordinary language immediately counter are ones that philosophizing is apt to produce. Austin is not particularly interested to say so because, I think, he does not wish to give the impression that what is in question are two modes or realms of discourse, the ordinary and the philosophical. His claim, largely implicit, is that the philosophical is not a special mode of discourse at all; it has no interests of its own (as, say, science or religion or sports or trades have), or it ought not to have. So its departures from the ordinary are not into specialties but, let me say, into emptiness. Compared with Wittgenstein, Austin has no account of this emptiness, beyond perhaps various casual suggestions about distinguishing species of nonsense, in itself important enough. While his avoidance here is part of my sense of the limitation of his philosophizing, it is still reasonably clear to me that with modes of discourse other than the supposedly philosophical Austin takes no particular issue.

Then why does Fish suppose otherwise? In what I have read of his work so far, there seem to be two causes. The first, perhaps of no significance beyond its curiosity, concerns Fish's use of the term "normative." When speech-act theory is used to arrive at definitions of literature and/or fiction, the enterprise, according to Fish, "necessarily begins with an attempt to specify what is *not* literature and fiction, or, in a word, what is normative. According to most of those who have worked on this problem, what is normative is language that intends to be or is held to be responsible to the real world" ("Austin and Searle," pp. 231–32). The ensuing quotations Fish presents from three such workers do not themselves contain the term "normative," and indeed I thought I had invented the idea of speaking of the normative in this connection, and, until I began reading Fish's recent collection of essays, I believed that I had remained alone. When in the title essay of *Must We Mean What We Say?* I come out with the assertion that "what is normative is exactly ordinary use itself," it is with a certain air of triumph, and what I felt (still feel) I was triumphing in was not the affirmation of a distinction between ordinary and some other kind of language; on the contrary, I felt I was winning freedom from such distinctions between the normative and the descriptive, say as instanced by that between the literary and the ordinary. The triumphant air was an expression of my relief in having discovered for myself what it was about the distinction that for ten years had had the power to make my flesh creep (I dare say a political emotion). Most probably my use of the term "normative" is irrelevant to the present coincidence of terms; but on the chance that it is not, my reversal or recapturing of the term seems to have defeated itself, seems to affirm precisely what it denies, and I do not understand why.

The second cause I mention for Fish to take Austin as opposing ordinary to literary language is that Austin all but says he does, in so many words. All but; but I think not really. Fish quotes what he calls Austin's classic formulation as follows:

> A performative utterance will, for example, be *in a peculiar way* hollow or void if said by an actor on the stage, or if introduced in a poem. . . . Language in such circumstances is in special ways—intelligibly—used not seriously, but in ways *parasitic* upon its normal use—ways which fall under the doctrine of the *etiolations* of language. All this we are *excluding* from consideration. Our performative utterances, felicitous or not, are to be understood as issued in ordinary circumstances. ["Austin and Searle," p. 233]

But why take a passage that says it is excluding something, as if guarding against being misunderstood here, to be presenting a classic formulation of a theory of that excluded thing, a thing about which the book has next to nothing to say? Moreover, in the examples Austin adduces here, he is egregiously, compared with his usual care about examples, his Austinian care, careless; he seems to have some wires crossed. When he says that a performative utterance will be in a peculiar way hollow or void if said by an actor on the stage, this is either false or too poorly described to assess. It is false to say, for example, that Horatio and Marcellus do not really or felicitously swear by Hamlet's sword never to speak of what they have seen and heard; and to say that the actors playing those roles have not really sworn would be as useful as to say that those actors are not really, except *per accidens*, in Denmark. Say that what actors do is imitate actions. Then the conditions of any act you can specify can be imitated. So you can imitate any way in which one of these conditions might fail and hence perfectly imitate an infelicitous act of speech. If Hamlet had no sword or if Horatio had crossed his fingers or winked aside to the audience, then he would not exactly have sworn on Hamlet's sword. But if Austin had in mind an actor speaking not to other actors but rather to us in the audience, then the case has to be imagined as one in which we or the other actors do not know that the actor speaking is on the stage or that we are members of an audience. And whatever it is to know this and however we might be imagined to fail to know it are matters that have nothing special to do with performative utterances. The question raised by Austin's passage is why he should be prompted at all to attempt such exclusions, what misunderstanding it is he takes himself to be guarding against.

I do not deny that Austin's speaking of roughly theatrical or fictional uses of language as nonserious and as parasitic on normal use is symptomatic of his cast of mind (as is the fact that he got some wires crossed in exemplifying it). But is this basis enough on which to build a confident description of this cast of mind? Is he, for example, contrasting the realm of the serious with the realm of play? Yet he more than once accuses philosophers of having robbed philosophy of its fun. No doubt he is suggesting that matters like promising and marrying and warning (as of fire in the theater) require restrictions on the realm of play. Don't they?

Most immediately, it seems to me, what he is guarding against is being taken as giving conditions for what he calls the seriousness of assertion, as if he supposed that seriousness were something added on, as it were, to what is said. (Wittgenstein discusses this philosophical temptation in considering Frege's sign of assertion.)[6] The difference between assertion and fiction is not going to be settled by any such signs. The difference as Austin puts it, in the sentence omitted from the citation of what Fish calls Austin's classic formulation, is the result of a "sea-change" of language, which is to say, a metamorphosis of the whole of a discourse, as into another mode. This is hardly clear, but it is surely not meant to do much more than mark the merest suggestion of an idea worth pursuing. (One way to pursue it might be to compare it with Fish's suggestion of ordinary language as undergoing "framing" in literature.) So another danger I see in Fish's summary of the philosophy of speech acts as telling us that ordinary language is extraordinary is that it takes Austin's theory of speech acts to express Austin's vision of language, a vision Fish sketches this way: "When we communicate, it is because we are parties to a set of discourse agreements which are in effect decisions as to what can be stipulated as a fact" ("Austin and Searle," p. 242). I share a sense of agreement underlying communication, or community. But Fish's words here make this agreement seem much more, let me say, sheerly conventional than would seem plausible if one were considering other regions of Austin's work, for example, the region of excuses, where the differences, for one small instance, between doing something mistakenly, accidentally, heedlessly, carelessly, inadvertently, automatically, thoughtlessly, inconsiderately, and so on are worked out with unanticipated clarity and completeness but where the more convinced you are by the results, the less you will feel like attributing them to agreements that are expressible as decisions. How could we have agreed to consequences of our words that we are forever in the process of unearthing, consequences that with each turn seem further to unearth the world? (I don't say there is no way.) I suggest in *The Claim of Reason* that it is skepticism that produces as a reaction to itself the idea of language as essentially conventional. But skepticism, as I have conceived it, is a repudiation

[6]See Wittgenstein, *Investigations*, par. 22, p. 10e.

of the naturalness of language (by means of the power of this naturalness itself), not a theoretical observation about it.

I would expect these dissatisfactions with certain of Fish's remarks
to find various measures of accommodation in further discussion. I
am less confident of this in my study to date of de Man's *Allegories of
Reading*. In this work the claim to philosophical rigor is repeatedly
made, but the work's discourse is one that pretty well, to my ear,
ignores the paradigms of comprehensibility established in Anglo-
American philosophy. Perhaps they should be ignored; it has occurred to me more than once over the years that they should. But I
have said that I remain, instead, in quarrel with them; to that extent
I cannot accept de Man's carelessness of them.

Take his prominent and recurrent invocation of a distinction between the constative and the performative. He sometimes, not always, associates Austin's name with these words, but so far as I understand his sense of what he wants the distinction to do, it contra-
dicts Austin's. A hint of this occurs in his last chapter, when he describes an excuse as a performative utterance on the ground that its
purpose is not to state but to convince.[7] But to say "I convince you"
is not (except by chance) to convince you, and so it is trivially not a
performative utterance. In Austin's more general theory, convincingness and persuasiveness are not illocutionary forces of utterances. They are perhaps the quintessential examples of what is not
illocutionary, since one of Austin's philosophical motives is to deny
that the alternative to stating something is to persuade someone of
something (a motive bearing on what is to be called rhetoric and
specifically on the claim that moral discourse is essentially persua-
sive).[8]

More generally, de Man wishes, I believe, to align the constative-
performative distinction with what he says about distinctions between grammar and rhetoric, or between the intraverbal and the

[7]See Paul de Man, *Allegories of Reading: Figural Language in Rousseau, Nietzsche,
Rilke, and Proust* (New Haven, Conn., 1979), p. 281; all further references to this
work will be included in the text.
[8]A fruitful study and amplification of Austin on speech acts may be found in Ted
Cohen, "Illocution and Perlocution," *Foundations of Language* 9 (1973): 492–503.

extraverbal, or between referentiality and nonreferentiality, or between assertion and action. He appears to take the distinction to turn
on whether a use of language refers to something outside language,
something in the world, and on whether a use of language has some
actual effect on others. But to defeat the idea that constative and
performative utterances differ in their responsibilities, or respon-
siveness, to facts and to distinguish among ways in which words
may have "effects" or "forces" just are Austin's purposes in arguing
against positivism and the later Wittgenstein. Perhaps de Man will
be defended on the ground that he is really denying the distinction,
not endorsing it, or rather really arguing, as he puts it, that there is
an "aporia between performative and constative language" (p. 131).
Then I might offer the following as a parallel argument. Someone
says that the difference between knives and forks is that you cut with
a knife and spear with a fork; a second objects that you can also cut
with a fork and spear with a knife; whereupon a third concludes that
there is an aporia between knives and forks, that there is no stable
distinction we can draw between them. Of course de Man may use
the words "constative" and "performative" for any purpose he defines, and maybe he has; but it must not be assumed that the distinction Austin goes to such lengths to clarify lends clarity to that purpose.

This is something that those who are interested in both Austin
and de Man will work out for themselves. There are much simpler
matters that discourage me from going on to work at what de Man
says. I would like to be able to because I find in his book wonderful
and sympathetic moments of insight, and about the texts he discusses at length it would, I think, be folly to deliver oneself without
considering what he has to say. It is in this spirit that I go on to take
up two of the principal examples he uses in his opening chapter,
"Semiology and Rhetoric," "to illustrate the tension between grammar and rhetoric," a tension which will flower into his theory of reading as deconstruction (p. 9). The examples illustrate that conjunction of grammatical and rhetorical constraints called the rhetorical
question.

The first example is an exceptionally elaborate gag about Archie

Bunker, the character in the popular television series "All in the Family." I cite only the preparatory part of the gag, which is probably unfair and ungrateful of me; but since the gag is meant, I take it, to soften me up, it seems to me worth explaining why it hardens me. De Man writes:

> Asked by his wife whether he wants to have his bowling shoes laced over or laced under, Archie Bunker answers with a question: "What's the difference?" Being a reader of sublime simplicity, his wife replies by patiently explaining the difference between lacing over and lacing under, whatever this may be, but provokes only ire. "What's the difference" did not ask for difference but means instead "I don't give a damn what the difference is." The same grammatical pattern engenders two meanings that are mutually exclusive: the literal meaning asks for the concept (difference) whose existence is denied by the figurative meaning. [p. 9]

To discover one and the same grammatical pattern used for different rhetorical effects was the stock in trade of ordinary language philosophers. (This is to be contrasted with the program of earlier analytical philosophy, associated with the names of Frege and Russell, in which the grammatical pattern of a proposition is shown in certain cases to falsify what was called its logical form.) Wittgenstein, for example, observes that "we could imagine a language in which *all* statements had the form and tone of rhetorical questions," like "Isn't the weather glorious today?," which is grammatically a question but rhetorically a statement.[9] I assume that this is what Austin's constative-performative distinction is about, that certain utterances that are grammatically statements are rhetorically something else. Shall we say that their rhetoric deconstructs their grammar, or is in tension with it, or that their grammatical pattern or their rhetorical function is somehow aberrant? But *why* say so?—as if the grammatical or rhetorical facts should be other than they are. You might as well say it is perverse or aberrant of the normally functioning human hand that it can grasp, and make a fist, and play arpeggios, and shade the eyes, and be held up to bless or to swear. Does one of these possibili-

[9]Wittgenstein, *Investigations*, par. 21, p. 10e.

ties repress or otherwise oppress the others? Or would the idea of a supposed aberrance in using a question for constative purposes, or in using an assertion for performative purposes, better be imaged as like using a fist to play arpeggios? Then it should be cause for amazement that so many people, and so young, with no special history of side-show virtuosity, can negotiate rhetorical questions so smoothly: The question "What's the difference?" evidently requires further analysis, or description. I should think one will want to include considerations along the following lines.

Let us to begin with be sure we remember that there are definite, practical differences between ways of lacing shoes, say between lacing them so that they crisscross and lacing them so that they are parallel. The former might be called lacing over, the latter lacing under. Apart from neatness of appearance, lacing under butts the edges better but takes a longer lace. If Archie knows this difference, then he is saying that he doesn't care how the laces on his bowling shoes are tied (which is a fair-sized assumption), and he is angry because he's being told what he already knows. If he does not know there is a difference, then he is saying that his wife therefore cannot know a difference, tell him a difference that could matter to him, and he is angry that she should think otherwise (which is something like a political position). In neither case does "I don't give a damn what the difference is" seem a fair paraphrase. This form of words is likely to be used either to mean "I'm not interested in the difference" (which in this case may be quite false) or else to mean "The difference won't change my plans" (which would make good sense if, say, Mrs. Bunker were trying to *prevail* on Archie to wear the shoes). And in both cases the rhetorical question remains why he expressed what he meant *this* way. But isn't that what literary critics and theorists have always asked themselves? In the present case, to determine the point of the expression "What's the difference?" we would do well to compare it with expressions such as "Who knows?" "Who cares?" "Who's to say?" "What did I tell you?" "Isn't it awful?" Like them, Archie's question is a hedge against assertion, and like "Isn't the weather glorious?" it is a statement that asks for a response. But while the difference between asking "What's the difference?" and saying, for example, "It doesn't matter" is that the question asks for a response, it may be that Archie at the same time does not want a response from his wife. This would show an ambivalence that many would take as the commonest characteristic of marriage, or of a comic marriage. But that is a fact about some Archie, not about the inevitable relation between grammar and rhetoric. The moral of the example seems to me to be that there is no inevitable relation between them. This seems to me the moral of ordinary language philosophy as well, and of the practice of art. Put it this way: Grammar cannot, or ought not, of itself dictate what you mean, what it is up to you to say.

The second example de Man uses to illustrate the rhetorical question is William Butler Yeats's perhaps too-famous "How can we know the dancer from the dance?" which concludes "Among School Children." De Man says, surely correctly, that this question should not, not simply, be taken as conventionally rhetorical, as if it implied that obviously there is no difference between the dancer and the dance but only an exquisite unity realized; and he goes on to say that taken as literal "How *can* we know . . . ?" urgently denounces, or turns upside down, the error of the rhetorical confidence. But de Man is assuming that what the question "How can we know . . . ?" asks, or means to ask, is how we can tell, tell something apart from something, tell the difference between them. If this were the question here, the literal version would become fairly incomprehensible; it is not clear what would count as literally telling the difference between a dancer and a dance, like asking for the difference between a knife and a cut. This makes the question into a kind of riddle, and certainly an important feature of the question "What's the difference?" is that one of its conventional rhetorical functions is to introduce a riddle. In this function it simultaneously gives great range to the inventiveness of possible answers and places severe conditions on anything that is to count as an answer, for example, that it must be witty. ("What's the difference between a schoolteacher and a railroad conductor?" The teacher trains the mind, the conductor minds the train.) Let us suppose that this piece of rhetoric is irrelevant here.

The cause of taking Yeats's question about knowledge to be asking about telling a difference is evidently that knowing and telling are intimately related epistemological concepts, indeed they share a significant grammatical doubleness: telling something from something either may mean telling things apart that are similar or on a par or it may specify how, by what signs or on what basis, you tell them apart. You can perhaps tell a goldfinch (distinguish it) from a goldcrest, and you can perhaps tell this from (by means of) the tailfeathers. *Knowing* something from something shares this doubleness, but it does not claim to go by differences; to know a hawk from a handsaw you simply have to know what is before your eyes, and from your own experience—it would be suggestive of madness not to know them apart, to take one for the other. But knowing from, in Yeats's line, goes altogether beyond telling. The line asks how we know the dancer from, meaning by means of, the dance; how it is that the dance can reveal the dancer. (If the dance and the dancer were, as it were, the same thing, then this would be no question. As things are, the question is simultaneously one of epistemology and of aesthetics.) But the line equally asks how we can know from, meaning know apart from, the dance; meaning know the dancer *away* from the dance. The doubleness, or ambiguity, persists still here, for who is imagined to be away from the dance, hence to have been dancing—we, or some other? I suppose both. Apart from the other's passion in the dance, the other is no longer transfigured: Is this the one who was there? Apart from my passion in the dance, my perception is no longer transfigured: Who am I (are we) to take such perception as valid? And now we have to consider afresh who or what the dancer is and who or what the dance. If the dance is the poetry, then the dancer is the poet and/or the reader, on the one hand, and, on the other, the world. Here the rhetorical reading courts doubt and despair (there is no reliable connection to or from the dance, hence none with the dancer), but the unrhetorical holds out hope (there must be some ground for our conviction, however shaken, that there is a connection). I suppose one may say that the reading of despair and the reading of hope are denounced by one another or turn one another upside down. But these seem to me overly melodramatic, or may I say overly literary, ways of characterizing what

Yeats's line offers, the enactment of the poise between hope and despair, a fair portrayal of a human life.[10]

The readings seem to me equally allegorical, equally (so far as I
understand the matter) referential and nonreferential, equally consistent, equally partial. I like the sort of move de Man makes when,
noting that Rousseau has had some silly things to say on a subject, he
adds parenthetically that silliness is deeply associated with reference
(see p. 209). I am more partial to this sort of thing from Wittgenstein's *Nachlass*: "Always climb from the heights of cleverness into
the green valleys of silliness." It depends no doubt on what one wants
from reading.

The importance to me of preserving in Yeats's words the asserting
and the questioning of knowing is that I am interested in the possibility of art as a possibility of knowing, or of acknowledging. This
means to me an interest in its confrontation with the threat of skepticism, with the possibility that the world we claim to know is not the
world there is. It may be that the issue of what I call the threat of
skepticism, the threat that perhaps our claims do not, let me say,
penetrate a world of things and of others apart from me, is the issue
de Man is raising in speaking of referentiality. I will just remark here
that the access of skepticism and poetry to one another means to me
that a theory of referentiality or textuality designed to explain, say,
our relation to Wallace Stevens's jar in Tennessee or to Heidegger's
jug in the Black Forest is of no use to me if it fails to explain my
relation to the chipped mug from which I drank my coffee this morn-

[10]I have registered my sense that my criticism of de Man's use of examples may be
unfair and ungrateful; notwithstanding, in one discussion of my remarks I was told,
in effect, that I mistook the spirit of the examples altogether. This is a serious matter.
It may, for example, point to the correct charge against Austin's attack on Ayer in
Sense and Sensibilia which, for all its brilliance in producing and in criticizing examples, seems persistently, even perversely, to miss the drift of the philosophy (say
skepticism) that it attacks. The particular defense of de Man offered me, directed
specifically to the case of Archie Bunker, was that its point just was the joke it prepared
about arché-debunking. But I find (I hope without undue solemnity) that the examples I cite from de Man are cases of inaccuracy, and I am assuming that for a critic to
choose between accuracy and wit is as fateful as for a poet to choose between reason
and rhythm. It gives up the game, or stacks it. I add this observation here as a way of
stating my sense that the underlying subject of what I take criticism to be is the subject
of examples. I suppose it is the underlying subject of what I take philosophy as such
to be.

ing, I mean explain its vulnerability to doubt, or say to imagination. It does not help to picture language as being turned from the world (say troped) unless you know how to picture it as owed to the world and given to it. I do not expect de Man disagrees with this.

Now we are back to what I called the underwriting of Austin and Wittgenstein by Emerson and Thoreau, in their ideas of the nearness to us, hence distance from us, of the world. To accept this underwriting incurs a political liability of a kind I have so far not mentioned. Before recording it, I should make explicit that I have also not mentioned what has struck me as the most obvious tension between the sort of view represented by de Man and that represented in what I do. This is caused by the claim, most familiarly associated with the name of Jacques Derrida and endorsed by de Man, that an appreciation of textuality, of its literariness, or rather of the originariness (or equi-originariness) of its writtenness, constitutes, or requires, a deconstruction of philosophy's bondage to a metaphysics of presence.

Such a claim sets up at once an intimacy and an abyss between the ambitions of the Anglo-American analytical settlement and the new French upheavals. The intimacy is that both define themselves as critiques of metaphysics, which just says that we are all children of Kant. The abyss I might express by saying that the continentals rather regard metaphysics as having come to the wrong conclusions where the Anglo-Americans (so to speak) think of it as having come to nothing at all, nothing philosophical (at least not yet—they may still long for it). A symptom of this intimacy and abyss is Derrida's sense, or intuition, that the bondage to metaphysics is a function of the promotion of something called voice over something called writing; whereas for me it is evident that the reign of repressive philosophical systematizing—sometimes called metaphysics, sometimes called logical analysis—has depended upon the suppression of the human voice. It is as the recovery of this voice (as from an illness) that ordinary language philosophy is, as I have understood and written about it, before all to be understood. I am prepared, or prepared to get prepared, to regard this sorting out of the issue of the voice as a further stage of intellectual adventure, for certainly I do not claim that it is amply clear *why* the procedures of ordinary language philosophy strike me (not me alone, I believe) as functions of voice, nor clear what voice is felt in contrast with; nor do I claim that this function cannot be interpreted as an effect of what might be seen as writing. What I claim is that no such interpretation will be of the right thing from my point of view unless it accounts for the *fact* that the appeal to the ordinary, as an indictment of metaphysics, strikes one, and should strike one, as an appeal to the voice.

In speaking of the point of intellectual adventure, I hope I will be forgiven a certain impatience at being repeatedly told—quite apart from assertions about phonocentrism—that Western metaphysics is a metaphysics of presence, without being told very much, if a word, about how one might usefully understand and responsibly make such a claim. If it is Heidegger from whom this claim has been taken, then I would not know how to assess it apart from some place in a long line of companion assessments, for example, of Heidegger's own enterprise in overcoming metaphysics, represented, say, in his *What Is Called Thinking?*, his effort to replace philosophy by what he calls thinking; and apart from an assessment of any philosophy's efforts to end philosophy, a task in the absence of which I would hardly understand an intellectual enterprise to add up to a work of philosophy; and apart from an assessment of what would constitute understanding Heidegger without a conversion to his way of thinking. Since he stakes his claim to his extraordinary understanding of sentences from Parmenides or Hölderlin or Nietzsche on his authority as a thinker, which means on his being drawn to thinking, which means on his claim to have inherited, for example, those sentences, then presumably we are to claim, if we wish to claim his inheritance, authority as thinkers. (Is this politics, or religion, or pedagogy, or terrorism, or therapy, or perhaps philosophy?) What authority I could claim—or what I claim instead of his inheritance—is the inheritance of Emerson and Thoreau, whose affinity with Heidegger I have elsewhere maintained.

This takes me to the further political liability I said I incur in my acceptance of Emerson and Thoreau, namely, their interpretation of what you might call the politics of philosophical interpretation as a withdrawal or rejection of politics, even of society, as such.

For Emerson and for Thoreau, what requires justification is not the form of philosophical discourse so much as the intention to achieve what you might call philosophical discourse altogether. The perception of the necessity for this justification will force a serious thinker into uncomfortable postures, as for example when Emerson remarks in "Self-Reliance," as he pictures himself going off to write, "Do not tell me, as a good man did to-day, of my obligation to put all poor men in good situations. Are they *my* poor?" Why raise this issue if you have nothing more or better to say about it? Because Emerson has already shown his writing to be something that, so to speak, replaces religion ("I shun father and mother and wife and brother when my genius calls me"), and because it was always the only reason a good man could give for seeking the kingdom of heaven that the poor you have always with you; that is, the knowledge that there is always humanly a reason to postpone salvation. But it is part of Emerson's gesture to claim that his genius is redemptive beyond himself. The implication is that if you are not willing to make such claims for your work, do not call it philosophy. And has he said so little? When he asks whether the poor are his, he is claiming that it is not he who keeps them poor; that is to say, that he would be willing to undergo whatever costs to himself to end their poverty and that going off to write as he does is his best way of contributing to ending it, and first by interpreting it. It is a tremendous claim, expressing tremendous faith in himself. It makes his going off an indictment of his fellow countrymen.

Thoreau's withdrawal is more elaborately dramatized, its rebuke more continuous. In my book on *Walden*, I find that the writer who inhabits it asserts the priority in value of writing over speaking (at least for the present) in order to maintain silence, where this means first of all to withhold his voice, his consent, from his society. Hence the entire book is an act of civil disobedience, a confrontation which takes the form of a withdrawal. But his silence has many forces, as in such a sentence as this: "You only need sit still long enough in some attractive spot in the woods that all its inhabitants may exhibit themselves to you by turns." This is a fair summation of the point of the book as a whole. At the moment I focus on Thoreau's way of saying that reading his book is redemptive. I take it for granted that the scene is one of interpretation, of reading and being read. The inhabitants exhibiting themselves "by turns" means many things, among them of course taking turns (readers come to a book one at a time), and turning pages, and revealing themselves completely (convicting themselves, Thoreau elsewhere describes it); and "by turns" also means by verses (that is, since this is not poetry, by portions) and also by conversions. So the writer's silence (that is, this writer's writing) declares itself redemptive religiously, aesthetically, and politically.

For most of us, I believe, the idea of redemption or redemptive reading and interpretation will not be credible apart from a plausible model or picture of how a text can be therapeutic, that is, apart from an idea of the redemptive as psychological. (Here Fish's admirable essay in *Is There a Text in This Class?*, "Literature in the Reader: Affective Stylistics," and the first chapter of his *Self-Consuming Artifacts*, "The Aesthetic of the Good Physician," are exactly to the point. I find a therapeutic wish in de Man as well, though he might not appreciate the description.) I will conclude these remarks by racing through a sketch of what I think such a picture would have to look like. (Of all the problems that beckon and seem to me worth following from the sketch, the one that is perhaps paramount in terms of my work on skepticism that I have mentioned—the work for which the transcendentalists underwrite the ordinary language philosophers—is one I only mention here, namely, why or how the same silence, or rather the stillness of the text, the achievement of which perhaps constitutes textuality, or a text's self-containedness, should be interpretable politically as rebuke and confrontation and be interpretable epistemologically as the withholding of assertion, on which I have found the defeat of skepticism, and of whatever metaphysics is designed to overcome skepticism, to depend—as if the withholding of assertion, the containing of the voice, amounts to the forgoing of domination. Of course there are withholdings that are manipulative. These are not silent. I expect this process will come to an understanding of philosophy's own involvement in therapy, one of its obligations that Plato did not banish from his republic. This understanding would be required of someone who has been helped as much as I have by Wittgenstein, who speaks of his methods not as bringing solutions to problems but as treatments of them, like therapies, for whom accordingly philosophy is always a recovery from, and of, itself. My thought here is that this conceives of philosophy as a kind of reading.)

I imagine that the credible psychological model of redemption will have to be psychoanalytic in character; yet psychoanalytic interpretations of texts have seemed typically to tell us something we more or less already knew, to leave us pretty much where we were before we read. It ought to help to see that from the point of view of psychoanalytic therapy the situation of reading has typically been turned around, that it is not first of all the text that is subject to interpretation but we in the gaze or hearing of the text. I think good readers, or a certain kind of reader, have always known and acted on this, as in Thoreau's picture of reading by exposure to being read. But it is my impression that those who emphasize the psychoanalytic possibilities here tend to forget what a text is, the matter of its autonomy; while those who shun psychoanalysis tend not to offer a practice of reading that I can understand as having the consequence of therapy.

The practice suggested to me by turning the picture of interpreting a text into one of being interpreted by it would I think be guided by three principal ideas: first, access to the text is provided not by the mechanism of projection but by that of transference (which is why the accusation that in one's extended interpretations one is turning a work of art into a Rorschach test is desperately wrong but precisely significant and deserving of careful response); second, the pleasures of appreciation are succeeded by the risks of seduction; and third, the risks are worth running because the goal of the encounter is not consummation but freedom. Freedom from what, to do what? In the picture of psychoanalytic therapy, casting ourselves as its patient, its sufferer, its victim (according to the likes of Emerson and of Heidegger, this is the true form of philosophical thinking), the goal is freedom from the person of the author. (So we might see our model in Emerson's "Divinity School Address," which seeks to free us from our attachment to the person of the one who brings the message, an attachment in effect according to Emerson, of idolatry. So what I am producing here, or proposing, might be thought of as a theology of reading.) Presumably we would not require a therapy whose structure partakes of seduction, to undo seduction, unless we were already seduced. (I imagine that reading, so motivated, will not readily lend itself to classroom instruction. Would this be because of the nature of teaching or because of the nature of classrooms?)

But what is a text that it has this power of overcoming the person of its author? We can learn this, many of us have been forever saying, only by letting ourselves be instructed by texts we care about. For someone who thinks this way, there lies in wait what you might call the paradox of reading: I was just saying in effect that you cannot understand a text before you know what the text says about itself; but obviously you cannot understand what the text says about itself before you understand the text. One way of investigating this is to ask whether "before" bears meaning in this formulation, and if not, whether there is a paradox here. Another is to say that what you really want to know is what a text knows about itself, because you cannot know more than it does about this; and then to ask what the fantasy is of the text's knowledge of itself.

The sentence I cited from *Walden* about sitting still long enough knows, for example, all about the seductions of this writing—its writer is sitting still, maintaining silence, in what he calls an "*attractive* spot in the woods" ("woods" being one of his words for "words," hence for his book, and [hence] for America). The text he is producing, for our conversion, is based, along with some other things, on an equation between morning (as dawning) and mourning (as grieving). The general idea is that we crave change (say therapy) but we are appalled by the prospect; that in our capacity for loss there is the chance of ecstasy. What bears here on the idea of a text as therapeutic is the structure of what I call in my book on *Walden* its "immense repetitiveness," something you might think of as a capacity for bore-

dom, which I say Thoreau learned from the Old Testament proph-
ets, together with his notation of endless detail. Now the repetition
of each fact in one's attachment to an object gone, an effort to undo
or release the ties of association strand by strand, is part of the work
of realization of loss that Freud and principally after him Melanie
Klein recognize as the work of mourning. They call it reality-testing,
a subjection to the verdict of reality that one's attachment to an object
is to undergo severing. For *Walden*'s writer I understand the morning of mourning, the dawning of grieving, to be the proposed alternative, the only alternative, to what he calls "our present constitution," which he says must end. He means our political constitution,
with its slaves, but he means more than this; he means what permits
this constitution in our souls. He means that mourning is the only
alternative to our nostalgias, in which we will otherwise despair and
die. He completes the building of his house by showing how to leave
it.

Listen again to the book's parting line: "The sun is but a morning
star." Surely this means that our prospects are brighter than we
know. But this must be taken as part of the news that the sun is a
grieving star, presiding over a world of mourning, in which we are in
mourning for the loss of the earth and for the loss of the sun's old
cosmic station. It is an image of skepticism. (This is reinforced by
the old pun of "sun" with "Son," which in this context signifies an
identification, or confusion, of Christ with Lucifer, as though we
still have not grasped the difference between heaven and hell.) If the
sun is an old symbol of the metaphysics of presence, of a concentric
centeredness of our orienting polarities (say between heaven and
earth, and past and present, and culture and nature), an American is
apt to be perplexed in being told that this metaphysics is to be undone, since he or she will conceive of literature and philosophy as
having begun with the knowledge and the tasks of its passing. If
deconstruction, as in de Man's recommendation of it, is to disillusion us, it is a noble promise and to be given welcome. Disillusion is
what fits us for reality, whether in Plato's terms or D. W. Winnicott's.
But then we must be assured that this promise is based on a true
knowledge of what our illusions are.

POSTSCRIPT: A REPLY TO GAYATRI SPIVAK

In taking me to task, Gayatri Spivak sketches what she calls "arguments" that she courteously says I "undoubtedly can anticipate" (p. 353).[11] I understand this as an invitation to say why, if I can, even did, anticipate them, I left myself unguarded with respect to them. I cannot now accept this invitation, so I submit this note of regret.

To leave myself in certain moments unguarded I can see as habitual with me, even a point of honor. In the present case I thought I had been guarded enough in, for example, my closing sentences. In pairing the names of Plato and D. W. Winnicott on the concept of disillusion, I was counting on getting a little credit, not exactly for a worthwhile joke (Spivak is certainly right to take the pairing seriously) but for a juxtaposition surprising enough to make us question what the concept of illusion is that it should be fundamental in the thought of figures so removed (it seems) from one another. So that when, in my final sentence, I say "we must be assured that this promise [of deconstruction, to disillusion us] is based on a true knowledge of what our illusions are," I was counting on being taken to put first, in investigating what our illusions are, the investigation of what our concept of an illusion is, what the uses of this word come to.—Why not just say so?

Here are some reasons. I am—I suppose we all are—always looking for ways to distrust words, and entrust them, further than we normally are prepared to do. Skepticism, and its ordinary language critics, in my view of them, live essentially on nothing else than these investments and withdrawals. I have learned from the prose of Austin and Wittgenstein and Emerson and Thoreau certain uses of devices like "what you may call" or "let us say" or "so to speak"; but even I get to feeling that they can be used only so many times. For all I know, the idea of using a word "under erasure" is applicable here. But for my purposes every word (just about) would have to occur so. For example, as in the teaching of Austin and Wittgenstein, when philosophers have said such things as "we do not know with certainty

[11]Page references to Spivak and to my original paper are to *The Politics of Interpretation*, ed. W. J. T. Mitchell (University of Chicago Press, 1983); references to my paper are to its occurence above.

that there are things like tables and chairs because we do not really or literally see them but only see appearances or parts of them," they have, unknown to themselves, removed the words "parts" and "appearances" and "see" and "literally" and "things" and "like" and "know" and "certainty" and "really" from their ordinary uses; they have modified their uses so to speak. But if modified, do they mean what they appear to say? Shall we say that those words are all occurring under erasure? (It used to be said that they are occurring in a philosophical language game. Naturally unspecified.) It has occurred to some people that a fitting way to do justice to one's impatience with the words at hand is to realize the idea of erasing all one's words by leaving one's pages blank (just about). This appeals to me. But not enough.

Again, I want the joke because I do not believe that any given theory has the key to our disillusionment, and I felt it a shortcoming of Paul de Man's practice that it seemed (to me) to claim to possess such a thing. Moreover, I felt I had implied this reservation in preempting the word "illusion" early in my paper to refer to one of Wittgenstein's perceptions of our philosophical attachments to theory, a perception of us as inhabiting structures of air (see p. 30).

Something similar should be said about Spivak's remark that "it is not surprising that . . . the one sense of 'turn' . . . that Cavell does not (cannot?) mention is 'trope,' the irreducible turn of figuration that is the condition of (im)possibility of any redemption of voice" (p. 354). I had earlier (p. 48) preempted the word "trope" as follows: "It does not help to picture language as being turned from the world (say troped) unless you know how to picture it as owed to the world and given to it." The point of preempting this concept was to register my dissatisfaction with the theories of figuration I am familiar with. In that context I was suggesting that, for example, the difference between describing something as in waking life and as in dreams (or "literature"?) may be a difference that is a function of voice but is not a difference that is a function of figuration. In the context Spivak cites, where I am reading a sentence of Thoreau's, the absence of the concept of trope signifies that my exhibiting of myself, or betraying of myself, leaving myself unguarded, by turns before the silence of the therapeutic text, is not taken by me to be a function necessarily of my expressing myself figuratively. Again, Thoreau's sentence about sitting quietly in some attractive spot in the woods is not, in my view of metaphor, metaphorical, because it has an ordinary literal realization. No account of its figuration could be right which did not account for that feature of it. (Perhaps such a consideration is irrelevant to Spivak's speaking of figuration. Then that would be part of my difficulty in understanding what she is saying about it.)

When I say that "it is as the recovery of (the human) voice (as from an illness) that ordinary language philosophy is, as I have understood and written about it, before all to be understood" (p. 48), I am not talking about all recoveries or all nostalgias of all voices. No doubt some claims made on behalf of the voice are themselves part of the illness (of subservience, of unctuousness) from which I have sought recovery. What I was describing was the sense of defending and pursuing ordinary language philosophy on the only ground on which there was (while there was) anyone close enough to it, intimately hostile enough, to require defending it against. This was in practice other analytical philosophers, those for whom Frege's and Russell's visions of a perfect language set out their philosophical hopes. And this perfect language was dominating of what was felt as philosophical Reason, and it was essentially intolerant of voice; it was a discovery of writing. As a development within one strand of the present of philosophy it will have consequences for philosophy as a human enterprise, but they remain unassessed. That they are related to recent discussions of writing I do not doubt; what it would look like to specify the relations I do not know.

Spivak's instruction that "to predicate reality as the death of illusion is to ignore the syntax or practice that passes from illusion to reality via dis-illusion" (p. 353) seems to me, to the extent that I understand it, to be traversing mutually important and fairly familiar ground. I take it to be the burden of Austin's excruciatingly painstaking effort to "dismantle," among other things, the so-called Argument from Illusion in his *Sense and Sensibilia* (Oxford, 1962). ("Dismantle" is Austin's word for what he is doing, in the last sentences of the book.) Austin was so much on my mind as I wrote the

paper in question that I perhaps took this too much for granted.
Spivak says: "Not to acknowledge that deconstruction distinguishes
itself from dialectics precisely by this attention to the syntax that is
otherwise ignored in the interest of the semantics of reality is not to
speak of deconstruction at all" (p. 353). I do not know about this; I
am not in a position to speak in these ways; my paper is about what
you may call this inability, even a beginning effort to assess it. Something I am certain of is that I had no intention of providing a "reading
of deconstruction" and no wish to "convince" anyone of such a thing.

I think it expresses my inabilities and my prospects here that when
I read Spivak's phrase "the semantics of reality" I thought of the
following passage from *Sense and Sensibilia*: "Many philosophers,
failing to detect any ordinary quality common to real ducks, real
cream, and real progress, have decided that Reality must be an *a
priori* concept apprehended by reason alone" (p. 64). And her speaking of "syntax that is otherwise ignored" reminded me of Austin's
passage a little further on: "Next, 'real' is what we may call a *trouser-
word*. It is usually thought . . . that what one might call the affirma-
tive use of a term is basic. . . . But with 'real' . . . it is the *negative*
use that wears the trousers. That is, a definite sense attaches to the
assertion that something is real, a real such-and-such, only in the
light of a specific way in which it might be, or might have been, *not*
real" (p. 70). (I do not know whether the imagery of trousers in this
passage requires an apology. I mean I do not know whether someone
will take offense and, if so, whether an apology would be accepted.
Such are the hazards of the politics of superficiality.)

Would it make sense to say here that Austin's "syntactic" attention
is, or is not, ignored in the interest of his "semantic" interest? If it
would not make sense, is he free, or not free, of "this ideological
requirement"? It may be an ideological matter, or attitude, that prevents me from understanding our misunderstandings here as ideological—as opposed, at any rate, to attributing them to impatience,
to neurosis, to vanity, to Wittgensteinian bewitchment, or to some
further set of cultural differences. (Any term of criticism may, none
need, be taken personally.) Suppose it is true, and significant about
the American "style of thought," that it has lacked the concept of

ideology, an idea Spivak cites approvingly on p. 347. Is this like lacking thirteenth-century cathedrals (also true, and significant, of American culture), or like lacking churches of any kind, or like lacking the concept of religion altogether? In the last case you may have a theory of human culture that tells you this is impossible, in which case one tack for you to take would be to look for what concepts "(do) duty" for the absent concept. I think a related cultural difference between American and European intellectual life is that the American (with isolated exceptions) has no sacred intellectual texts, none whose authority the intellectual community at large is anxious to preserve at all costs—no Marxian texts, no Freudian, no Hegelian, no Deweyan, and so forth. Every text stands at the level of professional journal articles, open for disposal. (I am not considering the Declaration of Independence as a candidate for such a text.) If the concept of ideology depends for its usefulness on its functioning with such favored texts, then its absence in American intellectual life would be explained by the absence of such texts, I mean texts so conceived. Since my paper rather deplores the absence of Emersonian and Thoreauvian texts as something like sacred common possessions, I should add here that this absence is not wholly, or just, deplorable. But it surely makes for drastic barriers to communication, both within American intellectual life and between American and European thinkers.

The last sentences of my paper toy with issues of illusion and reality of the sort cited by Spivak and Austin, but they do not address them, as though the time for addressing them has passed or not yet arrived again. The issue on my mind, thinking of de Man's book, was something else, namely, how to accept a therapy of disillusion (or of dismantling) without succumbing to disillusionment, I mean disillusionment as an attitude, something between discouragement and cynicism. (If we see that politics has been one cure for this, and philosophy another, then we should equally see that they have both, or their degradations have, been causes of it too.) It is in part to refuse this attitude, or refuse it as an attitude (as an ideology, may I say?), that I used old-fashioned phrases of encouragement like "noble promise" and "be given welcome."

◆

CORIOLANUS AND
INTERPRETATIONS OF POLITICS
("Who does the wolf love?")

◆

A version of the following essay was prepared and distributed at the invitation of Professor Janet Adelman, as one of a number of papers by different hands for discussion at a study group she was organizing for the Shakespeare Congress held at Stratford-upon-Avon in the summer of 1981. I was unable to attend the Congress and participate in its discussion, but I did profit, more than my several footnotes may indicate, from the discussion of the paper when it was delivered as part of a colloquium on Coriolanus *at The Humanities Institute during its meetings at Stanford University, September 10–12, 1982. This version is printed in* Representations, *Fall 1983. The postscript is delivered here for the first time.*

◊

Something that draws me to *Coriolanus* is its apparent disdain of questions I have previously asked of Shakespearean tragedy, taking tragedy as an epistemological problem, a refusal to know or to be known, an avoidance of acknowledgment, an expression (or imitation) of skepticism. Coriolanus's refusal to acknowledge his participation in finite human existence may seem so obviously the fact of the matter of his play that to note it seems merely to describe the play, not at all to interpret it. It may be, however, that this lack of theoretical grip itself proposes a moral, or offers a conclusion, namely that *Coriolanus* is not exactly to be understood as a tragedy, that its mystery—supposing one agrees to something like a mystery in its events—will be located only in locating its lack or missing of tragedy, hence its closeness to tragedy.

But systematically to pursue this possibility would require—from me—following out a sense that this play presents a particular interpretation of the problem of skepticism as such (skepticism directed toward our knowledge of the existence of others), in particular an interpretation that takes skepticism as a form of narcissism. This interpretation does not in itself come to me as a complete surprise since a book I published a few years ago—*The Claim of Reason*—begins with an interpretation of Wittgenstein's *Philosophical Investigations* which takes his move against the idea of a private language (an idea which arises in his struggle against skepticism) as a move against a kind of narcissism, a kind of denial of an existence shared with others; and my book ends with a reading of *Othello* as a depiction of the murderous lengths to which narcissism must go in order to maintain its picture of itself as skepticism, in order to maintain its stand of ignorance, its fear or avoidance of knowing, under the color of a claim to certainty.[1] What surprised me more in *Coriolanus* was its understanding of narcissism as another face of incestuousness, and of this condition as one in which language breaks down under the sense of becoming incomprehensible, of the sense of oneself as having lost the power of expression, what I call in *The Claim of Reason* the terror of inexpressiveness; together with the thoroughness with which Narcissus's fate is mirrored in the figure of Coriolanus, a figure whose every act is, by that act, done to him so perfectly that the distinction between action and passion seems to lose its sense, a condition in which human existence becomes precarious, if perhaps transcendable. I mention these connections with the philosophical issue of skepticism not because I pursue them further in the essay to follow but only to attest my conviction that a work such as a play of Shakespeare's cannot contribute the help I want from it for the philosophical issues I mention, unless the play is granted the autonomy

---

[1]*The Claim of Reason* (New York and Oxford, 1979). The subject was broached in "The Avoidance of Love: A Reading of *King Lear*" in *Must We Mean What We Say?*, reprinted Cambridge, England, 1976.

it is one's power to grant, which means, seen in its own terms. What does this mean? What is a play of Shakespeare's? I will try to say something about these questions.

Something else also draws me. The way I have been understanding the conflicts the play engenders keeps sending me back over paths of thought that I believe many critics have found to be depleted of interest, or conviction; three paths, or branches of paths, in particular: (1) those that look in a Shakespearean play for something like an idea of theater, as it were for the play's concept of itself; (2) those that sense Christian stirrings and murmurings under the surface of the words; and (3) even those paths of thought that anticipate something you might call the origins of tragedy in religious ritual. I am, I suppose, as drawn to critical paths that others find empty as some poets are to words that others find flat. But to say fully why one is drawn to a work, and its work of interpretation, can only be the goal of an interpretation; and the motive of an interpretation, like what one might call the intention of the work it seeks, exists fully only in its satisfaction.

I expect, initially, general agreement on two facts about *Coriolanus*. First, compared with other Shakespearean tragedies this one lacks what A. C. Bradley called "atmosphere" (in his British Academy Lecture on the play, the decade after his *Shakespearean Tragedy*). Its language, like its hero, keeps aloof from our attention, as withdrawn, austere, as its rage and its contempt permit. Second, the play is about the organization of the body politic and about how that body is fed, that is, sustained. I expect, further, that readers from opposed camps should be willing to see that the play lends itself equally, or anyway naturally, to psychological and to political readings: both perspectives are, for example, interested in who produces food and in how food is distributed and paid for. From a psychological perspective (in practice this has in recent years been psychoanalytic) the play directs us to an interest in the development of Coriolanus's character. From a political perspective the play directs us to an interest in whether the patricians or the plebeians are right in their conflict and in whether, granted that Coriolanus is unsuited for po-

litical leadership, it is his childishness or his very nobility that un-
suits him.

In the critical discussions I have read so far, the psychoanalytic
perspective has produced more interesting readings than the political. A political reading is apt to become fairly predictable once you
know whose side the reader is taking, that of the patricians or that of
the plebeians; and whose side the reader takes may come down to
how he or she sees Menenius's fable of the organic state, the Fable of
the Belly, and upon whom he or she places the blame for Coriolanus's
banishment. If few will consider it realistic to suppose that Coriolanus would have made a good political leader, fewer will deny that
in losing him the city has lost its greatest hero and that this loss is the
expression of a time of crisis in the state. It is a time of famine in
which the call for revolt is made moot by the threat and the fact of
war and invasion, followed by a time in which victory in the war, and
bitterness over its conduct, creates the call for counter-revolt by the
state's defender and preserver. In such a period of crisis everyone
and no one has good arguments, everyone and no one has right on
their side. In Aufidius's great description of Coriolanus at the end of
Act IV he summarizes as follows:

So our virtues

Lie in th'interpretation of the time; . . .
One fire drives out one fire; one nail, one nail;
Rights by rights founder, strengths by strengths do fail.

One might say that just this division of fire and right is the tragedy,
but would that description account for the particular turns of just
these events, as distinct from the losses and ironies in any revolutionary situation? Even the most compelling political interpretation—
in my experience this is given in Bertolt Brecht's discussion with
members of his theater company of the opening scene of the play[2]—
seems to have little further to add, in the way of interpretation, once
it makes clear that choosing the side of the plebeians is dramatically

[2]See Bertolt Brecht, *Collected Plays,* vol. 9, edited by Ralph Manheim and John
Willett (New York, 1973), pp. 378–94.

and textually viable. This is no small matter. It shows that Shakespeare's text—or what we think of as Shakespeare's humanity—leaves ample room for distinctions among the "clusters" of citizens, and it shows the weight of their common position in opposition to that of the patricians. And I take this in turn to show that the politics of the play is essentially the politics of a given production, so that we should not expect its political issues to be settled by an interpretation of what you might call "the text itself."

Exactly the power of Brecht's discussion can be said to be its success in getting us *not* to interpret, not, above all, to interpret food, but to stay with the opening fact of the play, the fact that the citizens of Rome are in revolt because there is a famine (and because of their interpretation of the famine). They and their families are starving and they believe (correctly, for all we know) that the patricians are hoarding grain. Not to interpret this means, in practical or theatrical terms, that we come to see that this cluster is of human beings, individual human beings, who work at particular trades and who live in particular places where specific people await news of the outcome of their dangerous course in taking up arms. This fact of their ordinary humanity is the most impressive fact that can be set against the patricians' scorn of them—a fact that ought not to be visible solely to a Marxist, a fact that shows up the language of the leaders as mysterious and evasive, as subject to what one may think of as the politics of interpretation.

Yet we also feel that the pervasive images of food and hunger, of cannibalism and of disgust, do mean something, that they call upon us for some lines of interpretation, and that the value of attending to this particular play is a function of the value to individual human beings of tracing these lines.

Psychoanalysts naturally have focused on the images of food and feeding that link Coriolanus and his mother. In a recent essay, " 'Anger's My Meat': Feeding, Dependency, and Aggression in *Coriolanus*,"[3] Professor Janet Adelman has given so clear and fair an account of some two decades of psychoanalytic interpretations of food

[3] In *Representing Shakespeare*, edited by Murray Schwartz and Coppelia Kahn (Baltimore, 1980).

and feeding in the play, in the course of working out her further contributions, that I feel free to pick and choose the lines and moments bearing on this aspect of things that serve my somewhat different emphases.

Twice Volumnia invokes nursing. Early she says to Virgilia, rebuking her for worrying about her husband:

> The breasts of Hecuba
> When she did suckle Hector, looked not lovelier
> Than Hector's forehead when it spit forth blood
> At Grecian sword, contemning.
>
> (I.iii.43–46)

And in her first intercession with her son:

> Do as thou list.
> Thy valiantness was mine, thou suck'st it from me,
> But owe thy pride thyself.
>
> (III.ii.127–29)

Both invocations lead one to think what it is this son learned at his mother's breast, what it is he was fed with, particularly as we come to realize that both mother and son declare themselves to be starving. It is after Coriolanus's departure upon being banished, when Menenius asks Volumnia if she'll sup with him, that she comes out with

> Anger's my meat; I sup upon myself
> And so shall starve with feeding.
>
> (IV.ii.50–51)

As Coriolanus mocks and resists the ritual of asking for the people's voices, his being keeps revolting, one time as follows:

> Better it is to die, better to starve,
> Than crave the hire which first we do deserve.
>
> (II.iii.118–19)

I say that mother and son, both of them, *are* starving, and I mean throughout, always, not just when they have occasion to say so. I take Volumnia's vision of supping upon herself not to be a picture simply of her local anger but of self-consuming anger as the presiding passion of her life—the primary thing, accordingly, she would have to teach her son, the thing he sucked from her, of course under the name of valiantness. If so, then if Volumnia and hence Coriolanus are taken to exemplify a Roman identification of virtue as valor, they should further be taken as identifying valor with an access to one's anger. It is "in anger, Juno-like," godlike, that Volumnia laments (IV.ii.52–53); and it is this anger that the Tribune Sicinius is remarking as, in trying to avoid being confronted by her, he says, "They say she's mad" (IV.ii.9). Along these lines, I emphasize Coriolanus's statement about deserving rather than craving not as

> Better it is to *die*, better to *starve*,
> Than crave . . .

as if he is asserting the rightness of a particular choice for the future; but as

> *Better* it is to die, *better* to starve,
> Than crave . . .

as if he is reaffirming or confessing his settled form of (inner) life. I expect that the former is the more usual way of emphasis, but I find it prejudicial.

Coriolanus and Volumnia are—I am taking it—starvers, hungerers. They manifest this condition as a name or a definition of the human, like being mortal. And they manifest this as a condition of insatiability (starving by feeding, feeding as deprivation). It is a condition sometimes described as the infiniteness of desire, imposing upon the finiteness of the body. But starving for Volumnia and her son suggests that this infiniteness is not the cause of human insatiability but is rather its effect. It is the effect not of an endless quantity, as though the self had, or is, endless reserves of desire; but of an endless structure, as though desire has a structure of endlessness. One picture of this structure is given by Narcissus for whom what is longed for is someone longing, who figures beauty as longing. Starv-

ing by feeding presents itself to Coriolanus as being consumed by
hunger, and his words for hungering are desiring and craving. And
what he incessantly hungers for is . . . not to hunger, not to desire,
that is, not to be mortal. Take the scene of interview by the people:

> CORIOLANUS: You know the cause, sir, of my standing here.
> THIRD CITIZEN: We do, sir; tell us what hath brought you to't.
> CORIOLANUS: Mine own desert.
> SECOND CITIZEN: Your own desert?
> CORIOLANUS: Ay, not mine own desire.
> THIRD CITIZEN: How not your own desire?
>
> (II.iii.66–72)

If you desire to be desireless, is there something you desire? If so,
how would you express it; that is, tell it; that is, ask for it? Coriolanus's answer to this paradox is to become perfectly deserving. Since
to hunger is to want, to lack something, he hungers to lack nothing,
to be complete, like a sword. My speculations here are an effort to do
justice to one's sense of Coriolanus as responding not primarily to his
situation with the plebeians, as if trapped by an uncontrollable disdain; but as responding primarily to his situation with himself, as
befits a Narcissus, trapped first by an uncontrollable logic. While I
will come to agree with Plutarch's early observation or diagnosis in
his *Life of Caius Martius Coriolanus* that Coriolanus is "altogether
unfit for any man's conversation," I am in effect taking this to mean
not that he speaks in anger and contempt (anger and contempt are
not unjustifiable) but that while under certain circumstances he can
express satisfaction, he cannot express desire and to this extent cannot speak at all: the case is not that he will not ask for what he wants
but rather that he can want nothing that he asks. His solution
amounts, as both patricians and plebeians more or less note, to becoming a god. What god? We have to get to this.

Let us for the moment continue developing the paradox of hungering. To be consumed by hunger, to feed upon oneself, must present itself equally as being fed upon, being eaten up. (To feed means
both to give and to take nourishment, as to suckle means both to give

and to take the breast.) So the other fact of Coriolanus's and Volumnia's way of starving, of their hunger, is their sense of being cannibalized.[4]

The idea of cannibalization runs throughout the play. It is epitomized in the title question I have given to these remarks: "Who does the wolf love?" Menenius asks this of the Tribunes of the people at the opening of Act II. One of them answers, with undeniable truth: "The lamb." And Menenius, ever the interpretative fabulist, answers: "Ay, to devour him, as the hungry plebeians would the noble Marcius." The other Tribune's answer—"He's a lamb, indeed, that baas like a bear"—does not unambiguously deny Menenius's interpretation. The shock of the interpretation is of course that it is from the beginning the people, not the patricians, and least of all Coriolanus, who are presented as lambs, anyway as food for patrician wolves. In Menenius's opening effort to talk the people out of revolt he declares that "The helms o' the state . . . care for you like fathers," to which the First Citizen replies "Care for us! . . . If the wars eat us not up, they will; and there is all the love they bear us." This fantasy is borne out when the general Cominius speaks of Coriolanus's coming to battle as to a feast (I.ix.10). And the idea of the warrior Coriolanus feeding on a weaker species may be raised again in the battle at Corioli in his threat to any soldier who holds back, "I'll take him for a Volsce / And he shall feel mine edge," allowing the suggestion of his sword as a piece of cutlery. The idea of an ungovernable voraciousness is furthered by Volumnia's association of her son with his son's tearing apart a butterfly with his teeth. On the other hand, when Coriolanus offers himself to Aufidius at Antium he expresses his sense of having been devoured, with only the name Caius Marcius Coriolanus remaining, devoured by "the cruelty and envy of the people" (IV.v.77–78). And Menenius, whose sense of justice is constricted, among other things by his fear of civil disorder, is accurate in his fears, in the consequences they prophesy for Rome, and he will repeat his vision of civil cannibalism:

[4]"There seems to be some question whether one's knowing oneself is something active, something one does . . . or rather something one suffers, something that happens to one . . . ." *The Claim of Reason*, p. 352.

> Now the good gods forbid
> That our renowned Rome, whose gratitude
> Towards her deserved children is enrolled
> In Jove's own book, like an unnatural dam
> Should now eat up her own.
>
> (III.i.288–92)

All readers of this aspect of the play will recognize in this description of Rome as potentially a cannibalistic mother an allusion to Volumnia; and the identification of Volumnia and Rome is enforced in other ways, not least by Volumnia herself when in the second and final intercession scene she says to her son:

> . . . thou shalt no sooner
> March to assault thy country than to tread
> (Trust to't, thou shalt not) on thy mother's womb
> That brought thee to this world.
>
> (V.iii.121–24)

It is very much to the point to notice that in Menenius's vision of Rome as an "unnatural dam" an identity is proposed between a mother eating her child and a mother eating herself: if Rome eats up all Romans there is no more Rome, for as one of the Tribunes asks, "What is the city but the people?" (III.i.198).

The paradox and reciprocity of hungering may be found registered in the question "Who does the wolf love?" If the question is asking for the object of the wolf's affection, the more nearly correct grammar would seem to be: "Whom does the wolf love?"[5] But this correctness (call it a patrician correctness, a refinement in which the plebeians apparently do not see the good) would rule out taking the question also in its opposite direction, grammatically strict as it stands, namely as asking whose object of affection the wolf is. (Who does love the wolf?) The answer given directly, "The lamb," does not rule out either direction, but as the ensuing discussion demonstrates, the direction will be a function of what or who you take the

[5]A point emphasized by the chairman of the *Coriolanus* panel at the Stanford meetings, Professor Harry Berger, in his remarks introducing my paper.

lamb to be, hence what the wolf. Both directions, the active and the passive constructions of the play's focal verbs, are operative throughout the action. I have mentioned this explicitly in the cases of feeding and suckling. But it is, I find, true less conspicuously, but pertinently, in such an odd moment as this:

> CORIOLANUS: Let them hang.
> VOLUMNIA: Ay, and burn too.
> > (III.ii.23–24)

One of the functions in providing Volumnia with this amplification here strikes me as suggesting her sense of the inevitable reflexiveness of action in their Rome: are hanging and burning actions done to someone, or something "they" are, or will be, doing?

The circle of cannibalism, of the eater eaten by what he or she eats, keeps being sketched out, from the first to the last. You might call this the identification of narcissism as cannibalism. From the first: at the end of Coriolanus's first long speech he says to the citizens:

> You cry against the noble Senate, who
> (Under the gods) keep you in awe, which else
> Would feed on one another.
> > (I.i.187–89)

And at the last: Rome devouring itself is the idea covered in the obsessive images of Coriolanus burning Rome. It was A. C. Bradley again who at the end of his British Academy Lecture pointed up the sudden and relentless harping, principally after the banishment, on the image of fire, of Rome burning. Bradley makes nothing further of the point but it is worth noting, in view of the theme of starving and cannibalism, that fire in this play is imagined under the description of it as *consuming* what it burns.

You may say that burning as a form of revenge is Coriolanus's projection onto Rome of what he felt Rome was doing to him. This cannot be wrong, but it so far pictures Coriolanus, in his revenge, to be essentially a man like Aufidius, merely getting even; the picture requires refining. Suppose that, as I believe, in Coriolanus's famous sentence of farewell, "I banish you!" (III.iii.123), he has already begun a process of consuming Rome, incorporating it, becoming it. Then when the general Cominius tried in vain to plead with him to save Rome, and found him to be "sitting in gold, his eye / Red as 'twould burn Rome" (V.i.63–64), he somewhat misunderstood what he saw. He took Coriolanus to be contemplating something in the future whereas Coriolanus's eye was red with the present flames of self-consuming. Consuming the literal Rome with literal fire would accordingly only have been an expression of that self-consuming. Thus would the city understand what it had done to itself. He will give it—horribly—what it deserves. Thus is the play of revenge further interpreted.

These various understandings of cannibalism all illustrate the ancient sentiment that man is wolf to man. (The Roman Plautus, to whom Shakespeare is famously indebted, is credited with being the earliest nameable framer of the sentiment. A pertinent modern instance occurs in Brecht's *Threepenny Opera*.) But the question "Who does the wolf love?" has two further reaches which we must eventually consider. First, there is the repetition of the idea that devouring can be an expression of love. Second, if, as I think, there is reason here to take the image of the wolf as the figure of the mythical animal identified with Rome, the one who suckled the founders of Rome (Volumnia is the reason), there is reason to take the lamb it is said to love (or that loves it) as the mythical animal identified with Christ.

Before this, I should make explicit a certain way in which the account of Coriolanus's motivation I have been driving at is somewhat at odds with the direction of psychoanalytic interpretation summarized and extended by Janet Adelman.[6] She understands Coriolanus's attempt to make himself inhumanly independent as a defense against his horror of dependence, and his rage as converting his wish to be dependent against those who render him so. A characteristic turn of her argument consists of a reading of some lines I have already had occasion to quote:

[6] In the essay cited in note 3.

> The breasts of Hecuba
> When she did suckle Hector, look'd not lovelier
> Than Hector's forehead when it spit forth blood
> At Grecian sword, contemning.

Adelman reads as follows:

Blood is more beautiful than milk, the wound than the breast, warfare than peaceful feeding. . . . Hector is transformed immediately from infantile feeding mouth to bleeding wound. For the unspoken mediator between breast and wound is the infant's mouth: in this imagistic transformation, to feed is to be wounded; the mouth becomes the wound, the breast the sword. . . . But at the same time as Volumnia's image suggests the vulnerability inherent in feeding, it also suggests a way to fend off that vulnerability. In her image, feeding, incorporating, is transformed into spitting out, an aggressive expelling; the wound once again becomes the mouth that spits. . . . The wound spitting blood thus becomes not a sign of vulnerability but an instrument of attack. (p. 131)

This is very fine and it must not be denied. But the transformation of Hector's mouth into a wound must not in turn deny two further features of these difficult lines. First, when Hector contemns Grecian swords, he is also to be thought of as fighting, as wielding a sword, so the mouth is transformed into, or seen as, a cutting weapon: the suckling mother is presented as being slashed by the son-hero, eaten by the one she feeds. Suffering such a fantasy would constitute some of Volumnia's more normal moments. Second, the lines set up an equation between a mother's milk and a man's blood, suggesting that we must understand the man's spitting blood in battle not simply as attacking but equally, somehow, as providing food, in a male fashion. But how? Remember that Coriolanus's way to avoid asking for something, that is, to avoid expressing desire, is by what he calls deserving the thing. His proof of desert is his valiantness, so his spitting blood in battle is his way of deserving being fed, that is to say, being devoured, being loved unconditionally. (War and feeding have consistently been joined in the words of this play. A Plebeian says: "If the wars eat us not up they will" (I.i.85–86). And

Cominius: Coriolanus "cam'st to . . . this feast having fully dined before" (I.ix.10–11); but again Cominius does not get the connection complete.) To be fed by Volumnia is to be fed *to* her. But since the right, or effective, bleeding depends (according to the equation of blood and milk) upon its being a form of feeding, of giving food, providing blood identifies him with his mother. His mother's fantasy here suggests that the appropriate reciprocation for having nourished her son is for him to become her, as if to remove the arbitrariness in her having been born a woman; and since it is a way of putting her into the world it is a way of giving birth to her. Her son's companion fantasy of reciprocation would be to return Rome's gift, to nurse Rome with the valiantness he sucked from it.

This fantasy produces contradictions which are a match for the fury of contradictions one feels in Coriolanus's position (for example, between the wishes for dependence and for independence). For he can only return his nourishment if Rome—taken as the people—deserves it. Hence the people's lack of desert entails his lack of desert, entails that he cannot do the thing that acquires love; he is logically debarred from reciprocating. The fact that he both has absolute contempt for the people and yet has an absolute need for them is part of what maddens him. (This implies again that I cannot understand Coriolanus's emotions toward the people as directed simply to, say, their cowardice, their being poor fighters. I am taking it that he needs their desert for, so to speak, private reasons as much as public.) The other part of what maddens him is that neither the people nor his mother—neither of the things that mean Rome—will understand his position. Neither understands that his understanding of his valiantness, his virtue, his worth, his deservingness, is of himself as a provider, and that this is the condition of his receiving his own sustenance. (This assumes that he shares his mother's fantasy of the equation of milk and blood—as if there is nothing in her he has not taken in.) The people, precisely on the contrary, maddeningly accuse him of *withholding* food; and his mother precisely regards his heroism purely as toughness, devoid of tenderness; or pure fatherhood devoid of motherhood; and as deserving something more than acknowledging what he provides, more than the delicate balance of his self-account, as if being made consul were indeed something more. ("Know, good mother, / I had rather be their servant in my way / Than sway with them in theirs" [II.i.107–09].) In these misunderstandings they have both already abandoned him, weaned him, before the ritual of being made consul comes to grief and he is formally banished. This prior rejection, not just once but always, inherently, would allow the understanding of his anger as his mother interprets anger, that is, as lamentation ("Anger's my meat . . . lament as I do, / In anger, Juno-like"). We may not contradict her interpretation, though we may interpret it further. We might go on to interpret it as depression.

I might characterize my intention in spelling out what I call these fantasies as an attempt to get at the origin of words, not the origin of their meaning exactly but of their production, of the value they have when and as they occur. I have characterized something like this ambition of criticism variously over the years, and related it to what I understand as the characteristic procedure of ordinary language philosophy. (One such effort enters into the opening pages of "The Avoidance of Love: A Reading of *King Lear*.") And do my spellings out help? Do they, for example, help comprehend Coriolanus's subsequent course—how he justifies his plan to burn Rome and how he is talked out of his plan by his mother? It is not hard to encourage oneself in the impression that one understands these things. To me they seem mysteries. I will sketch the answers I have to these questions and then conclude by indicating how these answers serve to interpret our relation to this play, which means to me, to understand what a Shakespearean play is (as revealed in this instance).

I pause, in turning to these questions, to make explicit an issue that at any time may nag our consciousness of the play. The mother-relation is so overwhelmingly present in this play that we may not avoid wondering, at least wondering whether we are to wonder, what happened to the father. The play seems to me to raise this question in three ways, which I list in decreasing order of obviousness. First, Menenius is given a certain kind of fatherly role, or a role as a certain kind of father, but the very difficulty of conceiving of him as Coriolanus's real father, which is to say, as Volumnia's husband and lover, keeps alive our imagination of what such a figure might look like. Second, Coriolanus's erotic attachment to battle and to men who battle suggests a search for the father as much as an escape from the mother. This would afford an explanation for an otherwise, to me, insufficiently explained use in the play of the incident from Plutarch's *Life* in which Coriolanus asks, exhausted from victorious battle, that a man in the conquered city of Corioli be spared slavery on the ground that Coriolanus had "sometime lay at the poor man's house," a man whose name Coriolanus discovers he has forgotten. The vagueness of the man's identity and Coriolanus's expression of confusion in the Shakespeare—distinct differences from the occurrence of the incidents in Plutarch—suggest to my mind that the unnamed figure to whom Coriolanus wishes to provide reparation is, vaguely, transiently, an image of his father.[7]

Third, and so little obvious as to be attributable to my powers of hallucination, Coriolanus's efforts at mythological identification as he sits enthroned and entranced before Rome is an effort—if one accepts one stratum of description I will presently give of him—to come unto the Father. (I will not go into the possibilities here, or fantasies, that a patrician matron is simultaneously father-mother, or that, in replacing his father, he becomes his own father.)

I was about to ask how we are to grasp Coriolanus's return and his change of heart. My answer depends on plotting a relation between him and the other sacrificial lamb I have mentioned, the lamb of God, Christ. I say plotting a relation between the figures, not at all wishing to identify them. I see Coriolanus not so much as imitating Christ as competing with him. These are necessarily shadowy mat-

[7]This is not meant as an alternative to but as an extension of the fine perception in the last note to Act I, scene ix by the editor of the Arden edition (Philip Brockbank) that "One name is found in the scene and another is lost." My thought is that both are names held by Caius Martius Coriolanus. I suppose I am influenced in this thought by a further change Shakespeare makes in Plutarch's characterization of the man. In Plutarch Coriolanus speaks of the man as "an old friend and host of mine"; it is at the analogous moment in Shakespeare that Coriolanus speaks of the man as one at whose house he lay. The opening words of Plutarch's *Life* are "The house of the Martians," where "house" of course means "family," a phrase and passage employed by Shakespeare at the end of Act I I where the Tribunes invoke Coriolanus's biological descent as if to their sufficient credit for having considered it but to Coriolanus's insufficient credit for election to consul.

ters and while everything depends on accuracy in defining this relation all I can do here is note some elements that will have to figure in
the plotting.

Earlier I spoke of Coriolanus's solution to the paradox of hungering not to hunger, of wanting not to want, of asking not to ask, as one
of becoming a god. Now we may see that Christ is the right god
because of the way he understands his mission as providing nonliter-
al food, food for the spirit, for immortality; and because it is in him
that blood must be understood as food. If one is drawn to this as a
possibility, one may find surprising confirmation for it in certain of
Coriolanus's actions and in certain descriptions of his actions. (I am
not interested in claiming that Coriolanus is *in some sense* a scapegoat, the way perhaps any tragic hero is; but in claiming that he is a
specific inflection of *this* scapegoat.)

First his actions, two especially. First is his pivotal refusal to show
his wounds. I associate this generally with the issue of Christ's showing his wounds to his disciples, in order to show them the Lord—
that is, to prove the resurrection—and specifically with his saying to
Thomas, who was not present at the first showing and who made
seeing the wounds a condition of believing, that is, of declaring his
faith, "Thomas, because thou hast seen me, thou believest: blessed
are they that have not seen, and have believed" (John 20:29).
(Thomas would not believe until he could, as he puts it and as Jesus
will invite him to, "put mine hand into his side"; Aufidius declares
the wish to "wash my fierce hand in's heart" (I.x.27). I make no
further claims on the basis of this conjunction; I can see that some
good readers may feel that it is accidental. I do claim that good reading may be guided, or inspired, by the over-excitement such conjunctions can cause.) The second action is the second intercession,
in which Volumnia, holding her son's son by the hand, together with
Virgilia and Valeria appear to Coriolanus before Rome. I take this to
invoke the appearance, while Christ is on the cross, of three women
whose names begin with the same letter of the alphabet (I mean
begin with M's, not with V's), accompanied by a male he loves,
whom he views as his mother's son (John 19:25–27). (Giving his
mother a son presages a mystic marriage.)

I do not suppose that one will be convinced by these relations unless one has antecedently felt some quality of—what shall I say?—the mythic in these moments. This is something I meant in calling these relations "shadowy matters": I meant this not negatively but positively. It is a way to understand Volumnia's advice to Coriolanus that when he makes his appeal to the people he act out the meaning of his presence:

> . . . for in such business
> Action is eloquence, and the eyes of th'ignorant
> More learned than the ears. . . .
>
> (III.ii.75–77)

I accept this as advice Shakespeare is giving to his own audience, a certain hint about why the words of this particular play may strike one as uncharacteristically ineloquent.

The second source of confirmation for Coriolanus's connection with the figure of Christ lies, I said, in certain descriptions of his actions. I specify now only some parallels that come out of Revelation. In that book the central figure is a lamb (and there is also a dragon), and a figure who sits on a special horse and on a golden throne, whose name is known only to himself, whose "eyes were as a flame of fire," and who burns a city which is identified as a woman; it is, in particular, the city (Babylon) which in Christian tradition is identified with Rome. And I associate the opening of Coriolanus's opening diatribe against the citizens, in which he rebukes their wish for "good words" from him—glad tidings—accusing them of liking "neither peace nor war," with the message Christ dictates to the writer of Revelation: "I know thy works, that thou art neither cold nor hot; . . . Therefore, because thou art luke warm, and neither cold nor hot, it will come to pass that I shall spew thee out of my mouth" (Revelation 3:15–16). (An associated text from Plutarch would be: "So Martius, being a stowte man of nature, that never yelded in any respect, as one thincking that to overcome allwayes, and to have the upper hande in all matters, was a Token of magnanimities, and of no base and fainte corage, which spitteth out anger from the most weake and passioned parte of the harte, much like the

matter of an impostume: went home. . . . " Whatever the ambiguities in these words, the general idea remains, indelibly, of Coriolanus's speech, when angry, as being the spitting forth of the matter of
an abscess.[8] This play about food is about revoltedness and disgust.
Coriolanus and Revelation are about figures who are bitter, disgusted by those whom they have done good, whose lives they have
sustained.)

Conviction, or lack of it, in these relations is something one has
naturally to assess for oneself. Granted that they are somehow at
work, they work to make comprehensible what Coriolanus's identification with the god is (they are identified as banished providers of
spiritual food) and what his justification for destruction is (the people lack faith and are to suffer judgment) and why he changes his
mind about the destruction. It is, I think, generally felt that his
mother prevails with him by producing human, family feeling in
him, in effect showing him that he is not inhuman. This again cannot
be wrong, but first of all he has his access of family feeling the moment he sees the four figures approaching (a feeling that does not
serve to carry the day), and second, his feeling, so conceived, does
not seem to me to account for Coriolanus's words of agony to his
mother as he relents and "Holds her by the hand, silent."

> O mother, mother!
> What have you done? Behold, the heavens do ope,
> The gods look down, and this unnatural scene
> They laugh at. O my mother, mother! O!
> You have won a happy victory to Rome;
> But, for your son—believe it, O, believe it!—

---

[8]I quote from North's translation of Plutarch's biography of Coriolanus, which is
given in an appendix to the Arden edition of *Coriolanus* (London, 1976). The "impostume" passage occurs on p. 133.

Coriolanus's sense of disgust with the people is more explicitly conveyed by Shakespeare through the sense of their foul smell than of their foul taste. Shakespeare does
use the idea of spitting twice: once, as cited, to describe Hector's forehead bleeding in
battle, and the second time in Coriolanus's only scene of soliloquy, disguised before
Aufidius's house: "Then know me not. Lest that thy wives with spits and boys with
stones / In puny battle slay me"—so that both times spitting is linked with battle and
with food. As I have implied, I understand Coriolanus's vision of his death in Antium
at the hands of wives and boys as a prophecy of the death he actually undergoes there,
spitted by the swords of strange boys.

Most dangerously you have with him prevailed,
If not most mortal to him. But let it come.

(V.iii. 182–89)

(I say these are words of agony, but so far as I recall, no critic who cites them seems to find them so. I feel here especially at a disadvantage in never having been at a performance of *Coriolanus*. But I find on reading this passage, or rather in imagining it said (sometimes as by specific actors; Olivier, of course, among them, and the young Brando) that it takes a long time to get through. Partly that has to do with the fact of the repetition of words in the passage; partly with the specific words that are repeated, "O," "mother," and "believe it." It has further to do, I feel sure, with my uncertainty about how long the silences before and within this speech are to be held—a speech which may be understood as expressing the silence with which this son holds, and then relinquishes, his mother's hand. Suppose we try imagining that he does not relinquish her hand until just before the last sentence, "But let it come"—as if what is to come is exactly expressive of their separating, or say that of Rome from Rome. Then how far do we imagine that he goes through the imagining of what is to come, and how long would the imagining take, before he takes upon himself the words that invite its coming?) What it means that she may be "most mortal" to him cannot be that he may be killed— the mere fact of death is hardly what concerns this man. He must mean somehow that she has brought it about that he will have the wrong death, the wrong mortality, a fruitless death. Has she done this by showing him that he has feelings? But Christ, even by those who believe that he is the Lord, is generally held to have feelings. Coriolanus's speech expresses his agonized sense that his mother does not know who he is, together with an agonized plea for her belief. She has deprived him of heaven, of, in his fantasy, sitting beside his father, and deprived him by withholding her faith in him, for if she does not believe that he is a god then probably he is not a god, and certainly nothing like the Christian scenario can be fulfilled, in which a mother's belief is essential. If it were his father who sacrificed him for the city of man then he could be a god. But if it is his mother who sacrifices him he is not a god. The logic of his situation, as well as the psychology, is that he cannot sacrifice himself. He can provide spiritual food but he cannot make himself into food, he cannot say, for example, that his body is bread. His sacrifice will not be redemptive, hence one may say his tragedy is that he cannot achieve tragedy. He dies in a place irrelevant to his sacrifice, carved by many swords, by hands that can derive no special nourishment from him. It is too soon in the history of the Roman world for the sacrifice to which he aspires and from which he recoils.

And perhaps it is too late, as if the play is between worlds. I know I have been struck by an apparent incorporation in *Coriolanus* of elements from Euripides' *Bacchae*, without knowing how or whether a historical connection is thinkable. Particularly, it seems to me, I have been influenced in my descriptions by feeling under Coriolanus's final plea to his mother the plea of Pentheus to his mother, outside the city, to see that he is her son and not to tear him to pieces. The *Bacchae* is about admitting the new god to the city, present in one who is returning to his native city, a god who in company with Demeter's grain brings nourishment to mankind, one who demands recognition in order to vindicate at once his mother's honor and his being fathered by Zeus; the first in the city to acknowledge his divine descent are two old men. My idea is that Coriolanus incorporates both raging, implacable Dionysus and raging, inconstant Pentheus and that Volumnia partakes both of the chaste yet god-seduced Semele and of the mad and murderous Agave. Volumnia's identifying of herself with Juno (specifically, with Juno's anger) may thus suggest her sensing herself as the cause of her curse. It is not essential to my thought here that Shakespeare knew (of) Euripides' play. It is enough to consider that he knew Ovid's account of Pentheus's story and to suppose that he took the story as Euripides had, as about the kind of son (one unable to express desire) to whom the failure of his mother's recognition presents itself as a sense of being torn to pieces.

What is the good of such a tragedy of failed tragedy? Which is to ask: What is this play to us? How is it to do its work? This is the question I have been driving at and now that it is before us I can only state flatly, without much detail, my provisional conclusions on the topic.

They can by now be derived from certain considerations about

Menenius's telling of the Fable of the Belly in the opening scene of the play. Every reader or participant has to make something of this extended, most prominently placed event. Until recent times most critics have assumed that Menenius is voicing a commonplace assumption of the times in which Shakespeare wrote and one that represents Shakespeare's view of the state—the state as a hierarchical organism, understandable on analogy with the healthy, functioning body. It is my impression that recent critics have tended not to dwell on the fable, as though the conservative way is the only way to take it and as though that vision is no longer acceptable, or presentable. But this seems to me to ignore what I take to be the three principal facts about Menenius's telling of the tale, the facts, one may say, of the drama in the telling. (1) The fable has competing interpretations. What the first citizen calls its "application" is a *question*. He and Menenius joke about whether the people or the patricians are better represented by the belly. (2) The fable is about food, about its distribution and circulation. (3) The fable is told (by a patrician) to citizens who are in the act of rising in revolt against a government they say is deliberately starving them, hence the patrician can be said to be giving them words *instead* of food. The first mystery of the play is that this seems to work, that the words stop the citizens, that they stop to listen, as though these citizens are themselves willing, under certain circumstances, to take words for food, to equate them.

Coriolanus's entrance at the end of the argument over the application of the fable confirms this equation of words and food: he has from the early lines of the play been identified as the people's chief enemy, here in particular as chief of those who withhold food; and his opening main speech to them, after expressing his disgust by them, is to affirm that he does withhold and will go on withholding "good words" from them. Accordingly every word he speaks will mean the withholding of good words. He will, as it were, have a sword in his mouth. There are other suggestions of the equation of words and food in the play (for example, the enlivening of the familiar idea that understanding is a matter of digesting) but this is enough for me, in view of my previous suggestions, to take the equation as part of the invocation of the major figure of our civilization for whom words are food. The word made flesh is to be eaten, since this is the living bread. Moreover, the parables of Jesus are characteristically about food, and are always meant as food. The words/food equation suggests that we should look again at Volumnia's intercession speeches, less for their content than for the plain fact of their drama, that they are much the longest speeches Coriolanus listens to, that they cause his mother to show him her undivided attention and him to give her his silence; he is as if filled up by her words. It pleases me further to remember that Revelation also contains a vision of words that are eaten: there is a book the writer swallows that tastes as sweet as honey in the mouth but bitter in the belly (10:10), as if beauty were the beginning of terror, as in, for example, a play of Shakespeare's.

My conclusion about the working of the play, about what kind of play it is, adds up then as follows. I take the telling of the Fable of the Belly as a sort of play-within-the-play, a demonstration of what Shakespeare takes his play—named for Coriolanus—to be, for *Coriolanus* too is a tale about food, with competing interpretations requiring application, told by one man to a cluster, call this an audience, causing them to halt momentarily, to turn aside from their more practical or pressing concerns in order to listen. Here is the relevance I see in the fact that the play is written in a time of corn shortages and insurrections. The fact participates not just in the imagery of the play's setting, but in the question of the authority and the virtue of portraying such a time, at such a time, for one's fellow citizens; a question of the authority and the virtue in being a writer. I see in Shakespeare's portrayal of the Fable of the Belly a competition (in idea, perhaps in fact) with Sir Philip Sidney's familiar citing of the fable in his *Defence of Poetry*, or a rebuke of it.[9] Sidney records Menenius's application of the tale as having "wrought such effect in the people, as I never read that only words brought forth but then, so sudden and so good an alteration; for upon reasonable conditions

[9]The following remarks on Sidney's tract were reintroduced, expanded from an earlier set on the subject that I had dropped from the paper, as a result of an exchange with Stephen Greenblatt during the discussion period following my presentation at Stanford.

a perfect reconcilement ensued." But in casting his partisan, limited Menenius as the teller of the tale, and placing its telling at the opening of the play, where we have minimal information or experience for judging its events, Shakespeare puts into question both the nature of the "alteration" and the "perfection" of the reconciliation. Since these are the two chief elements of Sidney's defense of poetry, this defense is as such put into question; but hence, since Shakespeare is nevertheless giving his own version of the telling of the fable, making his own story about the circulation of food, he can be understood as presenting in this play his own defense of poetry (more particularly, of plays, which Sidney particularly attacks). It is in this light noteworthy that Sidney finds "Heroical" poetry to be most "[daunting to] all back-biters," who would "speak evil" of writing which presents "champions . . . who doth not only teach and move to a truth, but teacheth and moveth to the most high and excellent truth." But since "the image of such worthies" as presented in such works "most inflameth the mind with desire to be worthy," and since *Coriolanus* is a play that studies the evil in such an inflammation, Shakespeare's play precisely questions the ground of Sidney's claim that "the Heroical . . . is not only a kind, but the best and most accomplished kind of Poetry."

What would this play's defense of poetry be, I mean how does it direct us to consider the question? Its incorporation of the Fable of the Belly I understand to identify us, the audience, as starvers, and to identify the words of the play as food, for our incorporation. Then we have to ask of ourselves, as we have to ask of the citizens: Why have we stopped to listen? That is, what does it mean to be a member of this audience? Do we feel that these words have the power of redemption for us?

They are part of an enactment of a play of sacrifice; as it happens, of a failed sacrifice. And a feast-sacrifice, whether in Christian, pre-Christian, Nietzschean, or Freudian terms, is a matter of the founding and the preserving of a community. A community is thus identified as those who partake of the same body, of a common victim. This strikes Coriolanus as our being caught in a circle of mutual partaking, incorporating one another. And this is symbolized, or instanced, by speaking the same language. A pervasive reason Coriolanus spits out words is exactly that they *are* words, that they exist only in a language, and that a language is metaphysically something shared, so that speaking is taking and giving in your mouth the very matter others are giving and taking in theirs.

It is maddeningly irrevelant to Coriolanus which party the belly represents. What matters to him is that, whoever rules, all are members, that all participate in the same circulation, the same system of exchange, call it Rome; that to provide civil nourishment you must allow yourself to be partaken of. This is not a play about politics, if this means about political authority or conflict, say about questions of legitimate succession or divided loyalties. It is about the formation of the political, the founding of the city, about what it is that makes a rational animal fit for conversation, for civility. This play seems to think of this creation of the political, call it the public, as the overcoming of narcissism, incestuousness, and cannibalism; as if it perceives an identity among these relations.

In constructing and contesting with a hero for whom the circulation of language is an expression of cannibalism, *Coriolanus* takes cannibalism as symbolic of the most human of activities, the most distinctive, or distinguished, of human activities. (Sidney cites the familiar conjunction: ". . . Oratio, next to Ratio, . . . [is] the greatest gift bestowed upon mortality.") Coriolanus wishes to speak, to use words, to communicate, without exchanging words; without, let us say, reasoning (with others); to speak without conversing, without partaking in conversation. Here is the conversation for which he is unfit, call it civil speech. Hence I conceive *Coriolanus* to be incorporating Montaigne's interpretation of literal cannibalism as more civilized than our more sophisticated—above all, more pervasive—manners of psychological torture, our consuming others alive.[10] Montaigne's "On Cannibals" is more specifically pertinent to

[10]Finding the words/food representation so compelling, I am ignoring here the path along which the circulation of words also registers the circulation of money (as in "So shall my lungs/Coin words" (III.i.77–78); and in "The price is, to ask it kindly" (II.iii.77)). The sense of consuming as expending would relate to Coriolanus's frantic efforts to deny that his actions can be recompensed ("better to starve than crave the hire"—for example, of receiving voices *in return*). Money depends upon the equating of values; Coriolanus on their lack of equation, on measurelessness, pricelessness.

this play: its story of a cannibal prisoner of a cannibal society valor-
ously taunting his captors by reminding them that in previous battles, when he had been victorious over them, he had captured and
eaten their ancestors, so that in eating him they will be consuming
their own flesh—this is virtually the mode in which Coriolanus addresses himself to the Volscians in putting himself at their mercy.
And more variously pertinent: the essay interprets cannibalism as
revenge; and it claims (in one of those moods of measured hilarity)
that when three men from a cannibal society visited Rouen and were
asked what they found most amazing about the ways of Montaigne's
countrymen, one of their responses was as follows (I will not comment on it but quote in Frame's translation):

> Second (they have a way in their language of speaking of men as halves
> of one another), they had noticed that there were among us men full
> and gorged with all sorts of good things, and that their other halves
> were beggars at their doors, emaciated with hunger and poverty; and
> they thought it strange that these needy halves could endure such an
> injustice, and did not take the others by the throat, or set fire to their
> houses.

Within the experience of such a vision of the circulation of language a question, not readily formulatable, may press for expression: To what extent can Coriolanus (and the play that creates him
and contests with him) be understood as seeing his salvation in silence? The theme of silence haunts the play. For example, one of
Coriolanus's perfectly cursed tasks is to ask for "voices" (votes) that
he exactly wishes not to hear. Again, the words "silent" and "silence"
are beautifully and mysteriously associated, once each, with the
women in his life: with his wife ("My gracious silence, hail!"); and
with his mother ("He holds her by the hand, silent"). Toward both,
the word of silence is the expression of intimacy and identification;
but in his wife's case it means acknowledgment, freedom from
words, but in a life beyond the social, while in his mother's case it
means avoidance, denial, death, that there is no life beyond the social. The ambiguities here are drilled through the action of the play
by the repeated calls "Peace, peace"—hysterical, ineffective shouts
of this particular word for silence. The play literalizes this conven-

tional call for silence by implying that speech is war, as if this is the
reason that both words and war can serve as food. But the man for
war cannot find peace in peace—not merely because he, personally,
cannot keep a civil tongue in his head, but because a tongue is inherently uncivil (if not, one hopes, inveterately so). Silence is not the
absence of language; there is no such absence for human beings; in
this respect, there is no world elsewhere.

Coriolanus cannot imagine, or cannot accept, that there is a way
to partake of one another, incorporate one another, that is necessary
to the formation rather than to the extinction of a community. (As he
cannot imagine being fed without being deserving. This is his precise reversal of Christ's vision, that we cannot in ourselves deserve
sustenance, and that it is for that reason, and in that spirit, that we
have to ask for it. Thus is misanthropy, like philanthropy, a certain
parody of Christianity.) The play *Coriolanus* asks us to try to imagine it, imagine a beneficial, mutual consumption, arguing in effect
that this is what the formation of an audience is. (As if *vorare* were
next to *orare*).

It seems to me that what I have been saying demonstrates, no
doubt somewhat comically, the hypothesis of the origin of tragedy
in religious ritual—somewhat comically, because I must seem rather
to have deflated the problem, implying that whether the hypothesis
is true depends on what is meant by "tragedy," what by "origin," and
which ritual is in mind.[11] I have, in effect, argued that if you accept
the words as food, and you accept the central figure as invoking the

[11]In the discussion period at Stanford, Paul Alpers noted that I seemed to find something like a comic perspective of the play to be more extensive than just here where I
am making it explicit, and he asked how far I wished to go in seeking this perspective.
I find this a true response to my reading, but it goes beyond anything I can explore
now. I mentioned then what I take to be a starting point to such an exploration,
Coriolanus's sense that as he and his mother stand silent together "The Gods look
down, and this unnatural scene / They laugh at." Does he feel the gods laugh because
mother and son are too close or too distant with one another? At least the scene is
unnatural because it is social, and because the social is the scene of mazes of meaning
as dense as poetry, in which its poor, prosaic, half-human creatures are isolated. The
comedic perspective I seek presents itself to me as a totalization, or a kind of transcen-
dentalizing, of dramatic irony—where the omen or allusion is not of some specific,
future event, but of the totality of the present, of events as they are, without our being
able to specify in advance what individuates or what relates these events.

central figure of the Eucharist, then you may accept a formulation to the effect (not that the play is the ritual of the Eucharist, but to the effect) that the play celebrates, or aspires to, the same fact as the ritual does, say the condition of community. Eucharist means gratitude, precisely what Coriolanus feels the people withhold from him. This is another way to see why I am not satisfied to say that Coriolanus is enraged first of all by the people's cowardice. Perhaps one may say that to Coriolanus their cowardice means ingratitude. As for the idea of origin, we need only appeal to Descartes's idea that the origin of a thing is the same thing that preserves it. What preserves a tragedy, what creates the effect of a certain kind of drama, is the appropriation by an audience of this effect, our mutual incorporation of its words. When the sharing of a sacrifice is held on religious ground, the ritual itself assures its effectiveness. When it is shifted to aesthetic ground, in a theater, there is no such preexisting assurance; the work of art has to handle everything itself. You might think of this as the rebirth of religion from the spirit of tragedy. A performance is nothing without our participation in an audience; and this participation is up to each of us.

To enforce the necessity of this decision to participate (a decision which of course has its analogue for the individual reader with the script in his or her hands) is the way I understand the starkness of the words of this play, their relative ineloquence, their lack of apparent resonance. The play presents us with our need for one another's words by presenting withholding words, words that do not meet us half way. It presents us with a famine of words. This way of seeing it takes it to fulfill a prophecy from the Book of Amos (8:12): "Behold, the days come, saith the Lord God, that I will send a famine in the land, not a famine of bread, nor a thirst for water; but of hearing the words of the Lord."

POSTSCRIPT

It may be felt, it should be felt, that my account of Coriolanus's disgust by language has studiously had to avoid a more obvious, or equally obvious, if less explicit understanding than I have given of it. I said that he has a horror of putting in his mouth what (as in his fantasy) comes out of the mouths of others, and I gave that as a reason it is irrelevant to Coriolanus whether the Parable of the Belly is interpreted with the patricians or with the plebeians as the belly, or as the tongue, or as any other part. What alarms him is simply being part, one member among others of the same organism. But there is a different way of characterizing his reason for alarm, a different manner of taking the Parable from the beginning.

This way is one that rather literalizes the Parable, one that takes its joking not to turn merely, or primarily, on an ambiguity over whom the belly represents, over who does the providing to whom, but on an ambiguity over what the product is that the belly provides, over what there is to be provided, on this organic view of the state. This further ambiguity concerns what we might think of as the direction in which the giving or returning done by the belly is imagined to happen. Is the belly's process and product directed back toward the body of which it is part, or out toward the earth which it shares, and of which it partakes? In the latter case disgust is a function of imagining that in incorporating one another we are asked to incorporate one another's leavings, the results or wastes of what has already been incorporated.

On this reading two features of the Parable of the Belly find a better home than I was able formerly, concentrating on words as food, to provide for them: the First Citizen's image or fantasy of the belly as "the sink o' th' body" (I.i.123), its sewer; and Menenius's offering as the Belly's taunting reply to the accusation against it of the rebel parts of the body, what he calls "a kind of smile, / Which ne'er came from the lungs, but even thus—"(I.i.108–10). I do not insist that you must conceive Menenius here to figure the answering smile as a noise, say a kind of laugh, or a cheer; but only that *if* you find yourself figuring it so, you must be unsure whether the noise comes from above or from below.

The outward direction of circulation is as familiar in this period of Shakespeare as the inward. From *Antony and Cleopatra*: The man at the beginning is saying, "Kingdoms are clay; our dungy earth alike / Feeds beast as man; the nobleness of life / Is to do thus . . . "; and the woman at the ending, "And it is great / To do that thing that ends all other deeds, . . . / Which sleeps, and never palates more the dung, / The beggar's nurse and Caesar's." These imaginings of the earth as feeding its inhabitants, in reciprocation with the imagining of its being nourished by the leavings and remains of those it feeds, for example, by us humans, are in each case here expressions of a mind in exaltation, hence somewhat reductive of its environment; minds in a mood that seeks transcendence of the common lot of humanity. But this means that neither Cleopatra nor Antony is seeking to deny—the thing it is Coriolanus's mission to deny—that this circulation *is* common, is even *what* is common, along the scale of living kinds and the degrees of human ranks. I suppose that these late Roman plays exist on this axis in what Norman Rabkin has called a relation of complementarity. It accordingly suggests itself that the two directions of the circulation of nourishment are kept, in healthier imaginations, in healthier appetites, from crossing; that the imagination of what the mouth receives as food is normally mediated by passing it through nature, so to purify the contribution made to the process by other, let us say, human beings.

In suggesting that in Coriolanus the imagination has collapsed upon itself, that his fantasy is that he is asked to feed directly on the leavings of others, I am not retracting, but further glossing, his sense of disgust at the words that exit from their mouths, glossing what it is he thinks words are, and what food is, or you may say, the chain of food. Keeping one's critical balance in this matter, not allowing one's imagination to collapse upon itself, could hardly be trickier. The very suggestion of the element this postscript invokes is apt to stifle what the body of my essay takes—correctly, I persist in thinking—as fundamental in the play, namely the circulation from mouth to mouth of language. The trick is to let this fact be challenged, and not overthrown, by the suggestion that language is at the same time something retained, which perhaps means hoarded, for expulsion, or banishment, a way of conceiving of writing, physically altering the world.

The suggestion makes its way, in the part of the world I know, mostly in slang, or jokes, as when E. E. Cummings has his Buffalo Bill say, "There is some s. I will not eat," and in expressions rejecting the words of others by asking what they are trying to hand you, or by naming the product as the droppings of horses or bulls. And the idea presents a link with the ideas associating the circulation of food with that of the circulation of words and with that of money (cited in note 10). Here the connection is primarily through the senses of "super-fluity," as for example when the First Citizen says, "What authority surfeits on would relieve us. If they would yield us but the superflu-ity while it were wholesome, we might guess they relieved us hu-manely; but they think we are too dear; . . . our sufferance is a gain to them" (I.i.15–22). And the connection of words through grain to money is enforced in the same citizen's longest speech after Mene-nius enters: "They ne'er cared for us yet. Suffer us to famish, and their storehouses crammed with grain; make edicts for usury, to support usurers . . . " (I.i.80–83). To my ear, Shakespeare's lines here cite usury not simply as a second historically accurate cause for a second (earlier) revolt, but put as it were the two revolts in apposi-tion, so that usury and hoarding are metaphors for one another. Without insisting on this, I wish to invoke here Marc Shell's rehabil-itation of the concept of "verbal usury," for his extraordinary essay on *The Merchant of Venice*, a concept he characterizes as referring "to the generation of an illegal—the church fathers say unnatural—supplement to verbal meaning by use of such methods as punning and flattering."[12] It is as if Coriolanus finds the barest use of words

[12]"The Wether and the Ewe," in Shell's *Money, Language, and Thought* (Berkeley and Los Angeles, 1982), p. 49. I knew that my debt to Marc Shell went beyond the writing of his I can cite, since, among other matters, he attended the seminar in which I first broached my sense of *Coriolanus* and it was often his questions that kept me moving. But not until after completing not only the body of this essay but also this postscript have I returned to complete my reading of the essays in his *Money, Language, and Thought*, and there I find that I have incurred, or would like at once to incur, a new debt. The second essay of the book, "The Blank Check: Accounting for the Grail," which for some reason Shell did not press upon me on hearing my *Coriolanus* mate-rial, suggests to my mind that the story I have told, including its extension into this postscript, has to be extended further to incorporate the scene and action of Shake-speare's *Coriolanus* into a telling of (hence, as suggested by my account, a competition with) the dearth and plenitude as recounted in the legends of the holy grail. I assemble a packet of quotations from Shell's essay to indicate my sense of the issue:

> *The infinitely large gift and the free gift (one given gratis, without intending to obligate the recipient to reciprocate and without making him feel obligated to do so) may well be impossible in everyday exchange. . . . The hypothesis of the*

usurious, while the citizens accuse him of a kind of verbal miser-liness, depriving them of all credit. The feeling in the citizens' speeches is not alone of their physical pain in suffering want, but of the insufferable *meaning* of this pain, that it is inflicted, that it communicates the contempt in which the patricians hold them. (In saying that grain forms a link between words and money, I take for granted the connection, on either Marxian or Freudian grounds, of money with excrement. The folk character of the connection, hence preparation for its convincingness to me, is present in a joke circulated my way by my father, who once remarked that they must be teaching me chemistry in college because I had learned so well to take money and make dreck out of it.)

In responding to Paul Alpers's query concerning a sense of the comic underlying my entire reading of *Coriolanus* (reported in note 11), I should have pointed to the belly's smile as well as to the Gods'

---

infinitely large gift, for example, appears as the cornucopia, and the hypothesis of the free gift, as Pauline grace. . . . [T]owards the end of the medieval era . . . the first widespread vernacular literature told of a cornucopian grail, an extraordinary gift both infinitely large and free, which was said to be able to lift men out of the ordinary world of exchange into a world in which freedom and totality were possible. . . . The grail legends depict a wasteland to which the limitless production of material and spiritual goods stands as a defining and conceptually unique limit. (pp. 24–25)

Chrétien is a poet-sower who must consider the relationship of the fertility of his seed both to the relative spiritual sterility of his audience and to the material sterility of the wasteland of which he would tell them. Spiritual fertility varies from person to person, so that Chrétien must speak on several levels at the same time. . . . All the grail tales claim the status of riddle. (p. 25)

*Like the apostle's inkhorn (*cornu*) . . . the word* graal *operates in the grail tales as a "cornucopia of words," just as the grail itself operates as a plentiful cornucopia of nourishing food. (pp. 26–27)*

At the beginning of Chrétien's Account, *for example, the hero Perceval is presented as a typical hungry adolescent who seeks food from his mother, expects food at the tent he mistakenly believes to be a chapel, demands food from the God he believes to live in the tent-chapel, and finally receives earthly food. Only divine nourishment, however, can satisfy the desire of this questing man. Perceval learns about the kind of food God provides when a hermit tells him on Good Friday that the food he failed to ask about at the grail castle was "real." (p. 27)*

The kind of men who do not have good food to go into their mouths do not have good words to come out of their mouths. (p. 29)

The free sacrifice of a woman helps to resolder the broken sword of the realm. . . . [T]here is in many stories this identity of sword and person. (p. 33, and note) laughter. Then what is the joke? Who could laugh at it? Freud has some helpful words:

> There are yet other means of making things comic which deserve special consideration and also indicate in part fresh sources of comic pleasure. . . . Caricature, parody and travesty (as well as their practical counterpart, unmasking) are directed against people and objects which lay claim to authority and respect, which are in some sense "*sublime*." They are procedures for *Herabsetzung* [degradation] as the apt German expression has it. . . . When . . . the procedures . . . for the degradation of the sublime allow me to have an idea of it as though it were something commonplace, in whose presence I need not pull myself together but may, to use the military formula, "stand easy," I am being spared the increased expenditure of the solemn restraint . . . the difference in expenditure . . . can be discharged by laughter.

> Under the heading of "unmasking" we may also include . . . the method of degrading the dignity of individuals by directing attention to the frailties which they share with all humanity, but in particular the dependence of their mental functions on bodily needs. The unmasking is equivalent here to an admonition; such and such a person, who is admired as a demigod, is after all only human like you and me.[13]

But the comic pleasure in discovering Coriolanus's vulnerabilities, to us who are neither Gods nor just bellies, does not get much beyond the cold comfort of an ironic awareness of the viciousness of his virtue, the uselessness in his usefulness. I think back to my suggestion that the formation of a society depends on there being, on our achieving, a partaking of one another that is beneficial, creative, not annihilating, as if our mutual cannibalism is a parody of what we might be, that we are standing jokes on ourselves, wishing to transcend what would no longer deserve to be transcended if we could mutually give up the wish (as if needing one another's hands meant that human beings are fated to accept what they have so far learned to hand one another). Instead we feel deprived, hence vengeful, feel fated as things stand not to get as good as we give. (The comic necessity in

[13] *Jokes and Their Relation to the Unconscious*, J. Strachey, trans. (New York, 1960), pp. 200–201, 202.

these feelings, or tragic contingency, will want pursuing into the bearing of the Parable of the Belly on the full appeal of the idea of the body politic, as though the belly is smiling at all theorizing that leaves the state, or say sovereignty, organic. And does political thinking know itself to be free of this appeal, of, let us say, the idea of the citizen's two bodies, or it may be more; or is it better to think of each of us as of two or more minds?)

In broaching the subject of this postscript, I said that the anality in the play is less explicit than the orality I had confined myself to in the, as it were, body of my essay, implying that its being mostly implicit in the words of the play is hardly a sufficient reason for leaving it inexplicit in a stretch of criticism. But one may well, as Kenneth Burke has, take the issue to be given full explicitness in the play's, and its hero's, name. In the section headed "Comments" that follows, or concludes, Burke's masterful essay "*Coriolanus* and the Delights of Faction," he remarks:

> Though the names are taken over literally from Plutarch, it is remarkable how tonally suggestive some of them are, from the standpoint of their roles in this English play. . . . And in the light of Freudian theories concerning the fecal nature of invective, the last two syllables of the hero's name are so "right," people now often seek to dodge the issue by altering the traditional pronunciation (making the *a* broad instead of long).[14]

But how are we to specify what is "right" about the name? Granted the intentionality of Shakespeare's play's attention to the name, he may in it be seeking a heavenly horse laugh at language's vengeance in distributing one and the same sound equally to a suffix that encodes a name's military honor and to the name of the shape of a sphincter; as if noting a kind of poetic justice. (Another point of justice is perhaps noted in Burke's suggesting "excess" as well as "pride" as a translation of *hubris*.)

Burke is immensely tactful in mentioning the subject, in his essay here and elsewhere, and while on the occasions of delivering versions of my essays as talks I would allude to the fecal issue as something to be considered, I did not see how to consider it well in unprotected prose. Whatever I wrote down seemed to me either too explicit or too implicit, brazen or hidden. I could understand part of my difficulty to be quite inescapable; one cannot readily rise above the level of one's civilization's sense of humor. As in other matters I take *Walden* as a touchstone for this issue. Thoreau's recurrent allusions in that book to eating and elimination are expressions of his bursting admiration for the capacity of (especially Indian) scriptures to name the organs and functions of the body as plain facts of cosmic rhythms; as facts; without invoking or evading attitudes toward them, as if to suppose them so much as good or bad were presumptuous. It is a capacity to name them, and to make recommendations with respect to them with, let me say, detachment; to name philosophically. Thoreau did not think us Westerners capable of this, as a culture, yet. You might think of philosophical naming as something the serious writing of a culture holds out to it.

It was in coming to see more unprotectedly that Shakespeare's *Coriolanus* is itself exactly in struggle with this question of explicitness and naming, or that it is internal to the way I have proposed taking the play, as a study of the shunning of voices, hence the craving of them, that I was shamed into making my embarrassment (of style, say) more explicit in this note. The implication is that to avoid risking one's critical balance in traversing this play is to avoid a measure of participation in the play's assessments of the balance civilization exacts. Call it the exaction of civility. To what extent can the powers of a city reciprocate in civility and remain powers? To what extent can they withhold reciprocation without naming a state of war, directed inward or outward?

I hope I have sufficiently indicated in my essay why a study of voices goes into a study of the formation of human society, of the recognition of others as, so to speak, *my* others. The idea of a social contract as expressing one's consent to be governed, to be civil, is a demand, as I have had reason to insist, for explicitness, however hard it may be to establish what must constitute an original explicitness. (I have in mind *The Claim of Reason*, pp. 22–28.) For think of it this way. The consent to be governed must express the desire to be governed, governed by consent, hence to participate in the city. To express desire inexplicitly is an act of seduction, hence one that exists only in a medium of prohibition and conspiracy. It may be that human sexual life will continue to require this medium and its struggles for the foreseeable future, say for as long as our politics does not create a more perfect public medium, unfailingly intelligible, reciprocal, and nourishing. Without this, we will continue to interpret privacy as inexplicitness, and on this ground the private will continue to look like the natural enemy of the political, as in opposite ways it is shown to be, to our distress, in *Antony and Cleopatra* and in *Coriolanus*. Who cares whether the unjust can be happy when we still do not know whether the demand for happiness is survivable?

And the idea of the recognition of others as mine, implying the acknowledgment of human beings as human, things that think, is a matter of putting body and soul together, of connecting perception and imagination I have sometimes said, whatever these are. Philosophers have made problems, as well they might, about what it is to know that others have minds. I am in effect taking *Coriolanus* to raise the question, as well we might, what it is to know that others, that we, have bodies. According to the line of thought in this postscript it is to know that, and perhaps know why, the body has (along with the senses) two openings, or two sites for openings, ones that are connected, made for each other, a top and a bottom, or a front and a back, outsides and insides. But what is the expression of this knowledge, what acknowledges it; I mean, what is the expression of a knowledge of its commonness, for example as between us? Harping on the idea (perhaps as Swift did) seems to miss its commonness, or ordinariness. But how do you know that remaining silent about it isn't denying it? And does Descartes's metaphysical insistence that we are essentially minds deny the universal accident that we are (connected to) bodies? And does Nietzsche's metaphysical insistence that we are bodies deny the grandeur of the mind?

If we say that noting the connection of the body with itself wants tact, we may say that Coriolanus traces the costs of the absence of this tact of civility. While his case is more extreme than ours, our satisfaction in ridding ourselves of him attests to our representation by him, that we make him our agent. Our differences from his case are that we demand less of our honor than he of his and that social divisions among us are less, differences which at best speak of our fortune, or belatedness, not of our credit. So I gather that no one is in a position to say what the right expression is of our knowledge that we are strung out on both sides of a belly. Then the issue is whether we have to know this before we can know the partaking that makes a city good, or whether the city, in its poverty of goodness, can provide itself with individuals, or clusters, who know such a thing, and whether it can then stop and take in what they have to say, whether it can tolerate the voice of its own language.

A COVER LETTER
TO MOLIÈRE'S *MISANTHROPE*

◆

This letter was begun as a way of justifying the inclusion of an essay on Othello *in an issue of* Daedalus *(Summer 1979) devoted to the topic of hypocrisy, led off by an essay of Professor Judith Shklar's. I am grateful to Judith Shklar and to the editor of* Daedalus, *Stephen Graubard, for comments that helped me improve the letter. My* Othello *essay, with minor modifications, constitutes the closing pages of* The Claim of Reason, *and needs no reprinting here. But I preserve the cover letter both because it grew into something that sees things together in a way nothing else I have done quite manages, and because I always thought of it not as a general introduction to what I had to say about* Othello *but as a specific response to the narcissistic or misanthropic elements of its central character. In the letter, I mention* Hamlet *as another case or function of misanthropy; and* Coriolanus *is surely another, about whom the letter is an equally pertinent introduction. In some obvious ways it is more fully pertinent to* Coriolanus, *especially as a link between the topics I cite that are shared by the play that bears his name and by the films of Makavejev taken up in the essay following this one. Anyway, I tell Alceste in my letter that I mean to write to him about Makavejev's work, and so I led myself on.*

◇

DEAR ALCESTE,

They're thinking about you again, the good ones. Can you imagine why? I will not disguise from you my conviction that your position is intellectually indefensible. What more really can you say on your behalf but that human society is filled with show, with artifice, with insincerity, with dissociations between the public and the private, between the outer and the inner? And what more really need be said in reply to you than to concede this, and whatever follows from it, as the nature of human society, as the very essence of the civilized; and then simply request that you—what? Let us not say either love civilization or leave it. The request is rather that you not be illogical: if you do decide to join the human race; or let me say, to take your place in society; then do not complain that you will not by that act have rejoined the world of nature. It need not be denied that in this decision something is lost. But need you deny that something is gained, something indeed human? To see these two sides is just to grow up, something you are heartily advised to do.

Why is this not the end of the matter? The fact that it is not the end is what I take the issue of hypocrisy to be about, what it is that keeps it an issue. The issue is not so much why you are not convinced by the better arguments of the others. That sort of impasse is hardly news in human affairs. The issue is rather why the others care that you are not convinced. You are without power. What is your hold upon them? What do you represent to them?

Perhaps you imagine that you represent purity to their compromise and corruption. I think it would be closer to the truth to say that you represent purity to their purity, or to their sense of their purity lost—not as if corrupted exactly but as if misplaced, thus still present somehow. Purity and innocence are no doubt dangerous ingredients in society, rarely making a bad situation as good as it can be, often making it as bad as it can be, unable to listen to reason. But like virginity itself, innocence ought to be put aside in its own good time; which is to say, in a time and place of its own consent. In a happy world purity will itself know its time and its place. But suppose it does not? Suppose that the world is not happy. Purity can only know by its own heart and by the encouragement of what draws it. So if I maintain the right of experience to its arguments for consent, I equally maintain the right of innocence to give and to withhold its consent without argument, on the basis of its feeling, its sense of itself. The world needs that sense, requires that you say, willingly, that the world is good enough to want to live in. And I assume that in general you, in general youth, wish to want the world; which is to say: you wish to be presented with a world you can want, to which you give yourself. Why would you not?

Let us leave aside the possibility that you are neurotic, or tyrannical. Let us assume that you may be right, that the world as it is, is not wantable, or not acceptable. Let us also leave aside the possibility that you are a victim of political injustice, either privately or as the member of a victimized class or race. In so much as acknowledging that there may be room left, beyond private or public injustice, for refusing the world, I am, you see, showing the side of me that sides with you. (This implies that there is a part of me that parts with you. I'll come to that.) Then what room is left? How could the world as a whole present itself, to one's feeling, as uninhabitable? *What* is the feeling?

Evidently it must be understood as a mode of disgust, a repugnance at the idea that your life should partake of the world's, that what it does, you do; or is it at the idea that the world's life partakes of yours, that what you feel, it feels? I am not going to try now to define further or to assess such ideas. I am writing merely to reaffirm that I believe in the potential epistemological significance of this mode of disgust (recognizing always, as one always has to add in our day, that the significance may only be psychological, as if we knew what distinction we had in mind). Like Hamlet before you (with his sensitivity to odor, to the rotting), and like the romantics and the existentialists after you, you represent the discovery of adolescence, of that moment at which the worth of adulthood is—except, I suppose, to deep old age—most clearly exposed; at which adulthood *is* the thing you are asked to choose, to consent to. Naturally your choice will be based on insufficient evidence. But woe to them that believe the choice is easy, that in forgoing adolescence you forgo little of significance. They have merely forgotten what they have lost, as they have forgotten the loss of childhood, a matter of comparable significance. (Freud, to whom you should be introduced, means something like this, or ought to mean it, by speaking of human sexual development as having two phases, the second of which, after a period of latency, recapitulates the first.)

The idea here, that when the world's legitimacy comes to rest upon consent—when the public world is something that each individual has at some moment to agree to join—that then adolescence is invented as the time of preparing for that agreement, and is ended by it; this idea is confirmed in the thought of hypocrisy, a word which says something about playing a role but which at the same time derives from a sense of measured separation from something, say a sense of dissociation. The hypocrite would dissociate himself or herself from a life of human vulnerabilities, call it human nature; the antihypocrite would dissociate himself or herself from a world of invulnerable pretenses. If adolescence will level the most unforgiving charge of hypocrisy at those ahead of it, it will level against itself an equally unforgiving charge of fraudulence—and the one because of the other. The world posed before it, beckoning it, is a field of possibilities, toward which curiosity is bound to outreach commitment. It is inherently a time of theater, of self-consciousness presented as embarrassment, of separation from the familiar, of separation from the self, as if something were tearing; of a scrutiny that claims to know everything directing itself upon feelings and actions that can claim to know nothing. It is a time containing the reversal of rites of passage: the tribe shifts the responsibility for its pain from its back onto yours; and instead of opening secrets to you, it informs you that it has none, that what you see is all there is to it. Hence to its recruits it is now reduced merely to *saying* "Grow up."

I have several reasons for wanting to be in touch with you now. First, my old friend Judith Shklar is saying publicly that you finally lost the woman you love. This implies at the least that Célimène is right to refuse your offer of marriage with its condition that she abandon the remainder of the world, that she find the whole world in you. So I have to tell you that I agree with this verdict and will say so publicly. I will, however, go on to claim that the more significant fact, the mystery of your misanthropy, is that Célimène loves you, that they all love you, Arsinoé as well as Philinte; that they do not give you up but end their play by going to seek you out. Quite as if they think you are right, even if placed in the wrong, and cannot want to live without the thing you mean to them. And yet what? They find you too difficult or too hard. Is that your problem or theirs?

Second, the side of me that sides with you has in recent years repeatedly found itself siding with those for whom the relation of innocence and experience is their life, call it the relation between their past of possibilities and the present actuality of the world, or between their memories of being disappointed and their fears of being disappointing. Thoreau is talking about this relation in this passage from the chapter "Spring" in *Walden*. "While such a sun holds out to burn, the vilest sinner may return. Through our own recovered innocence we discern the innocence of our neighbors. You may have known your neighbor yesterday for a thief, a drunkard, or a sensualist, and merely pitied or despised him, and despaired of the world; but the sun shines bright and warm this first spring morning, re-creating the world. . . . There is not only an atmosphere of good will about him, but even a savor of holiness groping for expression." Emerson, I now believe to his credit, can barely let the issue alone, the issue of consenting to the world. It is this fact of his perpetual youth, calling to the perpetual youth in us, more than his incessant sagacity about it, that keeps Emerson so annoying to good society. For example, in the Swedenborg chapter of *Representative Men*: "The human mind stands ever in perplexity, demanding intellect, demanding sanctity, impatient equally of each without the other. The reconciler has not yet appeared." We may have imagined that it is hard to be known for a sinner, and may have feared scandal from *that* quarter. It proves harder to be known for a saint, hard to forgive the one who knows it of us. This, I feel sure, is something Nietzsche loved Emerson for. Zarathustra says to the young man from whom he has elicited the confession that he has been destroyed by his envy of Zarathustra: "Yes, I know your peril. But, by my love and hope I entreat you: do not reject your love and hope! You still feel yourself noble, and the others, too, who dislike you and cast evil glances at you, still feel you are noble. Learn that everyone finds the noble man an obstruction. . . . Alas, I have known noble men who lost their highest hope. And henceforth they slandered all high hopes. . . . But, by my love and hope I entreat you: do not reject the hero in your soul! Keep holy your highest hope."

One day soon I mean to write to you about a film of Dušan Makavejev's he calls *Sweet Movie*. It is a work that attempts to extract hope from the very fact that we are capable of genuine disgust at the world; that this disgust is to be understood as our revoltedness, as our chance of cleansing revulsion, that the fight for freedom continues to originate in the demands of our instincts. It is a work powerful enough to encourage us to think again that the tyrant's power continues to require our complicitous tyranny over ourselves. I would expect you, dear Alceste, to be capable of tears when, at the end of Makavejev's film, he allows a young boy who is fictionally dead, wrapped in plastic sheets and laid on a river bank, to resurrect and to declare himself as the young actor playing this part, thus exhuming his younger self, his innocent sincerity. He then directs this figure to look out from the screen and hence to confront his older self, his artistry, his experience as a filmmaker, a consenting adult in a world of horrors (thus, as Rousseau and Thoreau perceive, a conspirator of that world, chained by partialities) confronting himself with the chance to forgive himself, hence with the chance to start again.

You see that I would try to tempt you back, to tell you that there are those in the world who have not forgotten what you know, hence who feel the rebuke in your taking offense. But it is up to you and to us in our separate ways; it is pointless to beg, and this is not the time to harangue. The final reason I write now is to provide a cover for showing you something I have been thinking about *Othello*.

My thoughts about it conclude a very long manuscript having to do principally with a topic close to your heart, namely whether, and on what basis, we must acknowledge the existence of other human beings. These thoughts picture Othello as, in various ways, a *semblable* of yours, one who demands being the whole world to the woman he loves, as some sort of price for his joining her in wedlock. My tale is cautionary. To you it warns that a mind and a character as pure and grand as Othello's may, in its isolation, fall to wallowing in littleness. Of the world my tale asks watchfulness over itself, over its ability to encourage and to protect the innocent. Say Othello's ugliness was to have gone the limit in murdering his love and his hope, the hero in his soul. But his beauty was to have had such a love and such high hopes. Like Lear, he confuses the private and the public, the erotic and the political, distorting both. But who finds himself in a position to correct them? Who is prepared to advise them to grow up? Halting the brawl on Cyprus, Othello asks how it happened, concluding: "What? In a town of war / Yet wild, the people's hearts brimful of fear, / To manage private and domestic quarrel? / In night, and on the court and guard of safety? / 'Tis monstrous. Iago, who began't?" (II. iii. 212–16). When these questions turn upon him, he will turn upon himself.

My thoughts also relate *Othello* to some passages from Montaigne, someone I have several times wanted to bring you together with. Montaigne is appalled by the human capacity for horror at the human. I think I know what he means and I think you do too. But the world during my lifetime rather shows that it is yet more horrible to lose this capacity for horror. Judith Shklar's essay is guided and colored by experiences of the world war of the forties and the local wars of the sixties. How could it not be? But aren't Nazis those who have lost the capacity for being horrified by what they do? They are our special monsters for *that* reason, monsters of adaptability. (Who knows whether what they did, apart from scale, was really that different from what others have done? Who knows whether the only real Nazis were created by a particular time and place and by a particular set of leaders and led? Who does not know that Nazism cannot succeed apart from the human capacity for *going along*? And what political thinker does not recognize that most of us will mostly go along with the tide of events, and even argue that we (mostly) ought to? But who does not see that there must be *some* limit to this? I am saying that Nazism specifically turns this human capacity for adapting into a mockery of itself, a mockery of being human.) And was hypocrisy really the charge that the students brought against America a few years ago? Their claim was to be in revolt because revolted, because horrified, by what they were asked to consent to. I do not raise the question whether their response was pure. My question here is whether one is prepared to credit revulsion and horror as conceivably political responses, as perhaps the only epistemological access to the state of the world; as possible forms of conscience. Or is every attempt to deny the political, deny it supremacy, as it has become, in human life, to be dismissed as (anti-) hypocritical?

If youth cannot over a period of time make itself clear to age, this is tragic for both. I once described this situation as one in which society cannot hear its own screams. The nation was living then in the dissociated state of a foreign and incomprehensible war and I was, at the time I speak of, trying, defiantly if unsuccessfully, to conclude a private essay about *King Lear*, another dissociated world. is is a play in which each of two fathers produces the image of parents cannibalizing their children. *Sweet Movie* is gorged with images of this fate.) Evidently I was going around in those days, as one did, subject to fits of hearing screams in my ears. Others sometimes may have thought me mad; I sometimes thought they were driving me mad. I did not, I believe, think they were hypocrites, though it is perfectly true that I thought something was wrong with them (even ones I loved, even ones I had tremendous hopes for, like Lyndon Johnson), and true that I did not want to hear their arguments again. What allowed me to continue writing my essay was the idea of including in it a love letter to America, though its anguish at the tragedy of America might have struck some to whom it was addressed as written out of hatred.

Montaigne seems, if I understand you both, to share your view of the exclusiveness of friendship, hence to be another of the most private of men; and yet somehow he puts this together with sociability. He invented, in inventing the essay, an intimate discourse for addressing strangers. He calls those whom he addresses his "relatives and friends," and so they are, after his discourse has made them so (which it does in part by showing its strangeness to them, hence their strangeness to him, so that they may understand that there is something yet for them to become familiar with). Isn't this a staggering thing when we remember our fathers? We may have known them not to have had the education they provided for us, and sometimes felt their heartiness as well as their melancholy to be bullying, to run roughshod over our subtleties. But I remember instances of my father in conversation with strangers—in a shop, a lobby, a train—animated, laughing, comparing notes, when the charge of insincerity fell from my grasp and I would gaze at his behavior as at a mystery. How can he care enough what the other thinks to be provident of his good feeling, and yet not care so terribly as to become unable to provide it? What skill enables him to be the one that puts the other at ease? Where can he have acquired it? He knew no more about the other than the other knew about him. He seemed merely able to act on what nobody could fail to know, and to provide what nobody could fail to appreciate, even if in a given moment they could not return it. Call it sociability. At such a time I felt I would be happy to have my father as an acquaintance, to be treated by him to a serious regard, if somewhat external, for my comfort and opinion; to count not as an intimate but as an equal. The very need of formality, of ceremony, would all at once seem to me freeing, and for a while I glimpsed a splendor, a tenderness, in the idea of the sociable.

If you want further communication after the *Othello* material, it is not as hard as some of my acquaintances make out to find where I am.

♦

ON MAKAVEJEV
ON BERGMAN

♦

In our times, from the highest class of society down to the lowest, every one lives as under the eye of a hostile and dreaded censorship. Not only in what concerns others, but in what concerns themselves, the individual, or the family, do not ask themselves—what do I prefer? or, what would suit my character and disposition? or, what would allow the best and highest in me to have fair play, and enable it to grow and thrive? They ask themselves, what is suitable to my position? what is usually done by persons of my station and pecuniary circumstances? or (worse still) what is usually done by persons of a station and circumstances superior to mine? I do not mean that they choose what is customary, in preference to what suits their inclination. It does not occur to them to have any inclination, except for what is customary. Thus the mind itself is bowed to the yoke: even in what people do for pleasure, conformity is the first thing thought of; they like in crowds; they exercise choice only among things commonly done: peculiarity of taste, eccentricity of conduct, are shunned equally with crimes: until by dint of not following their own nature, they have no nature to follow: their human capacities are withered and starved: they become incapable of any strong wishes or native pleasures, and are generally without either opinions or feelings of home growth, or properly their own. Now is this, or is it not, the desirable condition of human nature?

John Stuart Mill, *On Liberty*

These remarks were occasioned by an experiment and a paper presented by the Yugoslavian filmmaker Dušan Makavejev to a confer-

ence entitled "Bergman and Dreams" held at Harvard University in January, 1978. The experiment consisted of a screening made entirely of material from the films of Ingmar Bergman, chosen and arranged with the following ideas in mind:

At times, Bergman's films look more like a book than a movie. Often, they can be reduced to "talking heads" moving through rooms. However, the nonverbal sequences in Bergman's films are replete with inner meaning and dreamlike atmosphere. It is in these sequences that Bergman tells us of many subliminal processes occurring beneath the level of the verbal interaction.

The original intention for the format of the presentation was to compose a single reel of the strongest nonverbal sequences from several of Bergman's most famous films, arrange them in some meaningful order, and screen them without any introductory explanation at the conference. The order of the sequences was worked out so that various events would not only relate to and resonate with each other, but also that parts of a sequence would have significant juxtapositions with other parts of the same sequence.

I decided to project alongside the black and white sequences two more recent films of Bergman that were photographed in color. Not only were these additional sequences in color, but they were also widescreen, thus producing a stunning visual collage. Thus, the schematization of the program is . . . : I. A single-screen projection of eleven black and white nonverbal sequences (thirty minutes). II. A three-screen simultaneous projection of black and white sequences flanked by color sequences (twenty-five minutes). III. A single-screen projection of the final minute and a half of Persona.

These descriptions are taken from the paper Makavejev, in association with his student Matthew Duda, prepared for the publication of the proceedings of the conference. However, it was expressly not to be read at the conference. On the contrary, Makavejev wished to manifest his healthy doubts about the primacy, or say authority, of the verbal. In fact the similar document that appears in the proceedings is a later version of that paper, together with other matters, put together by Duda, who had also assisted in the selection and screening

*of the Bergman sequences. While my remarks were not written for the
conference, they are included (reprinted from the Winter 1979 number of* Critical Inquiry*), along with other postconference papers, as
part of its proceedings, issued in* Film and Dreams: An Approach to
Bergman, *edited by Vlada Petric (Redgrave Publishing Company,
South Salem, N.Y., 1981). I am, I trust, still learning from the talks I
have had with Makavejev about his work and from the times I have
listened to and watched him speak publicly about his films and about
film generally—about the practical, artistic, political, intellectual,
moral (though he may distrust that word) contexts of their making. I
am also indebted to Vlada Petric, who organized the conference as
well as edited its proceedings, for many exchanges about Makavejev's work as well as about other names and topics in the history and
theory of film.*

*Some sentences from the preceding essay, "A Cover Letter to Mo-
lière's* Misanthrope,*" for reasons implied in its introductory note, are
more or less lifted into this one.*

◊

I had been delayed and only arrived at Makavejev's Bergman compilation as the lights were going down for the screening to begin. I
would not be surprised later to learn that Makavejev had, to deliver a
few words of introduction, put on a black cape and a woman's bright
red hat. I mean that while I was taken by surprise in learning of the
particular objects he sported, I might have known that he had found
at hand some way of putting a seam in our experience, of joining it,
hence differentiating it, to and from what was to succeed our arrival
in the basement auditorium of the Carpenter Center; some way of
acknowledging that his experience was about to intervene, along
certain lines, in ours.

That opening acknowledgment was in effect continued by the beginning of his presentation at the close of the film, presenting himself for discussion, no hat and cape now, no words either, no business
at all, just standing at the front of the room, looking over the lec-
tern at us, awaiting our pleasure, or whatever it would be. When it
dawned on me that he would not speak first, and that I might have

known that too (since I had come to accept, over the previous couple of years, a philosophical ambition in his work), I tried both to stay in the experience and to be aware of the length of time lapsing. Makavejev later said that it had been three minutes, but in a group of some three hundred souls, at attention, the resulting magnification of time was immeasurable. So I might itemize for future reference the elements of Makavejev's presentation in this way: [1] his verbal/visual introduction; [2] the screening; [3] his silent introduction, or invitation to discussion; and his two documents, one of which preceded the former items, one of which followed, call them [0] and [4] respectively. Document [4] is the earlier version of the Makavejev-Duda paper from which my introductory note quotes; document [0] is interpolated, explicitly as such, into the later, published version of [4].

Makavejev variously declares his intention in running together nonverbal sequences from Bergman's films. For example, in the conference paper that I quoted from in my introductory note (document [4]) he says it is "to produce a singular experience for the participants at the conference"—quite as if he were composing his own film for them. I can testify that for this viewer the intention to provide a singular experience was realized. Makavejev goes on to say that his experiment addresses the question "Is it possible to construct a Bergman film that Bergman never made?" I cannot testify to the answer to this question because I still do not know what constitutes, that is, what individuates, "a Bergman film." Maybe Makavejev could make one; maybe out of images Bergman would or could not use; and maybe another filmmaker could not.

The question "Is it possible to construct a Bergman film . . . ?" serves to make us think again about the relation of film and theater, about the fact that plays have productions and performances whereas films, by comparison, have their awful integrity or finality: modifying them feels like mutilating them. I suppose this is the feeling that, at best, could have produced the outraged question that at last broke the silence following the screening. It was a question, a comment rather, rebuking Makavejev's irresponsibility toward the prints he would have used in order to piece together ("re-edit" would hardly have been the word) his Bergman film ("his" "Bergman" "film"). The outrage rather takes it that Bergman's films are (or had been) identical with the prints Makavejev used, and that those prints were not Makavejev's to use, and hence that Makavejev's artistic probing suggested that he may not know his social obligations toward the property of others.

Having reassured the group that the prints he used of the Bergman films are fully intact, Makavejev addressed the feeling I imagined to underlie the outraged question by heading it in the direction, as in his films, of the question of outrage. He proposed that an accurate description of what he had done to Bergman was to excerpt him, thus allowing us to think how little control film audiences have over the conditions in which they view films—almost as little as over the events they view on the screen, thus perfecting the state of passivity in regarding them. In contrast, members of an audience of a (live) performance are participants in it in varying degrees; writing can be read at any tempo, at any length, in any order, and a passage reread at will; music can in addition be practiced, for example, hands separately. Those who praise film as the realization of the idea of a total art work, incorporating the other arts, appear to me to miss the equally obvious fact that film does not reciprocate; it does not lend itself—with but minor exceptions—to incorporation by the other arts. It is the perfect consumer, with a stomach for anything.

The matter of passiveness in viewing films must be an especially poignant matter for Makavejev, partly because he is so natural a maker of film, so generous a lover of film, that film's liabilities are his natural inheritance; and partly because, no doubt for this reason, one of the great subjects of his films is the variety of human passiveness, as if his interest in making his Bergman film is to say to his *semblable*, and to say it in the form of an *hommage*: Yes, the passiveness of your men and women is one revelation of the nature of film (of viewing and being viewed, of victimization), but futher revelations are possible. You may have discovered only the passiveness of revenge, and revenge itself may be causing this discovery. But who says that revenge is the last of human possibilities?

Something Makavejev calls a hypothesis about his experiment is this: "A film in which all the images are . . . [Bergman's] own but put into a different structure would offer to the viewer a possibility of exploring the inner meaning of Bergman's narrative." When later he finds the experiment to have succeeded, he accounts for the success more specifically, or practically, by claiming again that his reconstruction stayed within Bergman's imagination while at the same time it "[destroyed] the most important features of Bergman's narrative films—the plot structure, forcing the audience to perceive other components of his directorial style, such as camera movement, light impulses, mise-en-scène, shot composition, use of objects as symbols, faces in close-up, and color interactions." Nothing, I feel, is more important—who could deny it?—than to get an audience to perceive the specific events on the screen. (To have to insist on something like this is an indictment of our film culture. Surely serious readers of novels or audiences of plays know that things beyond what you may call their plots go to make up their art. Do they not?) But to effect the perception of specific events in a human work, with the goal of offering a possibility of exploring the inner meaning of, let us say, a narrative, is just something I understand the work of criticism to be.

Then let us call Makavejev's screening experiment a work of criticism. (His suggestion that it may be called a film is apt to beg a significant question of criticism.) The liability of criticism in words is that words can be cheap, the product of what Makavejev in his opening sentence calls "talking heads": mere critics using themselves only from the neck up. The liability of criticism in images is that the juxtaposition of images can be cheap, the product of mumbling bodies: mere entertainers using themselves only from the neck down. In any case the point of criticism lies in its fruitfulness. Criticism in words might take you away from the object under attention, say by avoiding everything but plot, as though everything else were ornamental or arbitrary. Criticism in images might take you away from the object by avoiding the plot, suggesting that it is arbitrary or incidental (or worse: it may encourage a perpetual assumption of poor criticism itself, that you know what the plot *is*, and how to assess it, apart from the specific events on the screen). So the fruitfulness of criticism depends upon how it is taken, what appropriation is made of it. What is the plot of *Persona*? And is it useful to assume that the brilliance of its exploration of the hunger for words and the hunger for silence, or for emptiness and fullness, or for absence and existence, or for otherness and oneness, would have been feasible for Bergman apart from the banality and evanescence of what we may call its plot? Are banality and stultification of plot Bergman's price for his art, or essential ingredients of its medium? Or both? What form of criticism is best placed to give us an answer here?

How was Makavejev's experiment in criticism appropriated by its audience? The claim I remember being made out loud most frequently during the discussion was that the experiment was not shocking, as though there were some honor in not being shockable. Makavejev says that for the three minutes of silence that unpredictably greeted the end of his screening it seemed to him that the audience was still dreaming. I do not find this quite fits my experience of that silence. I was grateful for Makavejev's power in having created this experience, and while at first I was tempted to embarrassment, I was drawn back into the experience by the candor and interest I felt in Makavejev's presence as he looked silently back at us. It was a therapeutic passage, a time in which one's experience of another and of oneself seemed fresh, seemed capable of surprise, of instruction; in which one's experience of time seemed fresh.

There were, to my mind, two primary pieces of instruction in the freshness of the inner voices made audible in that silence. One voice spoke simply of the power and energy brought to one's experience by the sheer fact of being a member of something to call an audience— a massive fact that systematic study of film, with its enforced isolation and registered audiences, is prompted to ignore. Here was a chance, exactly because no one could predict what the normal reaches of the experience would be nor what the discussion might sound like, to discover or construct an experience in common; or, perhaps I should say, to possess not only an experience in common but a certain spiralling of interpretations around it; a chance, as with old comedies, to be grateful to one's strangers rather than resentful of their intrusions, their differences from us. While this opportunity was not improved, a chance for something else almost as good might have occurred to one, namely to recognize by oneself that one may have nothing to say in a given moment and that this need be no disgrace; a chance to see that it is no point of honor to make oneself a talking head, or machine, or monkey merely because someone (perhaps oneself) cannot bear silence and gives you a penny of attention.

A related voice of instruction spoke not exactly of having nothing to say but eloquently of not wanting to say anything, of wanting not to speak. This is another creative possibility that normal routines of education ignore or suppress. It may be true of any experience of significance that one is reluctant in a given moment to try to form words for it. Sometimes one feels violated in having to produce words that one is years away from being ready to say; sometimes one may be only minutes away, but that time is no less decisive for being short. Naturally such facts may serve as excuses for someone for whom the time for words never comes, for whom the cry for change is always awkwardly too soon, for whom discussions always end before the propitious moment for satisfaction (as though others somehow exist in different circumstances). If the audience of Makavejev's experiment was really still doing something like dreaming and for *that* reason silent, I would accept this as good evidence that the experiment had constituted the showing of a film, because a natural experience of involvement in a film (inhabiting in its own way the realm of art) is that afterwards one has to awaken to the world.[1]

While Makavejev offers his experiment as "not a definitive product, but only a research . . . a new kind of evidence in film studies," it should help us to perceive that an immediate kind of evidence for studying a film, a kind taking the form of what I earlier called "criticism by images," is the use of other films: significant films are inherently criticisms of other films. Otherwise, of course, Makavejev

[1] I see no help whatever in thinking about Makavejev's experiment in the light of a remark—which seemed to gain some currency at the conference—to the effect that "the primary motivating force for dreaming is not psychological but physiological since the time of occurrence and duration of dreaming sleep are quite constant, suggesting a preprogrammed, neurally determined genesis." You might as well conclude that the primary motivating force for kissing is not psychological but physiological on the ground that the places of occurrence and the duration of kisses are quite constant. (This vaguely sounds like something Chamfort might actually have said.)

could not have conceived of his research experiment as itself a film. But then it is worth going over again one's experience of the experiment to discover whether it is right to say that "the audience followed and accepted the new structure [of the single-screen projection] as a unique continuity, that is, as a 'single' film" (perhaps as in certain kinds of musical medleys, generally comic), or whether it is better to say that the single-screen projection rather worked like vertically "compressed cinema" in which the nine films, represented in the twenty-five sequences, each maintains an autonomy that works upon one another associatively as well as reflexively, that is, both as separate films may work upon one another and as the parts of a single film work upon one another.

The nature or natures of autonomy is something Makavejev's procedures as a filmmaker depend upon and reflect upon. He declares himself to be the author of *Sweet Movie* in the statement distributed beforehand to the participants at the conference (document [0])—written to "trigger the audience's thinking about the real meaning of Bergman's films." The statement was itself triggered, evidently, by Makavejev's having had to think about the real meaning of *Sweet Movie*. (It begins: "Recently, after a screening of my film, *Sweet Movie*, someone asked me. . . . ") I might add that even should some segment of the audience respond to these events as forming a single continuity, this would not prove that they have on their hands, in Makavejev's words, "a kind of psychological Frankenstein." The Frankenstein in question may rather be, to correct a familiar mistake here where it may make all the difference, not the depicted monster but the (in the case of film, generally undepicted) maker of the monster, a role we are thus invited to project ourselves into, or rather to incorporate, in order to be in a position to ask ourselves in the right way, Why are the events on the screen as they are?

It was also the author of *Sweet Movie* who was capable of the most memorable set of critical observations made in the course of my attendance at the sessions of the conference. During a discussion of the opening sequence of more or less explicitly autobiographical images and reflexive cinematic preoccupations that form the authorial prologue to *Persona*, Makavejev interrupted from the floor, saying, in effect, "Why speculate here? Science can be brought to bear and we can look at what the actual images show us. From Tausk's 1919 paper 'On the Origin of the Influencing Machine' we learn that each schizophrenic has his own all-powerful dictating machine. This machine is our genitals, projected and seen as foreign, determining our lives, the source of life. Bergman's depiction of the parts of a projector is his declaration of his machine, so conceived. Now by editing, the old woman *becomes* (is replaced by) the live young boy. The woman is magnified and blurred. In relation to her the boy is the size of a fetus. But what is the blurring for? The capacity for sight matures in the womb at about five or six months. So blurring suggests that the child in question is yet unborn." If you can think like this, nothing is beyond mattering to you. The implication I draw is not that it is necessary to be a significant filmmaker in order to be capable of such remarks but rather that some significant filmmakers are also born teachers and that this fact about them may enter into the experience of their films, yielding the ecstatic experience—perhaps therapeutic—of being encouraged genuinely to think.

I take this as my cue for saying that my appropriation of Makavejev's experiment was and remains determined by my acceptance of his corpus of films as a significant present in the history of the art of film, a place in which the future of filmmaking, hence of significant film theory and of film studies generally, will have to work itself out. I do not propose to discuss this achievement at much length here, but I wish to give a concrete sense of Makavejev's remarks about his experiment as issuing from an experience of, especially, *Sweet Movie*.

Makavejev's recurrence to the ideas of death and birth, in his critical remark about the opening of *Persona* and in his quoting (in document [o]) of Bergman's statement "Each film is my last" (commenting about this that "it is not only a statement about imminent death, but a testimony of an obsessive need to be reborn over and over again"), recalls the recurrence of the ideas of death and birth in *Sweet Movie*. The sound track opens with a song asking "Is there life after birth?" and the images end with a corpse coming to life; in between, the film is obsessed with images of attempts to be born. The question about life after birth—posing the question whether we may hope for mortality as prior to the question whether we may hope for immortality—has the satisfying sound of one of Feuerbach's or the early Marx's twists that turn Christianity upside down into socialism. (Compare this from Marx's "A Contribution to the Critique of Hegel's 'Philosophy of Right': Introduction": "Luther, to be sure, overcame servitude based on devotion, but by replacing it with servitude based on conviction. He shattered faith in authority by restoring the authority of faith. . . . But if Protestantism was not the real solution it at least posed the problem correctly. Thereafter it was no longer a question of the layman's struggle with the priest outside of him, but of his struggle with his own inner priest, his priestly nature. And if the Protestant transformation of the German laity into priests emancipated the lay popes—the princes together with their clergy, the privileged and the philistines—so the philosophical transformation of the priestly Germans into men will emancipate the people.") It is the great concluding moments of *Sweet Movie*, however, which bear direct comparison with the great opening moments of *Persona*. But even to describe those concluding sonorities relevantly requires a general idea of the film as a whole.

Sweet Movie is, at a minimum, the most original exploration known to me of the endless relations between documentary and fictional film, incorporating both; hence in that way an original exploration of the endless relations between reality and fantasy. Its use of documentary footage declares that every movie has a documentary basis—at least in the camera's ineluctable interrogation of the natural endowment of the actors, the beings who submit their being to the work of film. My private title for Makavejev's construction of *Sweet Movie* (his fifth film) and of (his third and fourth films) *Innocence Unprotected* and *WR: Mysteries of the Organism* is "the film of excavation." (WR means Wilhelm Reich, on whom the film is a meditation.) I mean by this of course my sense of his work's digging to unearth buried layers of the psyche but also my sense that these constructions have the feeling of reconstruction—as of something lost or broken. The search at once traces the integrity (you might say the autonomy) of the individual strata of a history and plots the positions of adjacent strata. I accept as well the implied sense—something the experience of Makavejev's last three films conveys to me—that these constructions are inherently the working out of a group's genius, its interactions, not of one individual's plans; though it is true and definitive of Makavejev's work that a group's interactions, or those of shifting groups, work themselves out into comprehensible forms because a given individual is committed to seeing to it that they may.

This so far says nothing at all about *how* these autonomies, adjacencies, and interactions are devised and directed. But all I wish to convey here is an intuition of the kind of differences there will be between works made by the director of excavation sites and by, let us say, the operator of a switchboard (I take the title of Makavejev's second film—*Love Affair; or, The Case of the Missing Switchboard Operator*—to give one description of the director of a film, hence to name his relation to this work). And I would like to encourage as well an intuition of the differences there may be between works made on the principles of Eisensteinian montage or of Surrealist juxtapositions and those which are made on the principle of what I am thinking of as the aligning of adjacent strata. The former seek to fix or to flout significance, perhaps to suggest that significance is necessarily private or public or arbitrary or infinite or nonexistent. The latter propose significance as the intersection of nature and history, as a task of a continuous and natural unfolding of interpretations, each felt as complete and each making possible the next, until a human form of life fits together. (This is how classical narrative may be understood to direct itself.) The analogue of archeological excavation would accordingly realize what Bazin wanted from continuous shooting and deep focus without having to invoke an a priori or fixed understanding of the general differences between montage and continuity. (Of course all these modes of abutment are employed by Makavejev. Just as any good film may be expected to require authors who are, in varying degrees, both excavators and switchboard operators. And of course I am not prepared to define what a continuous and natural unfolding of interpretations is. I propose an intuition for investigation, of which the discovery and justification of this phrase is a proposed first step.)

The conscience of *Sweet Movie* is most hideously captured in a sequence of literal excavation—the Nazi documentary footage of German troops exhuming bodies from mass graves in the Katyn Forest. A lifelong participant in a society of declared socialist aspirations, Makavejev is asking: Was my revolution capable even of this? Has it cannibalized everything that has touched it? Is it true that the Red Army committed a mass murder of the Polish officer corps? The film shows a card which contains Anthony Eden's response to this news: "Let us think of these things always. Let us speak of them never." For Makavejev, that conspiracy of silence, call it mass hypocrisy, is a prescription for self-administered mass death. Mere film alone cannot prove who caused and buried the corpses in the Katyn Forest, but this film directly refuses the conspiracy of silence about it.

The focal characters of *Sweet Movie* are two women, Miss World and Captain Anna Planeta, who respectively represent, more or less allegorically, the Americanized and the Sovietized forms of contemporary existence; though, as their names suggest, they are to be found everywhere. These women never meet, but their conditions intertwine under the tension of the representations and ideas of the film, especially of birth and death, of sexuality and seduction, and of food, of eating and being eaten. The muse of old revolutions, Captain Anna, living on memories, presides over a drifting boat named *Survival*; the North American Miss World, figure of an early republic and living on anticipation, is presided over successively by a mother-in-law, a husband, and a latin lover, types from farce and romance let loose. The film opens on the North American side with a burlesque beauty or sweetness contest and continues with a satiric honeymoon trip about Niagara Falls and a wedding night of apparently Swiftian ambition. The first problem with the film, for me, is in understanding why this ambition is so weakly realized; the opening jokes on America are too broad, too abstract. The beauty contest in the form of competitive pelvic examinations seems too corny an idea to bear the weight of the themes it takes upon itself. Anyone who has given a thought to beauty contests knows that the plain facts about them must be more fantastic than a ribald allegory will capture and knows most particularly that beauty contests *are* burlesque shows. Then perhaps the real target of this satire is the real burlesque show. But the pleasures, the sweetness, no doubt somewhat uneducated, in either the real or the artificial exhibition is not something one can imagine a thinker of Makavejev's aspirations criticizing by making abstract fun of them, distancing himself from such expressions of needfulness, from the victims and the victimizers in these entertainments. Indeed, one of the qualities you come to depend upon in his work is its generosity toward pleasures and aspirations not exactly his own. (The failure of this generosity may even be derived as a characteristic of what he would mean by tyranny.) This is especially true in his feeling for popular entertainments or exhibitions, represented in his first film, *Man Is Not a Bird*, and in his third, *Innocence Unprotected*, in images of the circus. But then here is a first answer to this problem of *Sweet Movie*: images of circus acts (of all but inhuman acrobatic feats; of the things human beings can train themselves to swallow—swords, snakes, fire) together with vaudeville science (sometimes a sensational lecture, sometimes a demonstration of the powers of hypnosis) at once represent the degree to which society trains us to be freaks and form Makavejev's declarations of the powers or sources or responsibilities of the fact and the art of film. Makavejev cannot then be exempting himself from the worlds he departs from and depicts. But I knew that without such evidence. The therapeutic effect that watching and thinking about his films seems to have upon me is possible only as a function of the sense of inclusion in an enterprise honestly in search of self-understanding.

Of course if those opening sequences are badly done, without interesting ideas or true feelings, then these considerations of mine will not save them. But these considerations do make me want to see those sequences again. Then I would ask what the participating gynecologist, and the instrument, I mean the camera, his interest directs, are looking for up there: a hymen? a fetus? a penis? Makavejev credits Bergman with having been "the first major contemporary filmmaker who publicly raised the essential question: 'Am I, indeed, a woman?' " Is the pelvic examination a way of confessing that we do not know what a woman, in oneself or others, is?

The film fully begins for me (the three times I have seen it) when the second narrative focus—the boat of the drifting revolution— begins being cut in periodically with the first. This experience suggests an asymmetry of interest between the external depiction of Americanization and the internal expression of Sovietization and suggests that the tissue of cliché in which the opening sequences are wrapped is itself a perception or confession that socialist criticisms of clichéd Americanized aspirations are themselves clichés. This is a problem for a socialist; for a liberal, let us say, it may be a relief. But why isn't the issue for both of them to understand what happened to the fact and the idea of liberty under Americanization and to understand what happened to the idea and fact of community under Sovietization? Why isn't it?

Simultaneous issues of individual liberty and of true community, issues forever compromising one another in liberalism and in socialism, come to a crisis in *Sweet Movie* in the documentary or quasidocumentary footage of members of the Muehl commune—the film's best-remembered feature—where individuals who claim to witness the absolute bondage in which social existence has secured them band together to permit one another something you might see as absolute freedom. This freedom is to be achieved by a transgression of social taboos as specific and systematic as Freud's transgressions of defense mechanisms when he accompanied his patients on their journeys back. Expressing themselves in spitting food on one another, in vomiting at will, pissing, shitting, in mock self-castrations, the members of the commune go further than one might have expected to see in turning themselves inside out. They regress to the condition of birth as if to give birth to themselves from their otherwise dead bodies, the group assisting as anagogic midwives, oiling, wiping, and powdering their huge, bouncing babies and praising their performances of the natural functions of living things. Thus is Makavejev's opening question of life after birth given one answer, and Bergman's opening fantasy of the dead woman and the fetus given one natural realization.

The center of the action of the commune sequence is a communal meal, a feast whose ritualization strikes me as possessing, for all its confusion of tongues, a working solemnity. I think of Marx's characterization of religion as the heart of a heartless world, and I ask myself what the things of acceptance and redemption might look like to those who would actually bring such concepts to earth—as if inventing them and giving them a heart. I had not liked Makavejev's complaint that Bergman's "conception of God, especially, the God who does not love people and who makes them unexplainably miserable, seems to me incomprehensible and gratuitous for a serious artist." If this is bad for a serious artist, I felt, it is bad for any human being; but is it a matter over which human beings have a choice? But I also felt that Makavejev is meeting Bergman at once on Bergman's ground and on Marx's: "The critique of religion is the prerequisite of every critique." What Makavejev sees in religion and how he effects his critique of it will come up again.

(Since in the working of this film and in the mode of thinking it exemplifies, apt conjunction is everything, allowing the mutual excavation of concepts, I shall quote from the early pages of C. G. Jung's autobiography, *Memories, Dreams, Reflections*, without comment (as if one might use a quotation within the body of a text, that is, after the text has begun, as what you may call an internal epigraph), some fragments from his interpretation of "the earliest dream I can remember, a dream which was to preoccupy me all my life": "At all events, the phallus of this dream seems to be a subterranean God 'not to be named,' and such it remained throughout my youth, reappearing whenever anyone spoke too emphatically about Lord Jesus. . . . The fear of the 'black man,' which is felt by every child, was not the essential thing in that experience; it was, rather, the recognition that stabbed through my childish brain: 'That is a Jesuit.' So the important thing in the dream was its remarkable symbolic setting and the astounding interpretation: 'That is the man-eater.' . . . In the dream I went down into the hole in the earth and found something very different on a golden throne, something non-human and underworldly, which gazed fixedly upward and fed on human flesh. It was only fifty years later that a passage in a study of religious ritual burned into my eyes, concerning the motif of cannibalism that underlies the symbolism of the Mass. . . . Through this childhood dream I was initiated into the secrets of the earth. What happened then was a kind of burial in the earth, and many years were to pass before I came out again. Today I know that it happened in order to bring the greatest possible amount of light into the darkness. It was an initiation into the realm of darkness. My intellectual life had its unconscious beginnings at that time.")

The sequences in the commune are, among other things, revolting. Placed in general adjacency with the sequences of the Katyn massacre, which is also revolting, we are asked to ask ourselves what we are revolted by. What is the meaning of revulsion? If rotting corpses make us want to vomit, why at the same time do live bodies insisting on their vitality? But the members of the commune themselves display images of revulsion, as if to vomit up the snakes and swords and fire the world forces down our throats. It is on this understanding that the sequence strikes me as one of innocence, or of a quest for innocence—the exact reverse of the unredeemable acts of tyrants, under whatever banner. (Look at this from *Walden*, the penultimate chapter entitled "Spring": "We need to witness our own limits transgressed, and some life pasturing freely where we never wander. We are cheered when we observe the vulture feeding on the carrion which disgusts and disheartens us, and deriving health and strength from the repast. There was a dead horse in the hollow by the path to my house, which compelled me sometimes to go out of my way, especially in the night when the air was heavy, but the assurance it gave me of the strong appetite and inviolable health of Nature was my compensation for this. I love to see that Nature is so rife with life that myriads can be afforded to be sacrificed and suffered to prey on one another; that tender organizations can be so serenely squashed out of existence like pulp,—tadpoles which herons gobble up, and tortoises and toads run over in the road; and that sometimes it has rained flesh and blood! With the liability to accident, we must see how little account is to be made of it. The impression made on a wise man is that of universal innocence." Our wisdom is being put to the test here, along with Makavejev's. For the commune can give an impression of innocence, and achieve it, only if the work it is doing is the work of nature. Yet just that claim of obeying nature is the perennial claim of the de Sades of history.)

The commune is perfectly or purely indecent. I recall that to allegorize modern totalitarianism, Camus wrote *The Plague*, claiming that the only power sufficient to rid us of plagues is ordinary decency. Makavejev, through the commune, suggests that our strategy against emotional plague will have to be or to include indecency. I recall as well that the original title of Camus's book translated as *The Rebel* is *L'Homme revolté*, man revolted. Camus speaks of every form of revolt save, apparently, the one Makavejev takes as fundamental, physiological revolt. This means something for which I take Zarathustra to have laid down the logic or prescription: "You say 'I' and you are proud of this word. But greater than this—although you will not believe in it—is your body and its great intelligence, which does not say 'I' but performs 'I' " ("Of the Despisers of the Body"). Beyond the images of the commune, the emotion in the film as a whole, in its horrors, in its longing, in its laughter, is to have us become less proud of saying "No" in order to let the intelligence of the body perform "No"—in preparation, of course, of finding something, that is, creating something, to which "Yes" can be said and be done. I think of this No in terms of Zarathustra's parable in "Of the Three Metamorphoses": "I name you three metamorphoses of the spirit: how the spirit shall become a camel, and the camel a lion, and the lion at last a child. There are many heavy things for the spirit, for the strong weight-bearing spirits in which dwell respect and awe: its strength longs for the heavy, for the heaviest. . . . To create freedom for itself and a sacred No even to duty: the lion is needed for that, my brother. . . . Why must the preying lion still become a child? The child is innocence and forgetfulness, a new beginning, a sport, a self-propelling wheel, a first motion, a sacred Yes."

This combination of physiological revolt, of revoltedness, of disgust, together with the quest for innocence which forms a particular epistemological access to the state of the world, is something I broached in an essay that introduces a reading of *Othello* with a letter addressed to Molière's Alceste, the misanthrope.[2] In that letter I tell Alceste of some later writers who have shared his revulsion with the ways of the world, his finding the world uninhabitable. The immediate cause for linking Alceste and Othello is that each, because of their perceptions of certain distasteful, metaphysical facts about human existence, demands to be the whole world to the woman he loves—which really means, demands that she provide an entire world for him. One woman declines and is abandoned; the other accepts and is suffocated. I tell Alceste that I mean to write to him about *Sweet Movie* as in effect the most concentrated work I know that follows out the idea that the way to assess the state of the world is to find out how it tastes (a sense modality not notably stressed by orthodox epistemologists but rather consigned to a corner of aesthetics)—which means both to find out how it tastes to you and how it tastes you, for example, to find out whether you and the world are disgusting to one another. Such an assessment is particularly suited to a time at which the individual is asked to consent to his or her world, to take his or her place in society, that is, to take responsibility for it. It is the time at which adolescence and adulthood are discovered, the one as what you are asked to forgo, the other as what you are asked to accept instead. I claim that Alceste, and Hamlet before him (with his sensitivity to odor, to the rotting) and the romantics and the existentialists after him, represent this discovery of adolescence.

The discovery of adulthood through disgust was something acted out in the student movement in the time of our war in Vietnam. To perform ugly and indecent acts was an expression of the rejection of a world that asked for consent to its disgusting deeds. This was not my way of expression, partly because I had already given my consent to this world and partly because I do not understand myself as performing ugly and indecent acts. But I understand that way, I felt the exactness of its spiritual accuracy. To say so was my way, and it has

---

[2]The letter to Alceste immediately precedes this essay in this book.

its own price. This is or was so obvious that serious films made during that period did not so much need to assert disgust with the world as to ask for its assessment, to acknowledge this fact of the world without letting it sap the motivation to work at this art, even if the art itself was the best context for the assessment. Makavejev's way in *WR* is to follow a sole poet-actor dressed in mock battle gear down New York streets, a diminished Quixote bringing the war home. Makavejev is letting the war show its threat to drive one crazy. Bergman's way in *Persona* is to have the woman of silence see on a television screen the unforgettable footage of a priest immolating himself in protest; as if she were witnessing an image of a dream of herself, as if she were the origin of the craziness of the world.

Alceste's interpretation of the uninhabitability of the world, that is, of his distaste, is to see the world as a scene of universal hypocrisy. *Sweet Movie* interprets this hypocrisy, as it were, by picturing the earth as full of corpses—buried evidence of mass murder, rotting ideals, corpses with souls still in them. The film attempts to extract hope—to claim to divine life after birth—from the very fact that we are capable of genuine disgust at the world; that our revoltedness is the chance for a cleansing revulsion; that we may purge ourselves by living rather than by killing, willing to visit hell if that is the direction to something beyond purgatory; that the fight for freedom continues to originate in the demands of our instincts, the chaotic cry of our nature, our cry to have a nature. It is a work powerful enough to encourage us to see again that the tyrant's power continues to require our complicitous tyranny over ourselves. (In the early paragraphs of *Walden*: "It is hard to have a Southern overseer; it is worse to have a Northern one; but worst of all when you are the slave-driver of yourself." That was never easy to say. It is always in danger of a merely literary appropriation.) In my earlier essay I more or less accuse both Alceste and Othello of inviting Montaigne's terrible rebuke to mankind in "On some verses of Virgil": "What a monstrous animal to be a horror to himself, to be burdened by his pleasures, to regard himself as a misfortune!" But I go on to say—something I take *Sweet Movie* to be saying—that the world during my lifetime rather shows that it is yet more horrible to lose this capacity for horror.

It is to the anarchic commune that the American Miss is brought (some successor of what in *The Philadelphia Story* is called the married maiden, the American female), in a wheelbarrow, as if we are to discover that there may be something beyond the rubbish heap of history. She proves unable, however, to participate in this invitation to rebirth, and in the next and final sequence that we see her (as in her first sequence and in her central scene of copulation and cramp on the Eiffel Tower with El Macho), she is in front of a camera, enlivened, say animated, by the condition of exhibition. (Is this all a camera can do after human birth—create animation, or liveliness, not life?) Her inability to participate is shown as an inability to be nourished. A lifelong force-fed consumer, she becomes anorexic; and she swiftly winds up as a piece of chocolate. (Sorority girls in my youth used to announce their engagement to their sorority sisters by passing around a box of chocolate-covered cherries.) As she writhes and then drowns in the vat of chocolate-mud-excrement, like an isolated female wrestler, we can see at last, though filtered through a film of chocolate, a sweet movie, the genitals denied our sight when she was first introduced to us. She is again food for the hungry movie camera, a responsibility accepted by Makavejev as his depicted cameraman says an excited "Beautiful!" in response to her dying. And the insatiable and deadly voyeurism of the camera is then more amply declared by alluding—in an extreme close-up of this woman's profile as her head touches the floor of the vat and we see one eye caught open by death—to the shower murder of *Psycho*.

The anorexia of Miss World is linked to Captain Anna Planeta's cannibalism, suggesting that this figure of the revolution is a further surrogate for this movie director and this director's camera; at once the projection of human desire and the potential death of it. The women are also linked, also in counterpoise, by the idea and representations of corpses, the one seduced into becoming a corpse, the other producing corpses of those she has seduced. We see Captain Anna kill only once, the sailor from *Potemkin* whom she has bathed like a child; she bites him to drink blood and then stabs him to death in a bed of sugar. We are given to believe that this is her habitual treatment of those to whom she grants her favors.

We are also given to believe that she kills the four barely pubescent boys whom she invites into her hold and seduces in a scene of private striptease that forms the most difficult passage, from the perspective of ordinary moral sensibility, of this difficult film. The primary direction or object of moral outrage here is the reverse of what it is in the commune sequence. There we must wonder what the justification is for Makavejev's subjecting his audience to these scenes; the actors are unharmed, they self-evidently are behaving in ways no one has dictated to them; the struggle of their freedom with the power of the camera is an equal one. In the seduction of the children, both actors and audience are being subjected to something that requires justification, but one's first concern is for the actors, I mean the children. The question of this concern is opened to criticism (treated dialectically, its question subjected to a question) by our finding that the experience of the scene contains tenderness and elicits from us a reluctant excitement preserved under its anxiety. We recognize our complicity in finding in a world of corpses a world whose common coin of relationship is seduction, and we recognize our complicity as seducer and as seduced. But is this lesson sufficient justification for subjecting these young boys to this treatment? The scene is also a brilliant and inescapable declaration of a fact essential to anything I have recognized as a movie I have cared about—that it contains projections of (photographic displacements of) real human beings, human beings subjected to the interrogations and the imposing transformations of the camera. But is the declaration of this fact sufficient justification for subjecting just these real young male human beings to exactly these ways of this particular older woman's presenting herself to them? She really is taking off her stocking *for* this boy; really placing her naked leg over his shoulder, her pubic hair tufting beyond the edges of the strip of fabric hanging loosely down her front; she really is unzipping *his* fly. . . . No serious artist could have risked this sequence who did not know in his or her bones that eleven- or twelve-year-old boys have *already* been seduced over and over and more intractably than any way in which this nice lady will affect them in providing them and herself for the camera. The artist knows this not in a spirit which would say that a little more seduction won't hurt but knows it out of a conviction that the process of going through these gestures—with friendly preparation and with explicit delimitations, for the comprehensible purpose of producing the communication in these matters for a film—is, on the contrary, potentially therapeutic. (It was perhaps not surprising that freedom in the direction of what will still be called the pornographic has made possible a further region in which film may acknowledge the human individuality of its human subjects. I believe some people have felt that the softcore freedom of *Last Tango in Paris* did this for Marlon Brando. I do not so much wish to deny this as to say that it seems to me to underrate other of Brando's self-revelations—from as early as the t-shirt in *Streetcar.* An altogether more important revelation of *Last Tango*, to my mind, lies in its softcore limitation. Given what this film seems to be about, this limitation acknowledges not a freedom but a limitation that we understand will persist however far the camera will be permitted to go with stars in the future. The camera's metaphysical limitation is that it cannot provide unshakable evidence of the *satisfaction* of desire any more than the plain eye or ear can provide it—not of the woman's and not, if you are serious about it, of the man's either. A realization of *this* limitation must have contributed to turning the camera to greater feats of violence.)

The therapeutic effort in reenactment conjoins the seduction dance with the project of the commune; so does the mood it reaches of attentive solemnity, another invocation of the religious. The sound track—a male chorus singing something I recall Makavejev's identifying as a piece of Russian Orthodox liturgical music—does not impose the idea of the religious on this dancing but reveals it there, shows that it is naturally to be taken there, however unpredictably. (Exactly *what* creates this experience is an obligation of criticism to discover.) This experience—call it an experience of seeing something as something, witnessing its presence—acknowledges a clear indebtedness to Surrealism's experiments in cinema but simultaneously acknowledges an absolute break with, or reinterpretation of, Surrealism's experience and ambition. The sequence is equally conjoined, by opposition, to two features in the opening sequences with Miss World: first, the striptease is another direct borrowing from burlesque; second, Captain Anna is dressed, to the extent she is dressed, as a bride, so this is a honeymoon for her. In comparison with the honeymoon to which the first woman is subjected—her brutish and foul husband, wishing to sully her, obsessed with his personal hygiene, urinates at her from his metallic penis (bronzed or gilded, I imagine, as if in sentimental and detached memory of itself)—Anna's dance for the young boy is progressive, humanizing, and gives seduction due praise as an origin and consequence of the human craving for beauty, for a genuine cleansing of the spirit.

One more identification within the complex crossroads of the seduction sequence and I can make good—as good as I can—on my claim concerning the richness of the ending of *Sweet Movie*. Children led into an out-of-the-way dwelling, made of and covered with sweets, by an old witch who means to roast them for a meal, is the story of Hansel and Gretel, hardly the only fairy tale in which children are in danger of being eaten. When the sailor from the *Potemkin* says poignantly, "I'm starved for love," Anna buries the image, which is true of her, under a callous ideological rhetoric: "Only those who starve know how to love." The film is about how children come to be eaten and thereby about how witches are created, with their terrible, human emptiness. (That the failure to acknowledge children, to grant them an autonomous existence, may present itself in consciousness as their being eaten by their parents, is attested to twice in *King Lear*, once by each father.)

It is in light of this fairy tale allusion that I call attention to one of Makavejev's perceptions of Bergman's silences: "The *nonverbal* sequences in Bergman's films are replete with inner meaning and dream-like atmosphere. . . . [They], however, are often 'covered over' by the banality of the plot, creating an ambiguous understanding of the characters' psychic tension. . . . This tension is presented in a dreamlike way, possessing that 'tender insecurity' which always appears when the unreal is presented as absolutely real. It seems to me that Bergman's frequent use of nonverbal sequences is due to his fear of laying bare this insecurity in a direct verbal manner." *Sweet Movie* contains three extended nonverbal sequences, the dance of seduction, the communal feast, and the Katyn Forest footage. The seduction is the most dreamlike, the commune the least, and that documentary footage somewhere between dream and reality. To think through this variation is an obligation for those who believe in the value of this film and in the value of the consideration of dreams. The seduction *could* be read as a dream, but it need not. How is this different from our less luxurious, hence less noticeable, waking seductions? If we dream of such seduction, what is our complicity in the trance of our waking life? Again, if the reality of Katyn Forest is unbearable, then what happens if we cannot put it out of our dreams? Isn't that forest a name for the region inhabited by regimes who no longer know that there is a difference between dream and reality, acting out the one, wiping out the other? Again, if the members of the commune so directly express their wishes, destroying for one another the censorship that comes between us and ours, then what need would they have to dream? Can they? Is the vanishing of dreams something that frightens us? And are we to be likened, as Freud implies and as Descartes says at the close of his First Meditation, to slaves who are struggling not to awaken from a dream of liberty?

All I call attention to here is that in each of these three sequences the cause or occasion of the silence—or rather of the absence of words—is clear, as clear as an initial broaching of the situations can make them; and the issues within the situations are clear, anyway clear enough to begin a course of thinking about them; and the demand for thinking is urgent, as urgent as this master of excavation and conjunction can make it; and the evidence we are given for thinking through our silences and our conjunctions—for supporting a course of meditation—is complete, anyway as complete as the movie is, yielding significance to genuine interest and meditation, perhaps willing to be known better than it knows itself, an inspirer of thought.

It seems to me a reasonable hypothesis (which I will not attempt to test here) that Makavejev's films are less closely related to the dreams of sleep than they are to the dreams of what we call waking life, to trances. We might call the former restoring dreams (stocking our memories) and the latter guiding dreams (stocking us with what we call perceptions). The former emphasize the private and hallucinatory quality of dreaming; the latter emphasize the public and hypnotic character of dreaming. The former relate dreaming, anyway something less than waking, to religion; the latter relate dreaming to politics.

The final sequence of *Sweet Movie* opens, tinted blue, with five corpses (the sailor and the four boys) wrapped in plastic shrouds and laid neatly side by side on a river bank. We got there this way. We had earlier seen the police board the *Survival*, take Captain Anna into custody, and lay the wrapped bodies on this bank. Then after the American Miss fails to find another birth of freedom in the continent of the commune, we find her succeeding in becoming a chocolate corpse. From there we cut for a moment back to the exhumations of the bodies in the Katyn Forest, the footage tinted blue as it was in its original occurrence for us; and it is from here, retaining the monochrome blue tinting, that we cut back to those corpses on the bank. I remember what then happens this way. The wrapped corpses, shot so as to recede from us, begin to stir, and the human beings we knew to be inside, call them the actors, begin removing themselves from their cerements or cocoons, exhuming themselves. The figure nearest us proves to be the boy who was the main object of the seduction dance. He turns his face toward the screen and looks out, toward the (invisible) camera, toward us. An elevated train enters the background of the frame, from right to left, its high whistle blowing. The boy's look, perhaps in conjunction with this intervention of the train, freezes the frame, which thus preserves the looking and stops the train in midpassage; the whistle continues to blow for a moment, from nowhere to nowhere. Then gradually the blue tint gives way and color comes back to the frame, upon which the film ends.

These final moments form a further nonverbal sequence which epitomizes the film's perception of the world as full of corpses and in need of salvation—call it unfreezing, or metamorphosis, or coming to life, or call it the possibility of putting off the old man, the possibility of being born. The sequence, as well, claims for itself the classical alliance of sleep with death, so that the boy, in shedding his character and being (re)born as the actor he is in actuality, seems to be awakening, as from a dream, as from a film. In this absence of words, Makavejev acknowledges himself as the maker of this film by declaring his choice over a procession of what I have called automatisms of cinema. He is implied by whether a particular image moves, by its duration, by exactly what is allowed inside any frame and what is excluded, by what is heard, its duration and whether it is in synchrony, by the relations achieved between characters and the live actors they inhabit for the film, by whether color is wished for.

Significant films are those which give significance to the conditions of the medium of film. These conditions cannot be known a priori but must be worked out in acts of criticism which undertake to derive the significance of particular automatisms, undertake even to say that a particular set of events constitutes a significant automatism. But deriving significance is a matter of seeing how just this automatism is invited by just this subject, given significance by its place in this film—for the subject is not defined before the way of discovering it is defined. To get these matters together for a particular film is to give a reading of it. I read the concluding sequence as follows.

The boy looks out. Which is to say, Makavejev directs the boy to look out, at him; not exactly in accusation, rather as with a question. Makavejev is asking himself: Is there life after the birth of my film? Am I, at the end of what I have made here, to see that I have given life to this creation, or have I worked with live human beings only to choke off their voices in midpassage, only to turn them into dead replicas of themselves, mummies wrapped in celluloid? The boy looks out at the man who has interrogated his life and subjected it to new seductions and interrogates him in turn: If I am the innocence from which your experience has grown, the ambition along which your art has developed, you, who are now a consenting adult in a world of horrors, what world have you made for me to want, or in what way have you instructed me in what to want and in how to want, or what beauty and honesty have you provided for me to tide me over into my own consent? That Makavejev risks his work by giving it over to these questions and that the boy accepts the bequest and forgives the older self that he has become is expressed by the flowering of the film from its ambiguous tint back into color. It is being returned back to life and to its author. To see that the actor forgives the director is to see that Makavejev is forgiving himself—for the fact that the world is not better than it is and the fact that those who would make it better have only themselves, products of such a world, to work with. It is the best basis in the world from which to look for a new beginning, a first motion.

I have said little about Makavejev's sense of humor, but that sense is as active throughout *Sweet Movie* (and *WR*) as its sense of outrage. Indeed his good humor and his outrage make one another possible. I do not know that I can yet say anything useful by way of characterizing his particular cast of humor, but I feel sure that the commune sequence, for example, hasn't done what work it can until we can see, for example, the fat rosy man, who is being bounced and oiled and powdered and who then, while lying on his back, pisses a mighty arc into the air—not at all to sully anyone—and thereupon rises to take a bow, as someone being accepted back into a condition of playfulness.

Sweet Movie's conjunctions of ideas and moods invokes *The Gold Rush*, which extracts hilarity from a threat of cannibalism. Chaplin contrasts the imagination of his brutish cabinmate, who hallucinates the little man to be a Thanksgiving turkey, with the imagination of that little man himself, who can turn a shoe into a piece of food and turn pieces of food into a pair of shoes, actions which prove genuinely life-sustaining. The former dreams as we imagine the brutes dream, as the dog dreams of the rabbit. Judging from *The Gold Rush*, to dream the dream of civilization, to elaborate dire necessity into a ceremonial feast and into art, requires an openness to one's childhood, or childlikeness, and an openness to the distance and the splendors of others. The art of the little man's dream here is depicted as dancing (making rolls dance), but the self-reflexive references in the concluding sequence (where the little man is told, by a man behind a camera, that he has ruined the picture, apparently by expressing his desire before the camera) make it clear that the actual work of art in question is this film. So this film, as explicitly as *Sweet Movie* but less concretely, accounts for its origins. The cabin fever of the brute expresses itself as cannibalism not simply because he is starving but because he cannot tolerate the incomprehensible imagination of the one he is starving with, the mystery of that other's difference from him. He would incorporate the difference.

The conjunction of hilarity with human nature stripped away occurs, again, in the figure of Harpo Marx, another type of the artist (depicted as a virtuoso on the instrument of angels). Here cannibalism seems bypassed in a general condition of insatiability—an id somehow escaped intact. Groucho's acceptance and appreciation of Harpo establishes one of the tenderest relationships in the history of theater and exacts of him a pure commitment to anarchy. I do not quite wish to say that Harpo and Groucho would be at home in the Muehl commune but rather that they treat so-called civilized persons as if those persons were living in the commune without knowing it or knowing much—not because Harpo and Groucho impose their imaginations upon others but because they can respond accurately to the veneer of hieroglyphs the others put upon their desires. Their humor would then represent an effort not to die of pity for the world. Wit, by contrast, is conservative, not penetrating the hieroglyphs of society but perpetuating their mode. And here one should recognize that Groucho's commitment to the pun is a profound trait of his character not because his puns are always funny (often they are not), but because it is a commitment, a pure commitment to *his* response, refusing the coin of what the world has given him to mean. Thus is humor a moral equivalent of heroism. (I think of two fine songs that treat the knowledge of our wish to incorporate others not with horror but with particular good humor: "Sweet Georgia Brown" ("She ain't colored, she was born that way") and "Honeysuckle Rose" ("You're confection, goodness knows . . ."). I come from a culture in which a preoccupation of Montaigne's is brought momentary peace in the strains of Fats Waller.)

I know of no one who has found humor in anorexia, unless Kafka's "Hunger Artist" can be seen to be funny. (Though it occurs to me that I do not understand why an impulse to vomit, the hand over the mouth and a hasty exit, is found funny (in America; in English-speaking theater more generally?) whereas an urge to defecate, to lose control *that* way, is not. In France, *On purge bébé*; but in America it is *Bringing Up Baby*.) The most explicit anorexic I know in film is the woman in Antonioni's *Red Desert*, whose refusal to partake appears as something between a fear of being polluted or poisoned, a terror of trusting, and a wish not to have a body. It also goes with difficulty in taking care of a child, as if this obligation blocked a wish to become small or thin enough to be seen to need taking care of. I find myself thinking in this connection also of the woman in Godard's *Two or Three Things I Know about Her*, who consumes or swallows everything but what requires literal eating. Does the fact that, after our American Miss fails to be taught by the commune to admit nourishment or comfort by her mouth, she then exposes her genitals to a camera mean that she has been brought to ask: "Am I, indeed, a woman?" (She has identified with an earlier aggressor, the chocolate man who carried her to a cave of milk, exposed himself to her, knocked her out, and then packed her off to let her see if she could be born. Her identification, though mistaken, was a sign of a will to health, since she knew this man to be real, knew what he was made of, having licked his cheek and found it tasted sweet, the last taste in her mouth. But she found out from this empirical investigation only what the world had already forced down her throat, that the darkness of his skin was not merely a color but a matter of substance.) Is this question of identity something a camera can answer? I have said that it seems to me a question the camera is asking—of her, of itself.

What is the question? Am I, indeed, . . . since I do not know the difference between men and women—or perhaps between activity and passivity—and hence can imagine that there is none? Am I, indeed, . . . since I am castrated (I lack something)? Am I, indeed, . . . since I am not castrated (there is nothing I lack; I was born this way)? This sequence represents Miss World's active participation in the reality of theater. It links her with the theater of the seduction dance and with the enactments of the commune. It also dissociates her, since the origin of her act lies in the old food for peep show booths, and hence isolates her rather than initiates her.

The image of an anorexic woman exposing her genitals—anyway, a woman who refuses the world without letting it go—takes me to the image of Ingrid Thulin in *Cries and Whispers*; it is I guess the most shocking moment of Makavejev's compressed Bergman film. To the conjunction of spiritual starvation and of exhibition, Bergman adds the woman's explicit cutting of something inside her vagina and then licking the blood from her fingers. Are we to be disgusted by this? Is she? Is her husband meant to be—the fictional audience for whose benefit this set of actions has been undertaken? She is, let us say, eating her heart out. Cannibalizing herself. She is perhaps doing this as a sign of remorse and surely as an expression of rage, of revenge. To wish to harm another by a gesture of self-castration, to bloody one's mouth as if it were a replication of the castrated genitals, is to turn oneself into Medusa. Then this woman means to turn her husband to stone, perhaps by demonstrating to him that he is stone. And since Bergman's screen in this film fades into red at the close of its sequences, we may take Bergman to be declaring his film screen to be a version or container of the severed head of the Gorgon, to contain that kind of assault upon us. But what would be his attitude to this possibility? We are quite certain that we are not turned to stone, are we not? If we are not stone, and if the power of the film image is nevertheless what I say it is, then the screen we see it on is a version of the shield of Perseus. Then a film director, like Perseus flying through the air, looking down upon the earth, has in his hands the power to put halls full of people to instant death, or to preserve them.

"Am I man or woman?" is characterized, by Deleuse and Guattari in their *Anti-Oedipus*, as "the hysterical 'question' " and is paired with "the obsessional 'question' " "Am I dead or alive?" (They refer at this point to an essay by Serge Leclaire which I have not read.) The *Othello* material alluded to earlier represents the closing pages of my new book, *The Claim of Reason* (Oxford, 1979), the fourth part of which contains certain lines of meditation on what philosophers in the English-speaking tradition of philosophy call the problem of (how I know) (the existence of) other minds. These meditations can be said, I believe, to discover this problem to raise the question, "Am I a human being or a monster?" They also suggest that the problem of the existence of the other can be seen to derive from or to replace an earlier philosophical stake in the problem of the existence of God. This would provide a conceptual realm within which to grasp the progress of a Bergman character as he or she moves from a quarrel with God to a quarrel with the existence of others. Could we come to understand this final narcissism as an analogue of the initial narcissism sought by the commune, even as a step toward it? After all, it attaches ultimate importance to ultimate matters. And it is equally unreceptive to the further corruption of the world.

I understand there to be two modes of sweetness of which *Sweet Movie* speaks and which it embodies; they project alternatives for us. Either to continue to aestheticize the world, put that form of distance between it and our experience of it, say by converting all our experience into a mode of viewing. Or to learn to taste again, so that we can learn to maintain our disgust more easily than we learn to maintain what disgusts us. But this will require a transformation of the five senses, a new perspective, a new aesthetics. For mankind, to adapt a form from Nietzsche, would rather take Nothingness to be sweet than find nothing sweet.

Take the idea of film as producing, or making possible, a particular form of distance—let me call this the distance of something which makes its presence felt only through absence, as absence; together with the idea that this distance makes possible a particular mode of sweetness or nearness—let me call this seductiveness (or suggestiveness, to capture the neighboring sense of the hypnotic); together with an awareness that a filmmaker is raising the question whether he or she is indeed a woman—and let me now specify this as a speculation that the screen acts as a woman acts. This crossroads of ideas I find summarized in a passage from Nietzsche's *The Gay Science* in which he specifies the particular action of women (I dare say he is reporting on the feminine side of human character,[3] as that has so far unfolded itself) in the following terms: "When a man stands in the midst of his own noise, in the midst of his own surf of plans and projects, then he is apt also to see quiet, magical beings gliding past him and to long for their happiness and seclusion: *women*. He almost thinks that his better self dwells there among the women, and that in these quiet regions even the loudest surf turns into deathly quiet, and life itself into a dream about life. Yet! Yet! Noble enthusiast, even on the most beautiful sailboat there is a lot of noise, and unfortunately much small and petty noise. The magic and the most powerful effect of women is, in philosophical language, action at a distance, *actio in distans*; but this requires first of all and above all—*distance*" (section 60).

In claiming Nietzsche's figuring of action at a distance as a kind of mythological description of the action of film on a screen, I invite for consideration the consequent ideas that our Newtonian universe required the discovery of gravity as magnetism, call it mutual attraction, and that the Cartesians, battling Newtonianism, found such a property, invoking action at a distance, to be occult, that is, extrascientific or magical. It is as if the philosophers who invented psychology as a metaphor or allegory of Newtonianism somehow took it that if you got laws of association in the role of laws of motion, the idea and fact of universal attraction—you may say libido—would take care of itself. From which perspective Freud and his predecessors in hypnotism and animal magnetism, looking as it were for the gravity in human constellations, are felt to be dealing in occult or magical properties. And in a sense that is true, too—so long as society remains a field of occult forces.

A chain of ideas reaching throughout this essay is condensed or displaced in the final image of the woman in *WR*. The last of her we see is her severed head, brought into an autopsy room and placed in

---

[3]The feminine side of human character is something I found (in "What Becomes of Things on Film?" reprinted later in this book) to be "a natural subject of film." It is to be discovered in certain films (among them *Persona*) that are built upon a particular procedure of conjoining waking with dreaming life.

a white tray. The facts are quickly told: "DOCTOR: 'No sign of a struggle. Therefore she received the semen willingly. Better check mental hospitals in case some sex-starved patient has escaped. Find the murder weapon?' INSPECTOR: 'Yes, these nickel-plated Champions. They're the finest made.' " While he unwraps the silvery skates from a newspaper, the head begins to speak. Now when she begins to speak we have before us a literalization of the "talking head" that Makavejev finds characters in a Bergman movie often look like. I take the image in *WR*, accordingly, as an acknowledgment of a condition of movie making, more specifically as a danger of movie making that serious filmmakers must face or outface. But for a filmmaker to acknowledge this *in this way* requires him or her to acknowledge that it is he or she who has called for the severance of *this* head from its body and directed its placement into just this white tray. But how has this Perseus received the authorization for such an act, the sword necessary to accomplish it (call it the camera) and the shield necessary to bear up under its consequences (call it the screen)? In the absence of gods, what *WR* tells us is that this woman lost her head to love because of a mortal who had already been turned to stone; that she was made a monster, a talking head without a body, or confirmed in monstrousness, by a man who interpreted his purity as demanding that he exempt himself from ordinary human desires, save himself for something higher. The woman's words for this— that is, the talking head's words, I mean of course Makavejev's words—are "He's romantic, ascetic, a genuine Red Fascist," a patriot. Makavejev's further identification with this murderousness, his refusal to exempt himself from recognizing it in himself (in accordance, no doubt, with his own romanticism and asceticism and his patriotism toward a still invisible fatherland) is his further interpretation of the man's self-exemption as the capacity for art. This is shown in the man's beautiful song of prayer as he walks lost along the river, comprising the closing sequence of this film. Makavejev thus discovers further adjacencies in the concept of art as we have it, art as decapitation or renunciation or alienation; and he bears out the knowledge that this art is at the same time the victim or martyr of the very circumstances that produce it. I take the implication to be that this condition of what we know as art is also a condition of what we know as thinking, or philosophy; or might know. (An image of the kind of art that adapts to this condition, extracting no acknowledgment or autonomy of its own, is something I see in *WR*'s footage of the plaster-caster of erections, whose object or product is a tinted plaster phallus, a sort of life mask, which I read as a further stand-in for a certain kind of film image and filmmaking and film viewing (and by no means only or especially a stand-in for the obviously pornographic).)

The head of the woman, smiling, succeeding or surviving the man's song, retakes the field of the screen; she is displaced by the smiling head of Wilhelm Reich or absorbed by it. In bequeathing the film to these figures, Makavejev acknowledges further his identification with the muse and the presiding genius of his film, that he speaks from them, for them, in the excavation of their visions, and like them executes nothing of which he is not also the victim. So Makavejev declares himself indeed both a man and a woman. And, like all of them, a talking head. How could it be otherwise? The possibilities of film in any period can reach no higher or lower than the possibilities of humanness in that period, no higher or lower than the possibility of using talking heads therapeutically. To the extent that our heads and our bodies are not joined, we are Gorgons. Like the gods, we precede the human.

◆

A REPLY
TO JOHN HOLLANDER

◆

In February, 1980, the editors of Critical Inquiry *sent me a copy of John Hollander's "Stanley Cavell and* The Claim of Reason," *asking whether I would like some reply to appear along with Hollander's statement in the Summer 1980 issue. I came up with the following few words which, along with those of the essay following this one, show the good I have found in publicly letting myself be encouraged by the writing of friends, and trying to reciprocate. An immediate good of it was its eliciting from me the acknowledgment that a good part of what I spend my life doing is writing—that I wish to express the effects of the world on my life that way, that I wish to make that kind of cause. But what good is that to acknowledge? Well it means, for example, that I look for the conviction of others in what I say only to the extent that I can manifest my own conviction by it. This seems always to have been my belated way of keeping faith with philosophy as, in Thoreau's sly distinction, something admirable to profess because it is, or was once, admirable to live. I know this intention offends, or maybe amuses, some people. I do not know why they would not be worried more, or amused more, by writing which claims at once to be philosophical and also to know something others do not know (that is, that it may as well be science), or by other writing which adopts positions, say of irony or of hilarity, from which it either imagines its own efforts to be exempt, or else regards itself as in such command, or*

straits, that it has no further need, or hope, of conversation—philoso-
ophy as attitude and as number.

◇

Having just read through John Hollander's brilliant and moving response to my book, my first response in turn is one of gratitude, for
the generosity of his taking of my intentions, allowing them room to
extend themselves; and of admiration, at the writing of a writer who
has original and useful things to say about the relations of poetry and
philosophy, of fable and argument, of trope and example, relations
at the heart of what my book is about.

It is greatly heartening to me that he finds a weight for "poetic"
with which my philosophizing may seriously be found poetic (a
sense that depends on seeing that in English we have major poetic
texts that have to be called philosophical), and that he accepts a certain "novelistic intensity and accuracy" in my exemplifications.
Without such perceptions of the fact of my writing, of a reality to its
ambitions, it would have no way to achieve the ground of conviction
it aspires to. I believe Hollander is right in finding my mode somehow essentially American, and I do not imagine a handsomer compliment than his taking the activities of philosophizing in *The Claim
of Reason* as generally parabolic for the activities of the rest of life
itself. I accept the compliment as meaning that the activities of writing in that book project activities of a life that is better than the one I
inhabit, that beckons to this one as its better possibility, let me say its
better angel.

There is nothing in Hollander's essay for me to respond to in the
sense of answer. Coming close together with the publication of my
book, the first serious public response to it I know of, it will become
a part of the way I think about the progress of the book in the world,
of how I assess its successes and its failures; of how, I would like to
say, I will conceive of the book's *placing* itself, which is a way of
saying, its understanding itself. For throughout Hollander's essay
there is a recurrence, carefully modulated, to a fantasy (or trope) of
a mode of writing (or genre) as a place—a location in a world of

writing, in what Hollander once names "the allegorical country of Thought." He describes me as wishing to survey that country and (perhaps consequently) as myself occupying a "poetico-philosophical no-man's-land," a territory, or realm, that he also pictures as "the buffer zone between poetry and philosophy." I share something like this fantasy, one in which I am forever trying to make out the geography of surprising adjacencies, inner and outer, regions or spots of thought and of feeling whose comprehension exactly lies in their adjacencies, in what lies before and after them. (In speaking of the filmmaker Makavejev, in an earlier issue of *Critical Inquiry*, as an excavator and as a missing switchboard operator, with the former becoming more and more dominant in his work, I felt I was being somewhat autobiographical, anyway about my ambitions.)[1]

This fantasy of surveying is a late version, as suggested in the contexts Hollander adduces, of a quest myth, in which the goal of the quest is an understanding of the origin of the quest itself, of the dream that dispatches you. I assume that a piece of writing able to accept itself within a known genre would not have to contain or project such a myth of its own origin. It is a quest for authority in one's speech in the absence of the authority of genre, of a shared present, a grant of history. This quest for authority naturally tends toward the autobiographical, and since the self in question is not given, it presents itself as lost. Therefore the landscape through which the journey progresses will present itself as something that is distant, gone. The issue is one of inhabitation, placing yourself. But placing a lost self in a land that is gone is an exercise of mourning. This is, I dare say, more directly a description of Thoreau's *Walden*, which I call a book of losses, than it is of *The Claim of Reason*. But the description is meant to suggest why I have tried in my work to claim *Walden* as part of my inheritance, to show its presence in my landscape—an unplaceable book that is about placement. If I say that this reveals something American in me, shall I say that a companion wish to inherit Wordsworth's *Prelude*—a work describable in the same terms

[1] That essay precedes this in this book.

I just used of *Walden*—reveals something English in me? And then my affinity for Wittgenstein something Austrian? I would have no objection.

I am reminded of W. H. Auden's foreword to his *A Certain World: A Commonplace Book* in which he recognizes that his compilation amounts to a sort of autobiography. He calls it, responding to a passage from G. K. Chesterton, "a map of my planet." The passage Auden quotes from Chesterton contains these sentences: "The original quality in any man of imagination is imagery. It is a thing like the landscape of his dreams; the sort of world he would like to make or in which he would wish to wander; the strange flora and fauna of his own secret planet; the sort of thing he likes to think about." I would like to accept the idea that I have revealed a secret planet in revealing myself, a certain errant wholeness, with the proviso that no one's planet contains anything anyone else's may not contain, or does not have the equivalent of; and that their contents are commonplaces, including an aspiration toward the better possibility, which I might call the life of philosophy. Philosophy, at any rate, must ask no less.

◆

FOREWORD TO
JAY CANTOR'S
THE SPACE BETWEEN

◆

The subtitle of Jay Cantor's book of essays is Literature and Politics*; it was published in 1981 by the Johns Hopkins University Press. What appears here has in a few spots been slightly amplified.*

◇

No other book I know puts things together quite in the way of Jay Cantor's *The Space Between: Literature and Politics*. Its essays, working against and for one another, are displaced from the usual haunts and habits of literary or political prose. I think I can most usefully provide an introduction to them by indicating how they have encouraged me to place myself with respect to them, in terms of them.

My sixties began in the early summer of 1964 in Tougaloo, Mississippi and ended in the late summer of 1974 at Truro, on Cape Cod, with the television coverage of Richard Nixon's farewell to his White House staff. Whether one considers those years to have been hopeful or hateful ones, there can be few periods in any nation's experience in which more of its people have questioned or revised its identity for themselves. Call such periods crises of imagination. I know of no such crisis that remains so poorly grasped. That poorness must itself be part of what constitutes this crisis.

One may describe Jay Cantor's *The Space Between: Literature and Politics* as an effort to imagine that time, and therewith an effort to grasp ours as a time for imagining. It is also about what must constitute such imagination, and about why it must consider that constitution, what kind of writing it is that shoulders it. It is about being born around 1950 (hence, having to grow through adolescence within the dates I called the sixties) and about conceiving and accepting the ambition, in those years, to be a writer. I understand this nesting of subjects in the way I would understand Wordsworth's *Prelude* to be simultaneously about being born in 1770 (hence, being nineteen in 1789) and about accepting the ambition to be a writer in those years of English writing. Each of these writers is claiming that ambitious writing in his time must shoulder the imagination and the acknowledgment of his time, where this is considered to mean not just knowing a thing or two about the time and about writing, but also seeing the public and his private history as one and the same nesting of subjects. Hegel, also born in 1770, expressed this knowledge another way, call it dialectically; Thoreau, sensing other revolutions, expressed it scripturally. All tend toward the autobiographical.

Accomplishing the conjunction of private and public history—call this composing the autobiography of your times—demands a healthy respect for your capacity to write. Jay Cantor is also the writer of a long novel in progress, two excerpts of which have been published.[1] The rim of the novel's subject is the life and works of Che Guevara, identified in *The Space Between: Literature and Politics* as the subject of one of its periodic pin-up posters, from whose journal the second excerpt of Jay Cantor's novel intermittently quotes. In one of these quotes Guevara appears, depicting himself in a conversation about how commitment to guerillas may be expressed, and he says to his journal parenthetically: "The basis of a first commitment is a very good imagination so you can at least dream the dangers you are entertaining. I need a batallion of dreamers?" Then a few dozen pages later in the novel the writer Regis Debray is saying to a fellow revolutionary that words have their time in a revolutionary process, and the fellow replies: "I came to understand what those

[1]*Tri-Quarterly* 45 (Spring 1979): 199–237; and *Canto* 1, no. 4 (Winter 1977): 1–18. The completed novel, *The Death of Che Guevara*, was published by Knopf in 1983.

feelings I had meant in my world. There's room for words. There have to be words, too. But that isn't the way it started for me. When I listen to you, I don't know. Can it start out as thinking?" That is a beautiful use of the Hemingway "it," meaning here the revolution, but no less meaning one's writing, and no less the seriousness, the thoughtfulness, of one's life, or the moment at which, as Conrad (I think) puts it, the possibility of a moral existence begins or ends.

It seems to me that Jay Cantor's writing is characterizing itself as the commitment "to dream the dangers we are entertaining." In writing, as in everyday life, these are not future dangers but present ones, ones inevitable if you are to demand thoughtfulness of your life. Thoreau says in *Walden*, "You may sit as many risks as you run"—you needn't look for moral adventure, it will find you if you are serious. Whether there will be what the world calls a revolution in a particular place is a function of whether there is a revolutionary situation in that place. This is never certain—already a key point for John Locke, our author of consent. What is certain is that the possession of oneself, the self's birth of freedom, now presents itself, as nations have presented themselves for two centuries, in terms of revolution, a splitting and struggle for one's own ground. I have expressed something like this thought as a matter of modern philosophy's availability to us only through conversion. But whether as the trope of political revolution or as the trope of religious conversion, the idea, variously expressed in the radical vision of every major philosopher since Bacon and Descartes, is that one finds one's own world only by turning, a turning away from the world (which therefore presents itself as appearance or fashion) that constitutes one's own turning toward a world (which accordingly presents itself, if in the future, as reality or permanence).

I suppose the development of the wish for change into a visionary craving for revolution or conversion is the work of two contrary pieces of knowledge, keeping one another alive: first, the knowledge of oneself, however affable, as enraged and desperate at the state of the world, a rage away from the violent and insupportable narcissism of those in power over us, a despair at one's powerlessness to matter; and second, the knowledge that change must be possible but that, since others will not change, one must make something happen, one must *make* a start, in thoughts, in words, in institutions however small, it may be in how you conduct a friendship, a greeting, a sale, so one must become a poet to survive.

Jay Cantor's vision leads through territories unpleasant and frightening to contemplate: Che Guevara, the Patricia Hearst story, the aesthetics of Harold Rosenberg and of Herbert Marcuse, the bits of truth in a hundred more or less, most and least, articulate places. But had one expected to find a better world without knowing the bad of this one, without knowing the bad in the good of it and the good in the bad of it? Then I recommend attention to what I understand as a climax of the vision of *The Space Between: Literature and Politics*, in a brilliant and convincing piece of, let me say, literary criticism. It finds, at the close of a chapter of "notes" on Beckett, that only after despair and equally only after hope can one discover what it is on which our existence—then dropping what may in our boredom have seemed the boring word in William Carlos Williams's poem about the wheel barrow after rain—depends.

And I recommend attention to the continuity of *The Space Between: Literature and Politics* with such a work as E. M. Forster's *Howards End*, which seems so congenial or genial by comparison. I wonder why people find Forster's epigraph to his masterpiece— "Only connect . . . . "—a profound sentiment. It is taken from the opening paragraphs of chapter 22: "Only connect! That was the whole of her sermon. Only connect the prose and the passion, and both will be exalted, and human love will be seen at its height. Live in fragments no longer. Only connect, and the beast and the monk, robbed of the isolation that is life to either, will die." That is not a prediction but a prophecy, a vision. Does it seem genial because it is imagined that the business of connecting is pretty, that it may not exact ugliness and violence in its achieving? The imagined sermon is directed to one who

> always had the sneaking belief that bodily passion is bad, a belief that is desirable only when held passionately. Religion had confirmed him. The words that were read aloud on Sunday to him and to other respectable men were the words that had once kindled the souls of St. Cath-

erine and St. Francis into a white-hot hatred of the carnal. He could
not be as the saints and love the infinite with a seraphic ardour, but he
could be a little ashamed of loving a wife.

The sixties is the name of a time in which for certain people, for quite
a large number of people at certain times, white-hot hatred and seraphic ardor seemed again practical emotions. If, as I do, you understand the religious sects of the seventies as fragmentary successors
of the fragmentary political sects of the sixties, and hence imagine
that there was from the beginning a religious ground in the student
movement—religious yearning, a religious purity, religious corruption and intolerance (there were riots of holiness on both sides, on all
sides)—then you may think you can spot the continuity of seraphic
ardor. But you must then ask what happened to the white-hot
hatred. Could Richard Nixon really have absorbed it all and carried
it away into the California desert?

Suppose you cannot, or can no longer, believe in the practicality
of these hatreds and ardors *and* you cannot, or can no longer, believe
in the practices and words that deny them, deny so much as their
fragmentary revelations (and these words are spoken not only on
Sunday but on every day and every night). Suppose you believe at
most in the merely human carry of your words, and you wish to lift
them merely to lift others, not to seek some transcendent orbit.
Then you will have, as befits philosophical prose, to distinguish, to
split, as well as to connect. And you will try, as I understand Jay
Cantor to do, to connect, to try to achieve a vision in which to connect
the prose and passion, of course (though now that connection
sounds rather like an invitation to write a novel—and perhaps,
understood usefully, one might after all get a grasp of one's life by
taking it as a tale in which you are the narrative voice), and in which
to connect the beast and the monk in yourself, of course (though now
you will suggest that to accomplish this you must connect the victim
and the terrorist in yourself, and the boredom and the poetry, and
the prisoner and the judge, and the patriot and the traitor, and the
immigrant and the American, and the ardor and the hatred and the
craving to write).

At Harvard in the spring of 1969 some hundreds of students were forcibly removed from an administration building by greater hundreds of police. It was several months earlier that I had become aware of Jay Cantor. He had written a feature for the Harvard *Crimson* in response to a student sit-in at a faculty meeting, arguing in effect that in a bad time people on opposite sides of a public issue are equally apt to behave badly, and that each side of the current issue still had an opportunity to turn the other cheek. His statement remains in my mind as the best public statement made in those times, but his eloquent appeal to the best on all sides went unanswered. By the following spring the situation had deteriorated. I was giving a course that spring on texts from Luther and Machiavelli and Shakespeare through Locke and Marx and Mill and Hume and Kant to Nietzsche and Beckett. Hundreds of students were enrolled in the course, some of whom would have been in the administration building the morning it was emptied, more of whom would have attended the meeting the night before the building was filled, at which a majority had voted—in the largest and most thoroughly democratic meeting of its kind I ever witnessed—not to mount an occupation. Accordingly, some half of the students inside the building the next morning were there to argue the other half into leaving. Did those who used the police know that? If they knew, would they have acted as they did regardless? Why? Because students have no business holding a meeting—however democratically conducted, even seraphically—to discuss a proposal to act illegally? Then why did they hold it, hardly a scene producible by everyday lawbreakers? Did my beautiful list of readings for my course contain terms in which to think this over? And if it did, were they terms that were common to those inside and those outside that building, so they might figure in an argument between them? If not, what does it mean to call a place a university?

The last of the major disruptions of that spring was a week-long strike of classes called by an organization of Teaching Fellows. The following week, as I was collecting myself to go to the classroom and resume the course, there was talk that some Teaching Fellows and some students in the course wanted to continue the strike. As had become second nature to us within the span of a few weeks, we gathered at once for a meeting. I said that for my part I was not prepared to discuss the issue of continuing the strike, that I was going to the classroom and that the other teachers present would have to decide without me what they had to do. One of the most fervent supporters of the idea of the strike then said that this course was certainly special, that it should not be struck any longer, because its reading had suddenly become amazingly relevant. The teacher's heart in me sank. I said something to the effect that I had been assigning roughly the same texts since the beginning of my involvement with the course, half a dozen years earlier, that these texts had always been relevant to our lives, as relevant as thinking about our lives, and that our present events did not serve to show that the world and these texts may illuminate one another but rather that they may eclipse one another.

Now I add that my heart had sunk under a sense of hopelessness of ever really connecting the prose and the passion, the idea of our history with our history as we are making it, of ever having a voice in our history. So our ideas and our histories, separated, fragmented, each eclipse us. We remain essentially uneducated. Those who may share this sense or vision, however intermittently, will require words for it. I am grateful for the words Jay Cantor has found. I expect him to be recognized as one of the significant voices of his generation. The appearance of his sequence of essays does for me what Emerson asked of the American scholar: it raises and cheers me.

◆

NORTH BY NORTHWEST

◆

Printed in Critical Inquiry, *Summer 1981, this represents my contribution to a colloquium on Hitchcock's film held at the English Institute in Cambridge, Massachusetts, August 31, 1980. The other participants were Professors William Rothman (who organized the colloquium) and Geoffrey Hartman.*

◇

Philosophy's all but unappeasable yearning for itself is bound to seem comic to those who have not felt it. To those who have felt it, it may next seem frightening, and they may well hate and fear it, for the step after that is to yield to the yearning, and then you are lost. From such a view of philosophy I have written about something called modernism in the arts as the condition of their each yearning for themselves, naming a time at which to survive, they took themselves, their own possibilities, as their aspiration—they assumed the condition of philosophy. What I found in turning to think consecutively about film a dozen or so years ago was a medium which seemed simultaneously to be free of the imperative to philosophy and at tne same time inevitably to reflect upon itself—as though the condition of philosophy were its natural condition. And then I was lost.

But this is said after the fact. Over and over I have had to find again my conviction in these matters, to take my experience over the same path, finding the idea of film's philosophical seriousness first to be comic, then frightening, then inescapable. To achieve this conviction in the films of Alfred Hitchcock is not something I can imagine apart from a continuing conversation about film and about philosophy with William Rothman, whose conviction in the precision of Hitchcock's self-consciousness and passionate exploration of that self-consciousness in his films has convinced me to find this for myself. My remarks on *North by Northwest* are guided, more specifically, by two ideas from Rothman's book on Hitchcock, *The Murderous Gaze: Readings of Five Hitchcock Films*: first, that Hitchcock's interpretation of the power of the movie camera—for example, its power of interrogation of its human subjects—is something Rothman calls its murderousness; and second, that the Hitchcock film, hence Hitchcock, is first fully formed in *The Thirty-nine Steps*, in its weaving of Hitchcock's interest in his themes of the murder thriller together with the themes of romance.[1]

In *Pursuits of Happiness* I put together seven Hollywood romances of the thirties and forties and claim that they define a particular genre, something I call the comedy of remarriage. It happens that Cary Grant is in four of the seven; Katharine Hepburn is the only other principal to appear in more than one. In my account of Howard Hawks's *Bringing Up Baby* (one of the seven films in question) I claim that Grant's saving Hepburn from falling, at the close of the film, by hoisting her hand in hand onto the ledge of a scaffold, a place that also looks like a crib or treehouse, upon which they embrace, is alluded to by the conclusive hoisting in *North by Northwest* from a ledge onto an upper berth. If I will not ask you out of the blue to believe this connection, still less will I ask you to believe an allusion from *North by Northwest* to *The Philadelphia Story*, another of

[1]Rothman's book was published by Harvard University Press in 1982. I am also indebted to Marian Keane's "The Designs of Authorship: An Essay on *North by Northwest*," *Wide Angle* 4, no. 1 (1980): 44–52. I should like to mention here Robin Wood's *Hitchcock's Films* (New York, 1970), an intelligent, literate statement about the films of Hitchcock, which, while comparatively early as these things go in English-speaking circles, continues to repay reading. For an account of *North by Northwest* at once more suspicious than mine (about the value of the film) and more gullible (about Hitchcock's remarks about it and about the film's apparently casual evaluation of itself, so to speak), see George M. Wilson's "The Maddest McGuffin: Some Notes on *North by Northwest*," *Modern Language Notes* 94 (1979): 1159–72.

the seven films with Cary Grant, when Grant (or rather Roger Thornhill) early in *North by Northwest* tries to make the police and his mother believe what happened to him at the mansion in Glen Cove, and the place of liquor bottles is shown to be occupied by books. Thornhill's drinking is the subject of much attention in the opening sequences of *North by Northwest*, that is, as long as his mother is present, and C. K. Dexter Haven (Grant's role in *The Philadelphia Story*) cured himself of alcoholism by reading books, a process apparently from which he acquired the authority to affect the destiny of his love. I will wind up saying that *North by Northwest* derives from the genre of remarriage, or rather from whatever it is that that genre is derived, which means to me that its subject is the legitimizing of marriage, as if the pair's adventures are trials of their suitability for that condition. Perhaps this only signifies that *North by Northwest* is a romance. It is in any case the only one of Hitchcock's romantic thrillers in which the adventurous pair are actually shown to have married. It is also the only one in which the man of that pair is shown to have a mother—a mother, needless to say, whom he is shown to leave, and to leave running (out of the Plaza Hotel, away from his abductors, but at the same time away from his mother, who shouts after him to ask whether he will be home for dinner). The fate of the mother in *The Birds* will complicate this story. And naturally certain of Hitchcock's villains, and certain of his heroines, are allowed to have mothers.

But let us begin as uncontroversially as we can. *North by Northwest* contains as one of its stars Cary Grant. It underscores this uncontroversial fact in two principal ways: first, by remark after remark about his nice-looking, vaguely familiar face and about his being irresistible and making women who don't know him fall in love with him, together with several double takes when strangers look at his face (a man going into a phone booth Grant is leaving, a woman who, after as it were seeing who he is, wants him to stop in her hospital room); and second, by allusions to each of the other films Hitchcock made with Grant. *To Catch a Thief* also has him at the end holding a woman by the hand over a precipice, and in that film he is comically shown to be irresistible; *Suspicion* climaxes with a wild ride down a coast road in a convertible driven by Grant, from which he seems to shove someone out and from which someone who might be poisoned almost falls over a cliff into the sea; and the basic situation of *Notorious* is gone over again (a loose woman's liaison with something like a foreign agent is exploited by an American intelligence agency; the assignment thwarts Grant's desire; it leads to the woman's mortal danger from which Grant rescues her).

There seem to be two immediate reasons in *North by Northwest* for insisting upon the presence of Cary Grant; first, to redeem him from certain guilts acquired in those earlier environments, especially in allowing him to overcome the situation of *Notorious*, as if film actors and their characters get stuck to one another, and as if he is being readied for something purer in this context; and second, to inscribe the subject of film acting, and acting generally, as a main topic of this film, which is to say, a main branch of its investigation of the nature of film. The topic is invoked over and over in *North by Northwest*: Philip Vandamm (James Mason) hardly says a word to Grant that does not comment on his acting; the Professor (Leo G. Carroll) asks him to act a part; Eve Kendall (Eva Marie Saint) compliments him on his performance in the scene they have just acted out for Vandamm's benefit. The theme of theatricality is generalized by the fact that the part Thornhill is asked and forced to play is that of someone named George Kaplan, who doesn't exist; but to play the part of a fictional character is just what actors normally do. It happens that in the fiction of this film this new fictional identity is imposed by reality, thus generalizing the theme further into the nature of identity and the theatricality of everyday life.

It is, I think, part of Hitchcock's lingo to be referring to these facts, and more, in the exchange on the train between Thornhill and Eve about the monogram on his matchbook. "Rot," he says, "it's my trademark." She asks what the "O" stands for. "Nothing," he replies. In a Hitchcockian context this means both that this man knows that the advertising game (and the modern city generally which it epitomizes) makes up words that are rot and also that it would be rot to think this is all he means. Thornhill and Eve have already questioned his identity and spoken about his familiar face. So in part what or who is "nothing" is the film character (here, Roger Thornhill) in comparison to the film actor playing him. Cary Grant would be more or less who he is if Roger Thornhill had never existed, whereas Roger Thornhill would be nothing apart from Cary Grant (a form of consideration broached as long ago as Erwin Panofsky's "Style and Medium in the Motion Pictures"). "Nothing" equally means that the film *actor* is nothing in comparison to the power of the camera over *him*. This is not so much in need of argument as of interpretation. *North by Northwest* interprets the actor as a victim, as if of foreign views of himself. This thought puts two figures in the film in the role of directors, the Professor and Vandamm, who create scenarios and make up parts for people.[2] On Vandamm's first encounter with Thornhill he draws some theatrical curtains across proscenium-sized windows, shutting the world out, and arranges for Thornhill to be killed, as if punishing him for acting; the Professor lets this go on until forced for the sake of his own script to intervene.

The "nothing," or naught, in the ROT monogram equally appropriately stands for origin, so its simultaneous meaning is that the actor is the origin of the character and also the origin of what becomes of himself or herself on film. The further thought that the human self as such is both an origin and a nothing is a bit of Cartesianism that is conceivably not called for in the context of this film. (To say that Hitchcock is up to it if he wants it is to say that Hitchcock is as intelligent as, say, Samuel Beckett and that he is as good at what he does as Beckett is at what he does.)

But I was trying to begin uncontroversially. The film is called *North by Northwest*. I assume that nobody will swear from that fact alone that we have here an allusion to Hamlet's line that he is but mad north-northwest; even considering that Hamlet's line occurs as the players are about to enter and that *North by Northwest* is notable, even within the oeuvre of a director pervaded by images and thoughts of the theater and of theatricality, for its obsession with the idea of acting; and considering that both the play and the film contain plays-within-the-play in both of which someone is killed, both

---

[2] A consequent moral equation between these figures is being drawn, another point I took away from a conversation with Rothman and Keane.

being constructed to catch the conscience of the one for whose benefit they are put on. But there are plenty of further facts. The film opens with an ageless male identifying himself first of all as a son. He speaks of his efforts to keep the smell of liquor on his breath (that is, evidence of his grown-up pleasures) from the watchful nose of his mother, and he comes to the attention of his enemies because of an unresolved anxiety about getting a message to his mother, whereupon he is taken to a mansion in which his abductor has usurped another man's house and name and has, it turns out, cast his own sister as his wife. (The name, posted at the front of the house, is Townsend, and a town is a thing smaller than a city but larger than a village, or a hamlet.) The abductor orders the son killed by forcing liquid into him. It is perhaps part of the picture that the usurper is eager to get to his dinner guests and that there is too much competitive or forced drinking of liquor. Nor, again, will anyone swear that it is significant that the abductor-usurper's henchmen are a pair of men with funny, if any, names and a single man who stands in a special relationship with the usurper and has a kind of sibling rivalry with the young woman that this son, our hero, will become attracted to and repelled by. These are shadowy matters, and it is too soon to speak of "allusions" or of any other very definite relation to a so-called source. But it seems clear to me that *if* one were convinced of *Hamlet* in the background of *North by Northwest*, say to the extent that one is convinced that Saxo Grammaticus's *Danish History* is in the background of *Hamlet*, then one would without a qualm take the name Leonard as a successor to the name Laertes.

We have further to go. In Saxo Grammaticus's telling of the story the son's enemies send a beautiful woman to seduce him; he is to believe that he and the woman meet by chance. When questioned about what happened between them he says he raped her; she has agreed to back his story since they had known one another in the past. This figure is, as editors have noted, a peculiar prototype for Ophelia, but we can take her as near perfect for Eve Kendall. Thornhill does not, it is true, say that he raped her, but he describes something happening between them, in the name of love, that they both call murdering her. Hitchcock here is following one of his favorite identifications, that of killing with intercourse, the other side of a metaphysical wit's identification of dying with orgasm. It is also to the point, thinking of Thornhill's attention to his clothes, that Hamlet's prototype in Saxo Grammaticus is pictured as covering himself with dirt. That Hitchcock has gone back to the source or origin of the story of Hamlet, as well as to the play, is a reason not to have the title *exactly* from Hamlet.[3]

I note two or three further echoes of the play. Thornhill's problem begins when he is confused with, so to speak, someone who doesn't exist, let us say it is a nothing, or let us say a ghost; and when the woman betrays him he finds her out by following the itinerary dictated by the ghost. And then the son protects himself, saves his life, by what I would like to describe as feigning madness—in the auction scene in which he pretends not to know how you join in bidding for things. The auctioneer at one stage says, "Would the gentleman please get into the spirit of the proceedings?" that is, be decorous, be socialized; but society has been forcing an identity and a guilt upon him that he does not recognize as his own, so the natural hope for a way out is to abdicate from that society. Thornhill's identifying "rot" as his trademark by now irresistibly suggests to me Hamlet's sense of something rotten.

Allow for the sake of argument that *Hamlet* is present in the film in some fashion. Of what interest is this, I mean of what interest to

[3]Subsequent to the original publication of this essay I looked up another document familiar in *Hamlet* scholarship that Professor Geoffrey Bullough, in Volume VII of his *Narrative and Dramatic Sources of Shakespeare*, describes as "the German prose play *Der Bestrafte Brudermord oder Prinz Hamlet aus Dännemark*, the degenerate version of an English play probably taken over to the Continent by English actors before 1626" (p. 20). Professor Bullough prints the play (among the Sources, Possible Sources, Probable Sources, Probable Historical Allusions, and Analogues; specifically as an Analogue) in an English translation entitled *Fratricide Punished* revised from one made for H. H. Furness's *The New Variorum Edition* of *Hamlet* of 1877. In this play the Laertes character is named Leonhardus.

I mention this not exactly to clinch my suggestion that the name Laertes may be seen to survive in the name Leonard; and not just to indicate a perfectly obvious place in which Hitchcock might have learned this change of name (Furness's famous editions and compilations), a source he may very well have meant to leave a clue for in his own change; but primarily to make explicit the question of when and how a matter of interpretation gets clinched in one's own mind. It *might*, I think, have happened to me on discovering Leonhardus; but in fact it came with the emphasis on "rot," as read in the paragraph following the one to which this note is appended.

Hitchcock? I have various speculations about this based on my claim that *North by Northwest* invokes *Hamlet* in conjunction with the source of the story of Hamlet and on my sense that *North by Northwest* plays a special role in Hitchcock's oeuvre, a summary role. I take Hitchcock, as it were, to be saying something like the following. Granted that it is not necessary for anyone, let alone a filmmaker, to disclaim the intention of trying to compete with the quality and the importance of *Hamlet*, it is nevertheless my intention, as the filmmaker I am, to compete with Shakespeare in his handling of sources and in this way, or to this extent, to show myself to do whatever it is I do as well as Shakespeare does whatever it is he does. It is with sources as Coleridge famously remarked about Shakespeare's stories: "My belief is that he always regarded his story, before he began to write, much in the same light as a painter regards his canvas, before he begins to paint—as a mere vehicle for his thoughts—as the ground upon which he was to work." But then of course (still speaking for Hitchcock) the question is what one means by "sources." The story is one source, lifted often from indifferent places that would not constitute sources unless I had been inspired to make them such. So is the past body of my work a source, as *North by Northwest* makes explicit. So are what some people call "locations," which for me are places whose genius I wish to announce or to become. So are what other people call "actors," whereas for me what is called "Cary Grant" is considerably more than what that may be taken to mean. So is what you might call the camera a source. . . . You see the point.

But why is it *Hamlet* about which this is all, according to my speaking for Hitchcock, being said? I think there are two reasons. First, *Hamlet* is perhaps the most popular, or famous, of the greatest works of world literature; the man who on the basis of his kind of thriller became perhaps the most famous director of films in the world, and for a longer period than any other, and whom just about any critic recognizes as in some sense brilliant, may well be fascinated by and wish to comprehend this fact. Surely the play's fame cannot be the result of its actually being *understood*. Second, *Hamlet* is the subject of what is still probably the most famous Freudian interpretation of a work of art, Ernest Jones's *Hamlet and Oedipus*.

Given the blatant presence of Freudian preoccupation and analysis in Hitchcock's work I see in his allusion to *Hamlet* a kind of warning to Freudians, even a dare, as if to say: of course my work, like any art, is subject to your interpretations, but why are these interpretations so often so obvious, unable to grasp the autonomy, the uniqueness, of the object? (Hitchcock would not be the first artist of this century to feel he has to pit his knowledge of human nature against the thought of the man who is said to have invented its science.)[4]

The origin of Eve Kendall in Hitchcock's own past work is explicit enough. She succeeds another good-looking, blonde stranger in *The Thirty-nine Steps* whom an earlier Hitchcock hero also met on a train, also as he was eluding the police to get to a person who could clear him of the suspicion of having put a knife in someone's back; and at the end of that train ride there was also a professor. But this time, over twenty years later and in another country, the woman *offers* rather than refuses him help. This proves initially to be treachery rather than salvation, but it affords a picture of a relationship to women that this man, now and in the past, had not known. This woman's apparent faith in him succeeds both Madeleine Carroll's early skepticism about his predecessor (Robert Donat), who spends much of *The Thirty-nine Steps* trying to overcome it; and her faith succeeds more immediately the skepticism of his mother, to whom he had said goodbye just before encountering Eve on the train. The effect of these substitutions is elaborate and paradoxical, and all in favor of Eve.

Aligning, in retrospect, the Madeleine Carroll figure with the present mother, doubt is cast on the picture of marriage in the final shot of *The Thirty-nine Steps*; the man puts his arm around the woman with the handcuffs still dangling from his wrist, a picture suggesting that marriage is a kind of voluntary handcuffing (a porta-

---

[4]Even Raymond Bellour's useful and sophisticated study of *North by Northwest* ("Le blocage symbolique," *Communications* 23 [1975]: 235–350), judging from one hurried reading, has not, it seems to me, cleared itself of this question. My remark is directed only to the first half of this monograph-length paper. The second half, devoted to a geometry of the crop-dusting sequence, I have not looked at sufficiently to have a judgment of.

ble version of the ball and chain). On the other hand Eve is made to incorporate both the good woman and the adventuress of *The Thirty-nine Steps*, that is, both the marriageable and the unmarriageable woman. The most delicious linking of them is made openly by Eve when she explains her interest in Thornhill to him by saying, "It's going to be a long night and I don't particularly like the book I've started. Know what I mean?" The Madeleine Carroll figure had been reading a book when Donat burst in on her. Thornhill knows what she means, as if seeing a dream coming true. And in that dream, and its responsibilities, the man's task will be not just to save himself and save his country's secrets from leaving it and thus win himself a suitable mate. He has first of all to save the bad woman, to rewrite the earlier plot which in effect began by killing her off, to rescue or redeem or resurrect her, that is to say, to put the good and the bad together. This is rather more like *creating* a suitable mate for himself.

Why is she his to rescue? Both the Professor and Eve tell him he is responsible for her condition, the one because he has cast suspicion on her, the other because men like him don't believe in marriage. But I think the film shows two further causes. First, in addition to her incorporating at least two of the women from *The Thirty-nine Steps* she also incorporates the mother, perhaps the mother he never had, protecting him from the police by hiding him in a bellying container that shows she holds the key to his berth. (This wasn't necessary: the fact that she subsequently hides him from the porter sufficiently well in the washroom proves that.) It is every bit this birth he is reciprocating in his closing gesture of the film. Second, he has passed some kind of ordeal at her hands in the crop-dusting sequence, and his survival here somehow entitles them to one another—as if his survival, or revival from a Frazerian cornfield, had given them the key piece of knowledge with which to overcome their unlucky erotic pasts, which accordingly would be the knowledge that ecstasy such as she invites is not necessarily death dealing. I am taking it that she is not purely reluctant to send him to meet Kaplan. She is not worried that he is a murderer but that she is. They are both about to undergo an education in these matters. Redemption for them both is underway. But it is not a simple matter to put such knowledge into the world—say, in the form of marriage—and there is danger ahead.

How is it that he is equipped to meet the danger, I mean how does he know that the attempt is the most important thing in the world? I must now put the uncontroversial aside and put forward a bunch of assertions.

I begin by reinterpreting, or interpreting further, Thornhill's survival of the attack by the plane. The attack is the central image of his victimization. I said earlier that this is the form in which his being an actor is to be declared; and just now I said that his sexual redemption depended on what you might call his survival of a kind of victimization by, or a willing subjection to, an assault of feeling. Something cataclysmic happened to Thornhill and Eve the night before, and I understand the attack the next day to be simultaneously a punishment for the night and a gaudy visual equivalent of it. Then I understand the crop-dusting plane, instrument of victimization, as a figure for a movie camera: it shoots at its victims and it coats them with a film of something that both kills and preserves, say that it causes metamorphosis. I claim evidence for the association of the prairie with the, let us say, inner landscape of the train compartment, in the way a close-up of Eve's face at the Chicago train station dissolves into the establishing aerial shot of the road and fields of the plane attack. That conjunction of color and mood I claim asks for an allegorical identification of the woman and this stretch of land, but this is just something further each viewer must try out on his or her own. It is on this ground that the man undergoes his Shakespearean encounter of nothings—the nothing of Thornhill meeting the nothing of Kaplan—the attack on his identity, as it were, by itself. The recognition of the plane sent by Vandamm as a figure for the camera accounts satisfactorily for his gathering his stolen secrets on microfilm. This, in turn, would be a way Hitchcock has of saying that film—anyway in his camera—is the recorder of state secrets.

Put this together with the other overt declaration of the movie camera, this time by synecdoche rather than metaphor: I mean the telescope on the terrace of the Mount Rushmore Memorial focused on the faces of the presidents. A lot is being woven together here. We have cut to the presidents' faces from a close-up of Grant's face, turned toward us and suddenly illuminated as for examination by a harsh light from what we understand fictively to be a plane turning in his direction, hence what we understand literally and figuratively as a piece of photographic apparatus. We are being told that this face belongs to just one person on earth and that we are going to have to think about what that means. The cut from that image to the image of the presidents evidently poses some matching of Grant's face with the faces of stone, a matching generally prepared of course by the insistent references to the familiarity of his face but prepared more specifically by his having shaved with the minuscule razor and brush. Letting the phallic symbolism alone for awhile the question is certainly being posed about the sizes things are. Thornhill and Eve have had an exchange about whether he is a little boy or a big boy, and now the issue is about what size the human face of flesh and blood is in comparison with faces on the face of a granite mountain and the size of both in comparison with the photographic projection of the human face. A question is thus raised about what Grant is (made of), about what it means that he has become a national monument, and hence about what a monument is. So at the same time a question is raised about what presidents are and about what it means to know and remember them. These comparisons are underscored when it turns out, directly, that our initial view of the presidents' faces is an image of them as seen through a telescope set up for the pleasure and instruction of tourists. The image is possessed for us by, let us say, Thornhill, but there is no reason to think that anyone present wouldn't see the same image, the one we have now. Its being Grant who looks through the telescope at the famous stone faces identifies the conditions of his existence as a screen actor and thus identifies the mode in which we see him and think we know him. And I would be willing to swear from the fact alone of the way Grant is standing behind that telescope that he is also meant as a surrogate for the one who is capturing these images for our pleasure and instruction. But the Professor is there with Thornhill as we cut to him standing before the telescope, so the matter of directorial surrogates must be complicated.

Let us run through the evidence for Grant/Thornhill as surrogate for Hitchcock. There is, first of all, the hint laid down by Hitchcock's having autographed himself in this film as someone who misses a bus: Thornhill is the only (other) character in the film before whom a bus shuts its doors and drives off. Again, however we are to understand Thornhill's participation in the killing of the real Lester Townsend in the United Nations building, we must understand him as what this moment visually declares him to be, someone who betrays by showing a picture, that is, a picture which is, or which causes, a knife in the back—a reasonable, or anyway Hitchcockian, description of Hitchcock's narrative procedure. Now take the telescope and the two men on the terrace. Thornhill's initial reaction to the view through the telescope is to say "I don't like the way Teddy Roosevelt is looking at me." And he will say, "I think he's telling me not to go on with this harebrained scheme." This could be a line Hitchcock is allowing Grant to use about himself, perhaps about his role in this strenuous film, perhaps about his career as an actor. (I wouldn't put it past Hitchcock to be alluding to the fact that Grant shares a name with a president of the United States, one famous for drinking, and one in particular that only Teddy Roosevelt among the four presidents figured at Mount Rushmore would have known was a president.) But the Professor's response suggests something else first: "He's telling you to walk softly and carry a big stick." This makes a certain amount of sense said either to Grant or to Thornhill. It makes much better sense said to Hitchcock, hence said as it were to himself, that is, by one directorial surrogate to another. The exchange about a harebrained scheme and walking softly, as behind a big camera, would express a moment of self-doubt on Hitchcock's part to be overcome by the course of this film; and since this film is a kind of summary or anthology of his mature career as a whole, the doubt must be about the course of his mature career as a whole. If one were prepared to believe this, one would be encouraged to take the title *North by Northwest* not as naming some unheard of direction but as titling a search for directedness, or sanity, a claim to have found it, as of the course of a career. (We will come to a more general reason for taking the title this way.) Hitchcock's identifying himself with the actor figure permits him a certain opposition to the two more explicit director figures, that is, permits him to claim opposition to the way other directors operate; his testimony is to show himself the victim as well as the inquisitor of his trade, the pursued as well as the pursuer, permitting himself to be looked back at.

This prompts me to collect one of the last of Hitchcock's inclusions in his anthology: his reference to *Rear Window*, whose hero (James Stewart) also looks through a telescope, now explicitly a telescopic camera lens and thus more explicitly conferring an identification as a film director, and whom someone or something eventually also looks back at through his telescope in a way he does not like. The Stewart figure has a kind of comic Hamlet derivation in that he sees everything and is debarred from taking action (by a broken leg in a cast). The thing that looks back at him, locking gazes with him, is the man whose murdering of his wife and dismemberment and disposition of the pieces of the body Stewart's camera has divined; and this too feels like an act of identification, between viewer and viewed, between director and subjects. Hitchcock's confession is a terrible one. (It may just be worth remembering that the Hamlet figure in Saxo Grammaticus dismembered the body of the figure that became Polonius and disposed of the parts in a sewer; and just worth putting this together with Thornhill's early dictation to his secretary of a note to accompany a gift of gold-wrapped candy: "This is for your sweet tooth, and all your other sweet parts.") The brighter side of Hitchcock's sensing an identification of himself with Hamlet claims his position as that of an intellectual, as possessed of a metaphysical imagination, and as unknown (partly because of the antic disposition he puts on).

What I just called Hitchcock's terrible confession—it is something I understand by Rothman's detection of Hitchcock's murderous camera—was going to be the guiding subject of these remarks, the thought that filming inevitably proceeds by severing things, both in cutting and, originally, in framing, and that Hitchcock is

fully sensible of this fact and responsible to it. While it is buried in
North by Northwest in the rarified reference to the original Hamlet
story it is, if you allow the subject, blatantly posed by the gigantic
heads of the monument and by the matching of Grant's head with
them. The suggestion is that these memorializations have required
acts of severing. This would be something else Grant does not like
when he sees something looking back at him through the telescope.
And it is this fate that Thornhill is saved from in earning the rescue
from the faces of the monument. So when I say that Grant's looking
through the telescope represents our perception of film, of something I mean by viewing, I am proposing that a theory of this mode
of perception will be given in a theory of the perception of part-
objects, as this is broached in the work of Melanie Klein. Such a
theory should be able to help account for a pair of familiar facts in
looking at film: that there may apparently be the most fantastic disproportion between what is actually shown on the screen and the
emotion this elicits; *and* that this disproportion can be resisted, the
emotion fail to appear. After all, many people think, or think they
think, that *North by Northwest* is a light comedy. But while I have
left the theme of severed objects as an undercurrent of these remarks
I decided against making it explicit (then I partly changed my
mind).

What is it that looks back through the telescope at Thornhill, who
presumably has no special relation to those heads (anyway not
Grant's relation)? It is puzzling that he should say it is Teddy Roosevelt since that head is, from the angle taken, quite retracted in comparison to those of Washington, Jefferson, and Lincoln and is not
facing in the right direction. We are in any case being asked to let
ourselves be puzzled by what it is we see when we are looking at the
results of a movie camera and also by what the Mount Rushmore
Memorial betokens. I figure what looks back through the lens not to
require eyes, not even images of eyes, but to be whatever it is that a
movie camera looks at, which is to say, whatever power it is that is
solicited from us in perceiving things on film. I once said that the
images of photography are of the world as a whole, and now thinking
of what looks back at a director—an image's original audience as

reciprocated by these mountainous heads of the presidents, cliffs turned into faces—I would like to say that what looks back, what reveals itself to the viewer's gaze, is the physiognomy of the world, say the face of the earth. To animate, or reanimate, or humanize the world and so achieve a reciprocity with it is a recognizable aspiration of some poetry and some philosophy, as for example when Thoreau writes in the chapter "The Ponds" in *Walden*: "A lake is the landscape's most beautiful and expressive feature. It is earth's eye; looking into which the beholder measures the depth of his own nature." Thornhill's capacity for beholding nature in this way—as unsevered—would be a sign that he is to be saved.

The Mount Rushmore Memorial is a crazy American literalization of this ambition of reciprocity with the world. More specifically it literalizes such an idea as Walt Whitman's that America's mountains and prairies are the greatest of its poems. It is as if the monument proposes a solution to an American ambivalence as old as the pilgrims about the land of America: that it is human, in particular female, a virgin and yet a nourishing mother, but at the same time that we have raped her, blotted nature out by wanting our mark upon her.[5] (I have suggested that the film *North by Northwest*, in the cropdusting sequence, invokes that ambivalence and calls for a solution to it.) The proposed solution of the monument is that if the mark is big enough and art enough and male enough, the doom of progress may be redeemed. Hardly a saving message to be drawn from the observation and memory of Washington, Jefferson, and Lincoln.

The *Encyclopedia Americana* notes that the faces of the monument measure some sixty feet from chin to forehead and adds, rather proudly I thought, that this is twice as high as the head of the Giza Sphinx. But what else is there to think about but their monumentality, and what more to conclude on their basis than that America has become twice the land of Egypt, twice as enslaving and twice as mysterious? Hitchcock shows that for a projected screen image to en-

---

[5]Two valuable accounts of the history of American attitudes toward the American land are Edwin Fussell's *Frontier: American Literature and the American West* (Princeton, N.J., 1965), and Annette Kolodny's *The Lay of the Land: Metaphor as Experience and History in American Life and Letters* (Chapel Hill, N.C., 1975).

compass the size of these faces is the work of an instant, and thus he at once declares his work in competition with Mount Rushmore as a monument to America, about America, and asks for a meditation on what can now constitute monumentality, on what can be made so as to show the value in commemorating. This is a reason that this film is at pains to anthologize the whole body of Hitchcock's mature, mostly American, work, to throw it all into the balance as a kind of rededication. Rededication is an appropriate mood before a monument, particularly in a moment of self-doubt. And even if this monument exemplifies competition and domination as much as it does commemoration, still it is about founding fathers, a wish, however awkwardly expressed, to get back to origins. Hitchcock has been careful to dissociate his attitude toward the monument from Vandamm's contemptuous dismissal of it with his opening question to Kaplan/Thornhill at the cafeteria: something like, "Now what little drama have you invited me to witness in these gay surroundings?" (*This* Englishman does not belong to the place but owns a structure mythically close to it, pitched out from the land, less a dwelling than a space station.) And what better rededication than to compete with this monument's way of remembering by showing your fellow inhabitants a better way—a way that does not attempt to petrify and sever the past but to revise the inheritance of it, to reinherit it?

Before giving the answer I have, I pause to note that we could loop back and recount the main topics of *North by Northwest* as topics of seduction—our seduction by one another, by beautiful women and beautiful men and beautiful things, by mothers, strangers, liquor, fame, monuments, politics, America, art, film. The present film asks us to consider our attachments to things less in the light of what things they are than in the light of what mode of attachment we take toward them—for example, fetishistic, scoptophilic, masochistic, narcissistic, or in general, to use a key word of Emerson's, partial. One result of such consideration might be the thought that a healthy suspicion and testing of our attachment to film should extend to our attachment to, say, literature as well and that film and literature are each capable of helping us in this extension.

The mountain-monument seems to have become just another

landscape of a cold war, the scene of an escape, as though we had lost the capacity for attachment altogether; but then it is the site of the playing out of one of drama's oldest subjects, the rights of love against the rights, anyway the requirements, of politics. We might come to think that the escape of this pair is seen by Hitchcock to be of national importance. Who are they, and what are they doing on this monument?

I will, as said, assert that they derive from, or from the same source as, the American comedy of remarriage, which I said means to me that their goal is the thing I call the legitimizing of marriage, the declaration that happiness is still to be won there, there or nowhere, and that America is a place, fictional no doubt, in which that happiness can be found. The structure of these comedies, making the goal achievable, takes responsibility over a longish, extendable list of features, two of the principal ones being the achieving of a new innocence and the establishing or reestablishing of an identity. These are pieces of an ancient Hitchcockian problematic. So are the two further features of remarriage comedies that I call the capacities for adventure and for improvisation. I mean by these capacities the virtues that allow you to become at home in the world, to establish the world as a home. The capacities permit, if necessary, living together on the road, as if loving were the finding of a direction, that is, of a directedness, just, as I mentioned, as Hitchcock's title *North by Northwest* names otherwise than a given direction. So important is it to get this capacity for adventurousness straight that in the middle of their escape down the monument the pair pause, comically, surrealistically, to discuss it (as silent comics used to pause, in the middle of chasing one another, to catch their breath). After his proposal to her she asks what happened to his two earlier marriages. He says his wives left him because they found he led too dull a life. For Hitchcock so daringly to mock the suspense he has been building up over this escape, virtually declaring that the two are now standing on a platform in a studio, must mean that he wants to illustrate the significance of this exchange, to enforce the assertion that dullness, taken as the opposite of adventurousness, where these are characteristics of human relationship, spiritual matters, is not something that run-

ning around the face of the earth proves or disproves, except allegorically. With those wives even this monumental situation of life and
death would have been, spiritually speaking, dull; whereas with Eve
the "importance" of the time and place is unimportant for the opposite reason, that anything and everything can be an adventure, however untellable as such from outside. (This is roughly the sentiment
of *Bringing Up Baby*.)

The candidates for remarriage must, further, not be virgins, they
must have a past together, and they must talk well and wittily about
marriage, especially about whether they believe in marriage. The
past the pair share in *North by Northwest* is just one night, but it
proves ample enough. And one or both of the pair must maintain an
openness to childhood, so it turns out to be to Thornhill's spiritual
credit that although in the course of the film he becomes big he remains a boy. (The childlike capacity of Grant's temperament on film
is stressed, I suppose discovered, in the comedies he made with
Howard Hawks.) The man in remarriage comedies is responsible for
the education of the woman as part of a process of rescuing or redeeming her from a state in which she keeps herself; this may be
characterized as a coldness or an inability to feel, and the education
typically takes the form of the man's lecturing or haranguing the
woman. In *North by Northwest* Thornhill identifies Eve as a statue
and accuses her of having no feelings to hurt, but we are shown by
her tears at this moment (at the auction) that what I earlier called the
education in his surviving her onslaught has taken effect; to begin
her physical rescue, he will later write on his monogrammed matchbook a note that contains information no one else in the world is in a
position to impart to her. We may also see in this successful delivery
his finally getting a message through to a woman, the difficulty in
doing which began this plot.

This is enough to let me outline what I take as the essential difference in structure between the romantic comedies of remarriage and
Hitchcock's romantic thriller. The goal of the comedies requires
what I call the creation of the woman, a new creation of a new
woman. This takes the form in the comedies of something like the
woman's death and revival, and it goes with the camera's insistence

on the flesh-and-blood reality of the female actor. When this happens in Hitchcock, as it did in *Vertigo*, the Hitchcock film preceding *North by Northwest*, it is shown to produce catastrophe: the woman's falling to her death, precisely the fate *averted* in *North by Northwest*. Here, accordingly, it is the man who undergoes death and revival (at least twice, both times at the hands of the woman) *and* whose physical identity is insisted upon by the camera.[6] Hitchcock is thus investigating the point that the comedies of remarriage are least certain about, namely, what it is about the man that fits him to educate and hence rescue the woman, that is, to be chosen by the woman to educate her and thereby to achieve happiness for them both.

But again, why is the rescue to be achieved from the face of this monument? I have called it the face of the earth, the earth itself become visible, as pure surface. These tiny creatures are crawling between heaven and earth, a metaphysical accomplishment, as if becoming children again. Hamlet, feeling like a child, claims this accomplishment for himself as he decrees that there shall be no more marriages. Thornhill proposes marriage as he and the woman hang from a precipice; a gallant concept, as if marriage were a presence of mind, requiring no assurance of a future. Close-ups of the pair on the surface of the monument faces show them as if on an alien planet. There is no longer nature on the earth; earth is no longer an artifact by analogy, intimating God; it is literally and totally artifact, petrified under the hands of mankind. To place your film in competition with such an achievement is to place it in competition with film's own peculiar power of preserving the world by petrifying it, or anyway fixing it in celluloid. The couple in remarriage comedies are isolated at the end, expected to legitimize marriage without the world, which has no help for pain. The surface of Hitchcock's Mount Rushmore strikes me as a place of absolute spiritual isolation, civilization engulfing even empty space. In one of his first American films, *Saboteur* (to name a final excerpt in this anthology), a man holds a villain

---

[6]That a given genre yields an adjacent genre by having one of its features "negated" in this way is something I give a little theoretical attention to in the introduction to *Pursuits of Happiness*.

from a ledge at the top of the Statue of Liberty, but the villain's sleeve comes loose and he falls to earth. To fall from Mount Rushmore, as I am imagining it, would be to fall off the earth, down the vast edges drear of the world.

Thornhill lifts Eve up directly from the isolation of the monument's ledge to the isolation of the marriage bed, as if identifying both places as the scene of cliffhangers and declaring that they are at home in both. At the lift Leonard is overcome and drops the statue Eve has been identified with, which breaks against the granite monument, opening to produce some film, I take it the present film. I in effect describe *The Philadelphia Story* as a film produced by a rescue which takes the form of the breaking of a statue in favor of a woman. I also claim that the remarriage is, using a repeated phrase of that film, of national importance. My ground is the thought that while America, or any discovered world, can no longer ratify marriage, the achievement of true marriage might ratify something called America as a place in which to seek it. This is a state secret.

♦

WHAT BECOMES
OF THINGS ON FILM?

♦

*These remarks, more or less, were read at one of the symposia of the
Modern Language Association Annual Convention held in Chicago,
in December 1977. The title of the symposium was "Chosisme and
the Cinema: The Perception of Physical Reality in Cinema and Literature." Its idea, as well as the invitation to me to comment on the
papers submitted to it, was the work of Professor Terry Comito. The
thoughts I put together for my contribution to that occasion have
played a role in my further thinking about film out of proportion to its
small size (it first appeared in* Philosophy and Literature, *Vol. 2 No.
2, Fall 1978). A principal place these thoughts are picked up explicitly is in the* Adam's Rib *chapter of my book* Pursuits of Happiness,
*where I read the presence of its film-within-the-film (fictionally a
home movie) as a demonstration that "no event within a film (say no
gesture of framing or editing) is as significant (as "cinematic") as
the event of film itself."*

◇

And does this title express a genuine question? That is, does one
accept the suggestion that there is a particular relation (or a particular system of relations, awaiting systematic study) that holds between things and their filmed projections, which is to say between
the originals now absent from us (by screening) and the new originals now present to us (in photogenesis)—a relation to be thought of

as something's becoming something (say as a caterpillar becomes a butterfly, or as a prisoner becomes a count, or as an emotion becomes conscious, or as after a long night it becomes light)? The title is, at any rate, the working formulation I have given myself for the guiding question of this discussion. Of the many issues and many levels of issue raised by the papers I have been invited to comment upon, I have picked two moments at which work of my own about film has been referred to, wishing to contribute to a conversation in the territory of film study.

The first moment is one in which I am quoted (or Heidegger and I jointly quoted) as saying that "The cinematic image accentuates the conspicuousness, obtrusiveness and obstinacy of things." I am sorry to have given such an impression. The background of what I said[1]—in the course of giving some examples of how thinking about films and thinking about philosophy have drawn upon one another in my work—was this: early in *Being and Time*, Heidegger characterizes the specific way in which the phenomenon occurs, in his terms, of the "worldhood of the world announcing itself"; it is a phenomenon in which a particular mode of sight or awareness is brought into play. What brings this mode of sight into play is a disruption of what Heidegger calls the "work-world," a disruption of the matters of course running among our tools, and the occupations they extend, and the environment which supports these occupations. It is upon the disruption of such matters of course (of a tool, say by its breaking; or of someone's occupation, say because of an injury; or of some absence of material) that the mode of sight then brought forth discovers objects in what Heidegger notes as their conspicuousness, their obtrusiveness, and their obstinacy. Now the foreground of what I said was this: it struck me that this perception or apprehension of the things of our world is part of the grain of silent film comedy; and, more particularly, that Buster Keaton is the silent comic figure whose extraordinary works and whose extraordinary gaze, perhaps the fundamental feature of his character, illuminate

[1]In "Leopards in Connecticut," *The Georgia Review* 30 (1976): 233–62. The passage now appears in the appendix to *Pursuits of Happiness*.

and are illuminated by the consequent concept of the worldhood of the world announcing itself.

While I take even this bare broaching of this idea to formulate one possibility of cinematic images of the things of our world, it is no more to be expected that *all* cinematic images carry this force, than it is to be expected that all are in the service of Keaton's species of comedy; any more than the idea of such images exhausts what there is to say about Keaton, or about Heidegger, or about any further relations between them. What the idea ought to do is to help us to see and say at once what it is Keaton permits us to laugh about and what concretely the nature is of the mode of sight from which Heidegger begins his analysis of Being-in-the-world. This laughter is not defined, for example, by a Bergsonian suggestion that the human being has become machine-like, or vice versa. Keaton is as flexible, as resourceful, as Ulysses, and his giant machines do exactly what they might be expected to do under their circumstances. We have here to do with something about the human capacity for sight, or for sensuous awareness generally, something we might express as our condemnation to project, to inhabit, a world that goes essentially beyond the delivery of our senses. This seems to be the single point of agreement throughout the history of epistemology, at least throughout the modern history of the subject, say since Descartes. The most common conclusion among epistemologists has been some kind of skepticism—a realization that we cannot, strictly speaking, be said to know, to be certain, of the existence of the world of material things at all. I understand Buster Keaton, say in *The General*, to exemplify an acceptance of the enormity of this realization of human limitation, denying neither the abyss that at any time may open before our plans, nor the possibility, despite that open possibility, of living honorably, with good if resigned spirits, and with eternal hope. His capacity for love does not avoid this knowledge, but lives in full view of it. Is he dashing? He is something rarer; he is undashable. He incorporates both the necessity of wariness in an uncertain world, and also the necessary limits of human awareness; gaze as we may, there is always something behind our backs, room for doubt.

Quickly compare Chaplin's knowledge and his world of things, say in *The Gold Rush*, made the same year as *The General* (1925). And take just the two most famous set routines from that film, the Thanksgiving dinner of roast shoe, and the dream-dance of the rolls on forks. In both cases one object is taken as, treated as, something it is not in fact. The ability so to regard objects is studied in Part II of Wittgenstein's *Philosophical Investigations*, through the concept of "seeing as," the concept Wittgenstein takes as the topic of his study of interpretation. To this human capacity for seeing or for treating something *as* something, Wittgenstein attributes our capacity for intimacy in understanding, for what we might call the innerness of the meaning we attach to words and gestures. That the Chaplin routines are in a sense opposites of one another allows them to suggest a complete world of such understanding—in the one case a shoe is treated as a food (a case of dire necessity), in the other a food is treated as a shoe (a case of dire luxury); in both, his imagination gives habitation to his ecstasy and to his grief. The madness of his meaning keeps him sane. (One could say that the worldhood of the world never reveals itself to the little man; he is both too far inside the world for that, and too far outside.)

Say that Keaton and Chaplin make a comedy of the fact that such a creature as a human being is fated to pursue happiness, and that they undertake to demonstrate that such a creature is after all, and to a certain extent, under very exacting conditions, capable of happiness. Then Keaton shows these conditions to be essentially those of virtuousness, or of conscientiousness—e.g., of courage, of temperance, of loyalty, and of an aptness of the body that Spinoza calls wisdom; an ability to maintain your poise no matter what happens to your plans (the outside of you). Chaplin shows these conditions to be those of free imagination, especially the imagination of happiness itself—an ability to gather your spirits no matter what has happened to them (the inside of you).

The logic of skepticism requires two things chiefly: that knowledge be discovered to fail in the best cases—in knowing, for example, that I am seated before my fire, or that two plus three is five; and that this failure be discovered in ways open to any normal human being, not something knowable only by experts. It requires only the willingness to know. The logic of the comedy that absorbs skepticism (in opposite ways in Keaton and in Chaplin) requires that we discover outer and inner aptnesses with objects to succeed in the worst cases, and by means of a precision and beauty of conduct in principle open to any normal human being. It requires only the willingness to care.

A second moment at which work of mine is mentioned occurs in Elliot Rubinstein's valuable discussion of Buñuel, when he questions Robbe-Grillet's remark that "the cinema knows only one grammatical mode: the present tense of the indicative."[2] Others, including myself, have in effect questioned what "present" means applied to filmed objects. Rubinstein interestingly extends the worry to the idea of the "indicative mode" more generally, characterizing *Belle de Jour* as exploring "the camera's possibilities in the realm of the subjunctive." What Rubinstein is registering here is not simply the general truth, shown since the beginning of cinema, that the camera can lend itself to the projection of fantasy as readily as of reality; but, more specifically, the discovery that screened events remain intelligible to us if, even without conventional (or grammatical?) warning—specifically, without changes in the sound track, or the acting, or the modes of filming—they alternate between the depiction of the real and of the fantasied, call it the alternation between the indicative and the subjunctive.

Rubinstein claims distinctly more than this minimal intellectual or technical amount; he claims that Buñuel's discovery in *Belle de Jour* constitutes an artistic triumph. Going on my memory of the film from one distant viewing, and guided by Rubinstein's shaping of it, I am inclined to agree with him. But I put the point minimally first to emphasize that the intellectual or technical discovery, and the artistic achievement, do not assure one another. This is the sort of very primitive point of aesthetics that has to be made again and again in speaking of the modern in art, where artistic achievement does so often seem to be a function of some intellectual or technical discov-

[2]Rubenstein's "Buñuel's World, or The World and Buñuel" also (with this of mine) appears in *Philosophy and Literature*, Fall 1978.

ery. An instance at hand is provided by Robbe-Grillet's *Trans-Europe Express*. It was taken by one of the panelists of this session as exemplifying roughly the procedure under discussion in *Belle de Jour*, that of unmarked juxtapositions of the actual and the . . . what? Call it the imaginary. (One already senses such a distinction giving way. And what it should give way to is a set of ideas I expressed in *The World Viewed* by saying: "It is a poor idea of fantasy which takes it to be a world apart from reality, a world clearly showing its unreality. Fantasy is precisely what reality can be confused with" [p. 85].) But *Trans-Europe Express* is, I find, a more or less uninteresting piece of work. And it is, for me, a matter of aesthetic logic that no procedure discovered in a particular work can be proven by that work to have greater artistic point than the work itself achieves, or some relevant part of it. (Of course the work may inspire a better or different artist to look more deeply into that procedure's possibilities. And of course we must not suppose ourselves to know yet whether, nor how, the procedures in question really are the "same.") Then shall we say that *Belle de Jour*'s superiority is *not* a function of any such procedure, but is due rather to the presence of such phenomena as Catherine Deneuve, and the camerawork of Sacha Vierney, and the genius of Buñuel? But I think one feels immediately that such an alternative is false to one's experience of the film, that the procedure in question is indeed integral to the artistic achievement of the film, and that the phenomena of actress, camera, and director are to be accounted for by determining how the procedure lends itself to them, and contrariwise. I would like to say: in Buñuel's film the procedure has found its natural subject; which, if we accept this film as a masterpiece of the medium of film, means: in *Belle de Jour* film has found one of its master subjects. What is this subject?

Buñuel says, or someone says for him: the masochistic nature of a woman's impulses.[3] Rubinstein says, or suggests: the balance between sadism and bourgeois domesticity. How could we convince ourselves that these are answers, good answers, to the question I formulated?

I note that there is another masterpiece of film made within a year

[3]Cf. the Introductory Note to the English presentation of *Belle de Jour*, prepared by Robert Adkinson (New York, 1971).

of *Belle de Jour* that employs the procedure of unmarked juxtapositions of reality with some opposition to reality, and which maintains their balance, the irresolution of them, through to the end: I mean Bergman's *Persona*. And that film, too, has as what we might call its subject something about the imagination of a woman, or of a beautiful woman, or perhaps of two women; which no doubt in part means: a man's imagination of the imagination of women, or perhaps a man's compulsion to imagine the imagination of a woman. More particularly, both films concern the meaning, or limits, or conditions, of female identity, hence no doubt of human identity. (I do not wish to disguise that I take the accurate statement of a work's subject to be an obligation of criticism.)

What is it about film that lends itself to such a subject? (The validity and pressure of such a question is what I take to demand so solemn a topic as "the ontology of film.")

Two further films—masterpieces of their own kind—might be allowed to have a bearing on the further specification of the subject we are seeking to formulate: Hitchcock's *Vertigo*,[4] from a decade earlier; and Capra's *It's a Wonderful Life*, from a decade before that.

The climax of the Capra is as subjunctive as a stretch of film can be, the realization of the wish that one had never been born; and it is filmed and acted in no special way and with no conventional marks to indicate its break with the larger body of the film. It is true that we as viewers are not in doubt about the shift of the plane of reality, but the character with whom we identify is tortured by exactly this doubt; it is an expression of this character's self-doubt, doubt about the worth of his existence. And since this worth is explicitly characterized as a matter of the difference his existence has made in the world, the doubt can be said to be about his identity—something amply registered at the climax of the climax as he turns in anguish from friends to mother to wife, accosting them with the demands: Don't you know me?; Tell me who I am.

In *Vertigo* we do not exactly move from a real place to a projected

[4]Robin Wood cites *Vertigo* as a touchstone for assessing certain matters of the viewer's distance or involvement with the events of *Persona* in "The World Without, The World Within," reprinted in *Ingmar Bergman: Essays in Criticism*, ed. Stuart M. Kaminsky (Oxford, 1975). Reprinted in this same collection, Susan Sontag's essay on *Persona* momentarily contrasts, hence compares, that film with *Belle de Jour*.

place, but we are made to share the hero's quasi-hallucinatory, quasi-necrophilic quest in the realm of the subjunctive for the woman he imagines dead. The confusion over the question whether there is one woman or two, or whether one woman is alive or dead, feels like a confusion within his own identity. His existence takes place elsewhere than in the world we see.

The point, at once critical and theoretical, of considering the procedure of juxtaposed realities is to enable us to do what any reading of a film must do—account for the frames of the film being what they are, in the order they are in, e.g., to say what motivates the camera to look and to move as and where it looks and moves. The Capra and the Hitchcock films make nakedly clear the power of film to materialize and to satisfy (hence to dematerialize and to thwart) human wishes that escape the satisfaction of the world as it stands; as perhaps it will ever, or can ever, in fact stand. (Whose wishes, a character's, or the viewer's? We would, I think, like to say both. But the justification of this answer will require an understanding of the nature of a viewer's "identification" with screened characters.) I think it cannot be an accident that the actor in both films is James Stewart, that both Capra and Hitchcock see in Stewart's temperament (which, of course, is to say, see in what becomes of that temperament on film, its photogenesis) the capacity to stake identity upon the power of wishing, upon the capacity and purity of one's imagination and desire—not on one's work, or position, or accomplishments, or looks, or intelligence. Call the quality Stewart projects a willingness for suffering—his quality Capra also records in *Mr. Smith Goes to Washington*, and that John Ford used in *The Man Who Shot Liberty Valance*. It is the quality that would admit him to the company of the women whose search for their identities seems to have traced the contours of the subject of film to which I have been wanting to give expression. Then call the subject the identifying or the inhabitation of a feminine region of the self, whether the person whose self it is be male or female.

(A comparison seems immediately called for with Mizoguchi's *Ugetsu*. I do not feel that I know the temperament or the environment of this male well enough to assay his photogenetic possibilities—e.g., his femininity. But I note that his wish, anyway his final wish, is not for translation into an opposed habitation, but for a particular figure to inhabit, or reinhabit, his own. This wish seems to me to have its source not in the woman in him, but in the child in him. Its materialization is of a woman moving about his familiar room, and it occurs as he is curled on the floor; our response to it is not that of a cry in the throat but of a break in the heart.)

That to be human is to have, or to risk having, this capacity to wish; that to be human is to wish, and in particular to wish for a completer identity than one has so far attained; and that such a wish may project a complete world *opposed* to the world one so far shares with others: this is a way of taking up the cause of Shakespearean Romance. If so, it is not surprising that a filmic procedure which taps this cause is one that juxtaposes modes and moods of reality as a whole, taunts them with one another. So romance in turn shares with skepticism the realization, in the terms of Descartes's First Meditation, that "there are no conclusive indications by which waking life can be distinguished from sleep." The consequence of this realization, Descartes goes on to say, is that "I am quite astonished, and my bewilderment is such that it is almost able to convince me that I am sleeping." In both skepticism and romance, knowledge, call it consciousness as a whole, must go out in order that a better consciousness can come to light. (The idea of modes and moods of reality altering together as totalities, or the idea that the concepts of consciousness and of the world as such are made for one another, in one another's image, is epitomized in Wittgenstein's remark near the end of the *Tractatus*: the world of the happy is quite another than that of the unhappy. To this remark we might add that the worlds may be juxtaposed within the same breast.)

With one final film admitted to this discussion I will be ready to draw a moral. Rubinstein quotes Susan Sontag on Godard's films as follows: "In Godard's films things display a wholly alienated character. Characteristically, they are used with indifference, neither skillfully nor clumsily; they are simply there. 'Objects exist,' Godard has written, 'and if one pays more attention to them than to people, it is precisely because they exist more than these people.

Dead objects are still alive. Living people are often already dead.' "
I know this quotation from Godard only from his voice, or half-
voice, as narrator of *Two or Three Things I Know about Her*. We know
that we are to be wary of granting the whole truth to any remark of
this narrator, for at least the reason that he recurrently questions his
own remarks. *Two or Three Things*, made the same year as *Belle de
Jour*, is also a film about a bourgeoise who spends afternoons as a
prostitute, and also explicitly links questions about her identity with
speculations about the nature and existence of the external world.
This film contains a juxtaposition of filmed objects to whose extraor-
dinariness the filmmaker Alfred Guzzetti has called special attention.[5] With shots of the woman, and certain others, in a café-bar, the
camera alternates, with progressively closer shots, a cup of coffee
just stirred, and at last peers over the cup's rim until the bubbling
liquid swirling as a whole fills the cinemascope rectangle; the sound
track rises to a poeticizing meditation that fits our willingness to
endow this image with the power to invoke the swirling of the universe, and hence the question of its origin and ending. Whereupon
we cut to an image of the rough barman filling a shot glass, then
drawing a beer from a machine of pull faucets which now fills the
rectangle. One possible reading of the juxtaposition of the cup-uni-
verse and the barman is as a rebuke to our willingness for a poetic
meditation on universal origins when we do not even know where
the beer and the coffee we drink on earth come from—that we drink
them in real places made by real people for just this purpose; and
that they are handed to us by real people whose livelihoods depend
upon their being bought. We might speculate, among other things,
upon whether the gleaming beer dispenser, worked by the barman
as he observes the scene of meditation, is a comment on the idea of a
movie camera.

The moral I draw is this: the question what becomes of objects
when they are filmed and screened—like the question what becomes
of particular people, and specific locales, and subjects and motifs

[5]In a long study of this film prepared for a meeting of the American Film Seminar in
1975. Revised, and with a full body of frame enlargements, Guzzetti's study of Godard's film was published by Harvard University Press in 1980.

when they are filmed by individual makers of film—has only one source of data for its answer, namely the appearance and significance of just those objects and people that are in fact to be found in the succession of films, or passages of films, that matter to us. To express their appearances, and define those significances, and articulate the nature of this mattering, are acts that help to constitute what we might call film criticism. Then to explain how these appearances, significances, and matterings—these specific events of photogenesis—are made possible by the general photogenesis of film altogether, by the fact, as I more or less put it in *The World Viewed*, that objects on film are always already displaced, *trouvé* (i.e., that we as viewers are always already displaced before them), would be an undertaking of what we might call film theory.

◆

THE ORDINARY
AS THE UNEVENTFUL
(A Note on the *Annales* Historians)

◆

On November 13, 1980, at one of the set of Lionel Trilling Seminars held each year at Columbia University, I was one of two respondents to the principal paper of the evening, given by Paul Ricoeur under the title "The Eclipse of Event in Modern French Historiography." Despite, or because of, my lack of expertise in the substance of the material Ricoeur offered for discussion, I produced a formulation concerning the concept of the ordinary, an equation of it with that of the uneventful, that decisively confirmed, or advanced, to my way of thinking, thoughts I had been having about the consonance of so-called ordinary language with the visions of other intellectual quests for the ordinary, in this case with what I understood of the project of the Annales *school of history. And that equation plays a key role in shaping the discussion of television which occupies "The Fact of Television," the essay that concludes this book. For these and other reasons I wish to preserve the identity of the occasion on which I delivered these remarks, and I give them here as read.*

An important other reason is that I have been unable to determine whether Ricoeur has published his Lionel Trilling Lecture as such. Through inquiries kindly made on my behalf by Ted Cohen at Chicago, who spoke to Ricoeur's student and translator David Pellauer, and to his editor at the University of Chicago Press, it is clear that at least portions of the material have been recast for inclusion in a two-volume work of Ricoeur's whose English translation (by Kathleen

184

McLaughlin and David Pellauer) is to appear under the title Time and Narrative. *The first volume is scheduled for publication by the University of Chicago Press in the spring of 1984. So while I do not know, and am not interested in claiming, that Ricoeur still holds to the specific formulations that I took exception to in my response to him, and while I regard the worth of my counter-formulations to be independent of their origins in a particular occasion, there seemed to me more to be lost than gained by removing the form of the occasion.*

What struck me as a misstep in Ricoeur's presentation is a step that was, in my experience, natural to take; it was not at all obvious to me for some time what I thought was wrong with it, however uneasy it made me; nor do I claim, beyond the purposes of this exchange, to assess Ricoeur's formulations. For anything I have said further they may, on other grounds, be true and important. I took and gave back what I could; what I took became something else. It is one of the ways things happen.

Ricoeur's paper was divided into four sections entitled, in order: "Toward an Eventless History"; "The Resistance of the Event"; "The Indirect Reference of History to Story"; "The Ontological and Epistemological Status of Event in History." Sketching an initial characterization of what Ricoeur called uncritical ontological and epistemological assertions implied in "what we tend to assume as defining historical events"—roughly that a historical event is something past, something done by or to human beings, and something unrepeatable—his paper covered such ground as the following. In his second section: "My contention here is that history cannot be radically eventless *because it cannot break its ties with the kind of discourse which is the original 'place' of the notion of event, i.e., narrative discourse. History keeps being about events, because it keeps being related, directly or indirectly, to narrative discourse." In his third section: "Our problem . . . will be to show in which indirect way history, as modern histories practice it, refers to the narrative understanding that is the original 'place' of the notion of event. I shall try to open a difficult path between the claim for a history without events and the claim for a history which would directly proceed from story." The fourth section suggests a "twofold extension of the concept of event to long time-spans and to social change as contrary to the two-fold denial of [i.e., proposal by] eventless history," an extension of the idea of narration by means of a "theory of emplotment." Ricoeur's attempt to locate his indirect relation to narrative understanding involves a very complex discussion of what he calls ontological and epistemological issues in the philosophy of history. These have not arisen for me.*

What concerned me, reading and hearing his paper, was his diagnosis, in its first section, of why it is historians would wish to deny the concept of event to the writing of history, hence his citing of his own reasons for opposing their rejection of the concept. In general he is satisfied that, in the "French historians' [hatred of] philosophy and epistemology," they have given no theoretical justification for their conviction that their practice requires the shunning, or demotion, of the concept of event, whereas he will undertake to provide theoretical justification for its necessity in historical understanding, hence its presence, if disguised, or extended, in the historical successes of the Annales *school. In particular he wishes to oppose their nontheoretical, "visceral" implications in imposing on historical inquiry a shift "from the old primacy of political history to the new supremacy of social history." One of these implications is the denial of the short-term dramatic event as the "ultimate atom of social change." And this is connected with another of their denials that Ricoeur wishes to challenge, the denial that the individual is "the ultimate atom for historical inquiry and analysis." "Thus [it is] the twofold denunciation of 'battle-history' and of 'event-history' [that] forms the polemical underside of the plea for a history of the total human phenomenon with heavy stress on economic and social conditions. In this regard the most noteworthy works of the* Ecole des Annales *are concerned with social history in which groups, social categories and classes, town and country, bourgeois, artisans, peasants, and workers become the collective heroes of history." What substantively concerned me in Ricoeur's remarks was the suggestion that a turning away from "short-term" events—unique battles, unrepeatable successions, famous deaths, major marriages—toward the long-term, endlessly repeated conditions of human life amounted to history's turning away from attention to the story of individual human beings in favor of attention to more or less anonymous collectivities.*

I felt this was wrong, or prejudicial, both about what events are (what our concept of an event is) and about what individual lives are; and wrong, or prejudicial, in a way that bears down on the sense of the ordinary that was becoming further developed and more explicit in my current work. (Ricoeur could still be right in what he spots as the polemical underside of the Annales *historians' practice, or rather as the reason for their developing that underside, that they wish to overcome history's attention to the individual. What work of theirs I know does not strike me this way, but I ask nothing for that. My argument can be taken as saying that* if *they hoped to deflect attention from the individual by deflecting or defeating the concept of the event then* this *was their error, and it would arise not because there is some extended concept of event they appeal to but because the concept of the uneventful invokes an unchanged or unextended concept of event. Polemics will then have to remain directed upon the question whether the event or the uneventful is the more significant hewer or shaper of human ends, and of whether, or when, or how, one of these is more interesting to the historical sense than the other; which I suppose implies that the question what is to be called history is not, as raised here, to be decided by what is called an event.)*

And I felt, in my American context, one more native to an impatience with royal family matters, that I had heard a similar call for a different history made in my locale a long time ago. (It may be because of this that I seemed to find striking affinities between my remarks and those prepared by the second commentator on Ricoeur's paper, Clifford Geertz.) This earlier call shared the Annales *historians' vision of dramatic political upheavals but, contrary to Ricoeur's perception of such historicizing, it claimed that the life of the ordinary man and woman would not be written, not perceived, so long as these traditional stagings of historical interest—in, let us say, high events—were not reassessed and reinvested.*

Such was the background of surmise and memory out of which I thought I had something to contribute to the issues raised in, and by, what Ricoeur was to say that night.

◊

About most of Professor Ricoeur's resourceful and instructive paper
I will have little to say directly. Reading it has intensified my guilt in
reminding me of the years I have failed to meet summer resolutions
to read more of the French historians of the *Annales* school. I console myself for my ignorance tonight with the thought that my presence here is justified by my wish first of all to participate in honoring
the name of Lionel Trilling, whose work has been so nourishing to
me, from the time I began searching for my way into the world of the
mind; and then to salute the remarkable and growing accomplishments of Paul Ricoeur, not only for the daunting extent of them but
for an inspiration in them that lends profit to professional American
philosophy every day, I mean his ability to write philosophy as
though the fiction that the Continental and the Anglo-American traditions of philosophy have not entered upon their lamentable course
of mutual shunning. His paper tonight clearly exemplifies this ability, and on the odd ground of the philosophy of history—odd because while Anglo-American analytical philosophy has worked
in the theory of history, that tradition refuses history, whether as a
mode of knowledge or as a repository of knowledge, as a source of
inspiration or of commitment in the remainder of philosophy. For
an analyst, philosophy of science is philosophy, philosophy of language is philosophy, but philosophy of history—like philosophy of
literature or philosophy of religion—is at most an application of philosophy. It is pertinent to what I will be saying to add that in recent
years my anguish over the rift between the traditions of philosophy
has been succeeded or joined by an anguish over the inability of
American philosophy to inherit the writing of Emerson and Thoreau—which means that a rift between cultures has been succeeded
or joined in my mind by a sense of rift within one culture—hence
within culture itself, as I have inherited it.

Ricoeur apparently does not quarrel with the craft of history as
practiced by historians associated with *Annales*, but only with their
self-understanding of their craft, especially with their antipathy toward something they refer to as events, their understanding of them-

selves in opposition to a traditional history characterized as, or so far as it can justly be characterized as, a history of events. Ricoeur seeks to show that there is a way to understand or to extend the concept of event so that the *Annales* historians can be seen themselves to be talking about events. His argument here, in outline, is that the writing of history cannot fully escape narrative discourse, and that since this discourse requires the concept of an event, the writing of history—if even of long time spans—cannot escape the thought of the subjects of those time spans as events.

Ricoeur cautions against taking him to be pleading for a more narrative kind of history. His idea is rather of what he calls an indirect relation of history to story. Here he follows Fernand Braudel's articulation of history into three temporal layers and then proposes that what characterizes the history of long durations as history is its relation to the history of short durations, a relation he calls "emergence." But how does Ricoeur know that the level of long durations *requires* such a provision of what he calls historical intentionality? Why does he assume that this level has no way of justifying itself as history autonomously? In his closing pages he seems to speak of his conception of the historical as related to a conception of the human being, of what it is to know a human existence. But then isn't it plausible to assume that the rival conception of history has its rival grasp of human existence? I take it that it has, and that this is something Braudel means when he speaks in his inaugural lecture to the Collège de France of narrative history as "an authentic philosophy of history,"[1] for he goes on to say: "To the narrative historians, the life of men is dominated by dramatic accidents, by the actions of those exceptional beings who occasionally emerge, and who often are the masters of their own fate and even more of ours." Braudel calls this a "first stage of history" and declares it the task of history to get beyond it—away from the "monotonous game" of intercrossing and singular destinies, toward the tackling of "the social realities in themselves and for themselves." Surely this alternative history, however briefly and polemically stated, extends its own, competing philosophy of

[1] In *On History*, essays of Braudel's translated by Sarah Matthews (Chicago, 1980), p. 11.

history, a competing conception of the human being and of the knowledge of human existence. And if so then whether the levels of long span and short span are to be seen to emerge or to derive from one another, or whether each is to be understood as autonomous, depends upon confronting those philosophies of history with one another. How you conceive of history will then determine how you conceive of an event, not the other way around. Braudel's opposition is evidently to a concept of event one of whose negative features is that it theatricalizes human existence. Is the force of Ricoeur's *tu quoque* that the *Annales* historians likewise theatricalize human existence, that this is an inevitability of history's grounding in narration? If not, what assurance have we that he is speaking of the same concept?

While I have already implied that I am not in a position to elicit and assess what may be the actual contours of the *Annales* historians' self-understanding, I can still go on to do something philosophers typically do in the absence of a command of the facts: I can ask what such a self-understanding might look like, and I can do that in the guise of asking myself what I would mean if I claimed that there is a history of the human being to which we are blinded by the traditional histories of flashing, dramatic events. I can do this, moreover, by taking the opening three criteria of an event Ricoeur articulates— that it is of something past, something done by or done to human beings, and something unrepeatable—and then instead of going on to appeal with Ricoeur to the idea of narrative as placing, hence maintaining, the concept, I shall appeal to a fourth criterion of what I understand our ordinary concept of an event to be—at any rate, our concept of something we are likely to regard as an historical (as opposed say to a meteorological) event.

My fourth criterion is that an event is something to which some fairly definite public already attaches some fairly definite importance. Obvious examples are the things high schools in my day used to call current events, the things newspapers call news (as opposed, say, to human interest stories), the things that appear on calendars of events (and that will vary specifically according as the institution the calendar serves is a church, a university, or a court). (The phrase "a blessed event" is hyperbolical not because a private moment is being called blessed but because it is being called an event.)

This criterion about attaching importance seems, I believe, to note a trivial or weak feature of the concept of an event, all but negligible. If so then if it serves to elicit the self-understanding I seek, the result will be strong, since I will not have imported a prejudicial element into the concept. The self-understanding suggested by an attempt to escape or to depose events so construed would then be an attempt to escape the dictation of what it is interesting or important to think about and write history about, a dictation by the precept and example of what a fairly definite public already attaches a fairly definite importance to; a demand to let one's own discourse determine its interest for itself.

But escaping dictation seems a negative goal, saying only what these writers will try not to do. Does the idea of escaping the event contain in itself some hint as to a positive goal, saying something about what these writers are trying to do? Immediately, the turning away from events as made by exceptional individuals proposes that history turn to an interest in a different set or class of people, call them the unexceptional. Beyond this, it suggests that history, that the human being thinking historically, is *to interest itself differently* in human existence, whatever individual or class it turns its attention to.

To say how I would express this difference of interest I must make a little detour and indicate that the refusal of the dictation of importance, the wish for one's discourse to establish its own interest, points to a philosophical site which, to my mind, locates perhaps the most fruitful point of intersection of Anglo-American with Continental philosophizing. I mean the point concerning the issue of what it is worth saying, the discovery that much of what is said, especially by philosophers, i.e., by the human being philosophizing, is empty, say bankrupt, the result of speaking not meaninglessly, as the positivists used to like to say, as if words themselves had insufficient sense, but rather speaking pointlessly, as if we had nothing in mind, or nothing at heart to say. I have described this state as a mild and intermittent form of madness, of self-stupefaction. In Heidegger this is sometimes raised as a matter of what it is worth questioning (and it is worth noting in the present context that one of the guiding terms he questions in questioning Being is that of *Ereignis*, one of whose meanings is *event*); in Wittgenstein the issue is sometimes put as a matter of finding the home language game for an expression, a way of understanding its role in everyday language. For Heidegger our stupefaction results from an insufficient capacity to leave the ordinary language of everyday or average talk; for Wittgenstein— and on this point he and J. L. Austin are at one—our stupefaction results from an insufficient capacity to cleave to the everyday, which in this context may be thought of as holding on to comprehensible reasons for questioning ourselves.

It was always being said, and I believe it is still felt, that Wittgenstein's and Austin's return to ordinary language constitutes an anti-intellectual or unscientific defense of ordinary beliefs. While this is a significantly wrong idea it is hard to say what is wrong with it. I think it takes Wittgenstein's whole philosophy, at least, to say what is wrong with it, which really comes to presenting the right alternative. I will simply assert, for present purposes, that Wittgenstein's and Austin's return to ordinary or everyday language is, before anything else, a formidable attack on skepticism, epitomized by the difficult thought that it is not quite right to say that we believe the world exists (though certainly we should not conclude that we do not believe this, that we fail to believe its existence), and wrong even to say we know it exists (while of course it is equally wrong to say we fail to know this). And if one convinces oneself of the truth of such observations, it is then at issue, and much harder, to determine *what* it is right to say here, what truly expresses our convictions in our relation to the world. The idea is less to defend our ordinary beliefs than to wean us from expressing our thoughts in ways that do not genuinely satisfy us, to stop forcing ourselves to say things that we cannot fully mean. What the ordinary language philosopher is sensing—but I mean to speak just for myself in this—is that our natural relation to the world's existence is—as I sometimes wish to express it—closer, or more intimate, than the ideas of believing and knowing are made to convey. And I am for myself convinced that the thinkers who best convey this experience, or aspiration, of closeness, convey it most directly and most practically, are not such as Austin and Wittgenstein but such as Emerson and Thoreau. This sense of, let me say, my natural relation to existence is what Thoreau means by our being *next* to the laws of nature, by our *neighboring* the world, by our being *beside* ourselves. Emerson's idea of the *near* is one of the inflections he gives to the common, the low, as in the passage from *Nature* beginning: "I ask not for the great, the remote, the romantic; what is doing in Italy or Arabia; what is Greek art, or Provençal minstrelsy; I embrace the common, I explore and sit at the feet of the familiar, the low. Give me insight into today, and you may have the antique and future worlds."

That was my detour, meant to afford me a formulation of what I called the positive interest that a history may have whose self-understanding proposes an escape from events. Now I will say that such a history is interested not in what Ricoeur calls the *eventless*, as though it seeks, as it were, what is not happening; such a history is interested rather in the *uneventful*, seeking, so to speak, what is not out of the ordinary.

The uneventful, so conceived, is an interpretation of the everyday, the common, the low, the near; you may call it an empirical interpretation, still pre-philosophical. What is uneventful at one date and place is not the same as what is uneventful at another date and place, so that the translations of one to another may be knowable only to something we will call history. One might still maintain that there is a sense of the concept of event in which the *Annales* historians write about events indirectly; what I have wished to indicate is that there is a sense of the concept of event—apparently the sense they care about, a sense I find in what I permit myself to call our concept of event—in which they definitively do not write about events. While Ricoeur does not deny that the craft of the *Annales* historians is one that produces history, while indeed his effort can be taken as one of showing why it is history, still the most he has shown is that their craft *can* be looked at as he proposes, not that it must be.

So *can* you look at human beings through the concept (perhaps extended) of a machine; that does not show that human beings are machines.

Braudel writes, in the lecture I cited a few moments ago: "There is . . . a history slower still than the history of civilizations, a history which almost stands still, a history of man in his intimate relationship to the earth which bears and feeds him; it is a dialogue which never stops repeating itself, which repeats itself in order to persist, which may and does change superficially, but which goes on, tenaciously, as though it were somehow beyond time's reach and ravages." It is not for me to say whether such a vision inspires good history, but it strikes me as expressing the thought of an ambitious philosophy. In confessing that it sounds to me like a thought of Emerson's or Thoreau's I mean to register that while the opening essay of Emerson's first volume of *Essays* is entitled "History," the position of it is an indictment of what we know as history, of what this history takes the human creature to be; and the indictment carries the implication that what *he* writes is what should be known as history: "I am ashamed to see what a shallow village tale our so-called History is. How *many* times we must say Rome, and Paris, and Constantinople! What does Rome know of rat and lizard? What are Olympiads and Consulates to these neighboring systems of being? Nay, what food or experience or succor have they for the Esquimaux seal-hunter, for the Kanàka in his canoe, for the fisherman, the stevedore, the porter?" But now we may consider that when and where Emerson was writing, under the influence of what he knew of Kant and Hegel as much as of anything else, there was little possibility of understanding history as an autonomous discourse that might investigate empirically, in its own way, those very features of the human adventure Emerson spent his life getting what he sometimes calls the meaning of; little possibility of imagining a new rapprochement between the ambitions of history and of philosophy. This is where we came in.

♦

EXISTENTIALISM AND
ANALYTICAL PHILOSOPHY

♦

In collecting the essays that make up Must We Mean What We Say?,
*I chose, for a number of reasons, to leave out the present piece of work.
But it hits on, if sometimes prematurely, expressions for some things
that matter to me that I have not been able to improve; and sometimes, for those who share its preoccupations, it is illuminating in its
very primitiveness, its recurrent inabilities to formulate intuitions
that seem right over its shoulder; and in any case it continues to be
cited, I believe with increasing frequency. Recently it has been given
a role in a valuable set of conjunctions and reflections (with and on
Michael Fried and with Paul de Man and Jacques Derrida) by Stephen Melville in his "Notes on the Reemergence of Allegory, the For-
getting of Modernism, the Necessity of Rhetoric, and the Conditions
of Publicity in Art and Criticism," which appeared in* October, no.
19, Winter 1981. *So, awkwardness and all, and imperfectly remembering the circumstances that could have induced me to undertake
the assignment of comparison, I am glad for the chance to make this
piece more readily available. It was published in the Summer 1964
issue of* Dædalus.

*One reason for my earlier reluctance to reprint was my having
named in it a certain duplicitousness of language—certain of its
exchanges between the literal and the figural, or between the direct
and the indirect, or between the grammatical or logical and the rhetorical or semantic—as a function or expression of irony. While I*

went on to claim that irony is not Wittgenstein's stance toward these exchanges, I did not know how to express my contrary sense that irony is as much his enemy as his aspiration. I knew that the laughter he used in philosophical diagnosis is more good-humored than it is in the spirit of irony; perhaps more sociable, and certainly more self-catching. But I was not yet ready to see this comedy in relation to the tragedy that philosophy observes or enacts, call it the tragedy of skepticism. Wittgenstein is speaking of this, as I have come to see it, in noting that in philosophy (I mean, in the risk in any taking of thought) our words get away from our real need, from our (everyday) lives. You may also speak of this, I find, as the world's receding from our words, as the withdrawal of the world (of religion, of politics, of art, of philosophy). So that now, when sometimes it seems that irony has become yet more fashionable as an attitude to strike on the issue of language's duplicity, it is something that I feel my work well enough past, or better able to shake off.

The academic exercise of the several pages on logical analysis and logical positivism are worth retaining not only for the use of those who have so far avoided those two philosophy courses they know they should have brought themselves to take, but also as an example for those more sophisticated now, who know just about everything, to remind them of the rote and repetitiveness that is the price of one's having, of course for good and sufficient reasons, to control material to which one can make no contribution in return; of presenting oneself as a victim to learning. So much of education seems fated (while the necessity gets lost in the shadows of our institutions) to the turning of bread into stones. Of course if it is worth it to you to study philosophy it should be worth it to you to study, for example, Russell's Theory of Descriptions, hence possibly to postpone it. But nothing is worth hearing such a theory repeated, as if a password, at the beginning of a good half of the courses taught one under the rubric of philosophy, say two or three courses a year, for four years (I transferred in the middle of graduate studies and virtually began again), with no hope of making the thing one's own to divine with. No real science would accept so unprogressive a hold on its paradigms, I mean would treat its paradigms as passwords, their fruitfulness exhausted in their cor-

rect saying. Science hasn't that kind of guilty conscience. One has not learned the love of philosophy until one has despaired of, even in a sense learned to treasure, its awful stubbornness. At such a time one can sense the implacable sternness just under the elation of a thinker like Austin, not unlike the elation of an escapee.

So I am reminded that the inner history of the development of analytical philosophy is only now being composed, as if only now is analytical philosophy, in its late development, disposed to oppose its internal opposition to history, no doubt a version of philosophy's internal opposition to time, you may say logic's opposition to rhetoric. I mention examples of the work of three young analytical philosophers from which I am glad to be learning, to whatever degree my resources will permit, who have started, as I have in this matter, from the lectures and the conversation of Burton Dreben of the Harvard Department of Philosophy: Warren Goldfarb's "Logic in the Twenties: The Nature of the Quantifier" (Journal of Symbolic Logic, Vol. 44, 1979); *Peter Hylton's "The Nature of the Proposition and the Revolt against Idealism" (to appear in R. Rorty, J. Schneewind, and Q. Skinner, eds.,* Philosophy in History, *Cambridge University Press); and Thomas Rickett's "Objectivity and Objecthood: Frege's Metaphysics of Judgment" (forthcoming in* Synthèse*). In addition, Hylton's doctoral dissertation, or its successor, is slated for publication by Oxford University Press, under the title* Russell and the Origins of Analytic Philosophy. *For another inner judgment, none better earned, this time that the program of analytical philosophy in its logical or constructivist form has come to an unsuccessful conclusion, I recommend the recent writing of Hilary Putnam.*

And I mention in this connection Richard Rorty's frequently cited Philosophy and the Mirror of Nature *with its claim to be recording, among other things, the failure of much of what I suppose is to be thought of as professional or academic philosophy, especially its analytical version(s). Compared to the work of the philosophers I was just citing, Rorty's strictures are external to the discourse they would undo—or rather, if this is so, Rorty would, I think, regard it as a proud feature of his achievement. In his recent collection of essays,* Consequences of Pragmatism, *Rorty includes a review-essay of my* The

Claim of Reason *in which, after some gratifying praise of the second two parts of that book, he spends almost all of his space (understandably) on his disagreements with the first two parts. His counter-diagnosis of skepticism and counter-proposals concerning the problem of other minds demand and deserve full and specific discussion. Here I want to pick up just Rorty's more general charge, which I express for the moment in terms of questions like the following: If the portion of professional philosophy I am concerned with is as bankrupt as I seem to find that it is, then shouldn't I think of giving up my quarrel with it? Why spend hundreds of pages to understand, often in its own tortured terms, why philosophy is bankrupt? Why not just give it up for lost and get on with whatever good you have in mind?—It has occurred to me. But then it never fails to reoccur to me that to find philosophy's loss of itself is my good; at any rate, I see none apart from that.*

Rorty is, I think, assuming that (what I am calling) the professionalization of philosophy—at least in its English-speaking reaches—is external, simply foreign, to what philosophy is, or to what philosophy's successor might be; as if what is professionalized—say as in a university (analytical) philosophy curriculum—is just something else. It strikes me otherwise. That there is so much as an issue here I take to show that philosophy is neither science nor poetry—matters people keep trying to turn philosophy into, matters philosophy more or less resembles, or competes with. But there is no analogous issue of academic professionalization in science or in poetry. No one wonders, or not many do, whether what is taught in the physics and mathematics departments of major universities really is, in general, how physics or mathematics is done: if there is an issue in a given place, someone had better call in experts to take things in hand. If the experts divide, you have an intellectual crisis on your hands; new institutions will form. And no one wonders, or not many do, whether what is taught in the literature departments of major universities is really, in general, how poetry is made: that just is not, it seems plain, the mission of a literature department, what it professionalizes is something else, say scholarship, or say criticism. If some such depart-

ment happens to think that its own valuable mission is enhanced by, or somehow owes, support to contemporary practice, it may see fit to hire a practitioner to teach it in his or her own way. (This outsider may, by chance, also be an insider, also an academic.) If there is doubt about whether it is poetry that a given practitioner exemplifies, a reasonable way to handle the problem is to hire another practitioner of a different stripe. (The foreword to Must We Mean What We Say?, "An Audience for Philosophy," further defines such matters and acknowledges them as internal to my practice, or to its aspirations.)

From saying, or implying, that it is internal to philosophy that it can be professionalized, and that its professionalization, in one of its versions, looks like this (say a large American department of philosophy), it does not follow that philosophy exists only as professionalized (what indeed could that mean?). What I have said here is only that this is an issue. And it is an ill-defined one. To what extent is the issue one of assessing the vicissitudes of an aspiration that cannot have, or has lost, institutionalization—like religion outside churches? or perhaps politics outside governments? or maybe like love outside marriage, or outside society? And what if the fundamental fact of philosophy lies in its recognition of a certain social role, as in Plato's image of the philosopher as gadfly, or Locke's of the philosopher as under laborer in the commonwealth of learning; a role for which, perhaps, a given society has no particular professional preparation. Perhaps "gadfly" is the name in philosophy of what in it forever resists professionalization. (Who but a gadfly would undertake to show the fly the way out of the fly bottle?) And perhaps "under laboring" is now the name of whatever it is that philosophy, to proceed in its clearings, forever has to undermine.

When the professionalization of philosophy has most seemed to me a desert of thought (they make a desert and call it a clearing), the thought appears to me that the desert is—to some as yet, by me, unassessable degree—mine, or rather philosophy's, and I find it to have a value the world would be a greater desert if it lost. So a quarrel with professional philosophy remains mine to conduct, and hence my discourse is in part controlled, pent, by a wish to stay within reach of the *discourse of that profession. Could I perhaps cease claiming philosophy for my writing in favor of claiming that it is (merely) continuous with philosophy? That might be all right, but how much of a shift that would be would depend on how you understand such continuity to be managed (it may present itself, for example, as discontinuity), hence on what you take philosophy to require itself to manage; perhaps it has to manage its continuity with itself.*

Accordingly, I should emphasize that the impatience I was expressing in using the teaching of Russell's theory as an example of professional instruction was not a response to this theory's asking for, and exemplifying, a technical *discourse. I do not assume that we have a good sense of what this idea of the technical comes to, nor do I assume that the technical is the only way, or the chief way, or a sure way, in which philosophy may be lost. Say that my impatience was directed to the manner of my inhabitation of that discourse, to my being its prisoner. I do not assume that the technical is the only, or the main, discourse within which one can imprison oneself, or perhaps comfort oneself.*

Such possibilities are under observation in Walden *when Thoreau is accounting for his departure back to civilization after his better than two years in the woods, and he remarks that after just a week at the pond he could note the paths, or ruts, that his tracks, repeated treks, were cutting into the new territory. And this confinement, don't forget, came from his pleasures, not his fears (if you get the distinction). Let us not underestimate such pleasures or fears. For what is an alternative to subjecting oneself to a standing discourse, and letting it stand? Perhaps you forever question the ground your discourse occupies and forever try the routes it proposes—call this philosophical dialogue, Emerson calls it our antagonism to fate. (I go further into this in "Genteel Responses to Kant?," in* Raritan, *Fall 1983). Or perhaps you give up the effort to buy into intellectual currency and settle into the use of a kind of scrip, good for all the essentials the country store has to offer, but worth next to nothing on the international market. It is a standing temptation for American literary theorists. I think at the moment, beyond the figures of Emerson and*

Thoreau themselves, of the theoretical writings of Kenneth Burke and of Paul Goodman, whose admirers know to be rich out of all proportion to their current circulation.

So when I spoke of primitiveness at the start of these introductory words, I was thinking not alone of what was perhaps unnecessarily rudimentary in my education, but of what was more rigorously closed off by it. I had, for example, got through hardly more than a small handful of pages of Being and Time, *fighting for every inch of lost ground, as I wrote the piece of work I am introducing here. The piece can be said to be about, or to enact, I imagine to its credit, the difficulty, in the era in which it was written, of finding one's philosophical hands and feet, let alone voice—a place to stop and work. This sometimes presents itself as having been cheated by one's education, not exactly as having been lied to, but sometimes as having not fully been taken into the confidence of one's teachers. How otherwise, except in blessed science, would we come to feel that we have to begin all over again? Not everyone has the feeling, or has use for it, and I assume that it did not become a characteristic feeling about one's education until, on the American calendar, the time of Emerson and Thoreau, whose warnings to scholars against reading too much in books, which seems a crazy warning to a people with hardly a literature to its name (though that was doubtless part of the point of the warning), is as much as to say: no one knows any longer what it is we must know in order to say what we have it at heart to say. Out of such a sense it is understandable that one's education, or edification, should become the subject of major Romantic works, say, beyond* Walden, *of* The Prelude *and of the* Biographia Literaria—*works in which the quest for one's own question, and for what it takes to pose it, are entered on together. One is not a preparation for the other, the madness and the method are the same. (There is no metaphilosophy.) I gather this is not true of science, even definitively not true. So if a distinction between, say, discovery and justification defines what science is, and you think philosophy is essentially science, then what I was just saying in connection with philosophy should have no interest for you. Perhaps it is because I am thinking these days of the out-*

cropping of Romantic texts and preoccupations in the last part of The Claim of Reason *(some lines of Blake, the Boy of Winander, Coleridge's "Ode on Dejection," Thoreau on neighboring, or nextness), and certainly because, as I have had occasion to note before, I understand the* Philosophical Investigations *as, whatever else, a work of instruction, that I am not much moved to assert philosophy's distance from the aspirations and scruples of the Romantics, for example from their willingness to see the entanglements of poetry with philosophy.*

So the difficulty in finding one's own work (supposing for the moment that one has been able to find work) is not quite expressed in the familiar picture of our critical powers as growing out of proportion to our creative acumen. There are even people now, with reason, who undertake to deny this distinction between the critical and the creative. The further twist in the difficulty is better pictured not as the pressure of a familiar criticism hostile to one's creativity, but as the pressure of another creativity, a foreign creativity, on a par with, and apparently hostile to, one's own. Or you may say that one knows the contempt each side of the philosophical mind harbors of the other earlier than one knows the accomplishments of both or the possibility of managing both modes. Then to the extent that one becomes and remains in some memorable way struck by both, a standing possibility is that one will be made unready for learning either. It is my sense that in the years this conflict was most virulent philosophy failed to keep its share of the talented young attracted to its study. Which means to me that the mutual shunning of the English and the German traditions of philosophy (one way of putting the issue) represents a genuine rift in the spirit, or intelligence, of philosophy, hence a genuine expression of the present of philosophy—some late expression of the relation Emerson wished to see in taking England as the noon and Germany as the night of the daily cycle of philosophy.

The outcome of this conflict is unsettled. More talent, maybe deeper, is responsive to it now than in the era of this reprinted piece, but the issues are correspondingly harder to see, harder to say. Our

*danger is, as elsewhere, of a state of primitiveness sophisticated, like
the pair of officers on duty at the console of a Minuteman silo wearing
pistols, not against intruders, but in view of one another. Dreaming
these dangers seems to me worthy of a philosophical discourse.*

*One mode of this dreaming in any field is simply to imagine where
everyone is residing at this moment, what it is they are ready for, and
getting ready for. And the nearest danger is from those who feel themselves ready for anything.*

◊

Hopeless tasks are not always thankless. I have tried to make the task
of comparing analytical philosophy and existentialism in a few thou-
sand words less thankless by organizing my remarks in the following
way. In a brief opening section, I indicate a few general comparisons
of these philosophies in order to discover *why* a general comparison
between them is hopeless. In Section II, I sketch a history of the
main movements within analytical philosophy, something I do not
attempt for existentialism. The excuse for this disparity of treatment is that a history of existentialism would entail a history of European literature since Goethe and Hegel, whereas the stages or
strands of modern analytical philosophy are at once fairly definite
and widely unknown. (This difference of density in their histories is
itself a significant difference between them as philosophies.) If my
effort puts an end to anyone's referring to what is called "ordinary
language philosophy" as positivism, and makes him or her recognize
that he or she should know more about positivism before dismiss-
ing—or adopting—its program, it will have been worth its pains.
This historical sketch also prepares for the specific comparison, in
Section III, of the later philosophy of Wittgenstein with the writing
in Kierkegaard's *Concluding Unscientific Postscript*. It may appear
that in choosing these particular writings as representative of analytical philosophy and existentialism I have made matters of comparison too easy for myself, may even have changed the subject. I should
say, therefore, that I certainly hope the comparison does seem easy,

and that while Wittgenstein and Kierkegaard may be untypical representatives of the philosophies for which I am making them stand, they are hardly peripheral to them. Any general comparison which could not accommodate these figures would also, if differently, risk irrelevance.

I

The most hopeless aspect of any undertaking to cover our subject lies not merely in its vastness, or in the fact that neither philosophy is simple or single; it lies more particularly in the fact that both are live and therefore open to change through self-discovery, and that their relation to one another may alter with fresh insight and result. At the moment, analytical philosophy is the dominant mode of academic philosophizing in America and England, while existentialism (together with phenomenology) dominates the philosophizing of Western Europe; and there seems to be no trade across the English Channel. Mutual incomprehension and distrust between them are among the facts of contemporary philosophical life.

The task of comparing these philosophies is more specifically a comic one. It is, in the first place, something of a logical, or metaphysical, jest to suggest simultaneously that these intellectual positions are incomprehensible to one another, that one is inevitably reared to speak from within only one or the other of them, and yet that one is going to comprehend both. Second, and more important, to summarize either of them counters the spirit of the philosophies themselves. For any of the philosophers who could be called analytical, popular discussion would be irrelevant; for the existentialist, it is betrayal. For the analyst, philosophy has become a profession, its problems technical; a nonprofessional audience is of no more relevance to him than it is to the scientist. The existentialist has not relinquished philosophy's traditional audience—namely, everybody, regardless of any technical competence, philosophical or other; but his entire animus is against the idea that what philosophy has to say can be *told*, not, as for the analyst, because philosophy has no content of its own, but because the very content of his philosophy is that significant content cannot cognitively or discursively be articulated, but must be communicated, if at all, in some other way.

This characterization may seem, and should seem, less faithful to the work of Heidegger than it is to Kierkegaard's, to which this paper is restricted. Before concluding, however, that it is not at all true of Heidegger, one would have to consider the following points: (1) While Heidegger is the most important of contemporary existentialists, he is not the purest; so the characterization may still be true of him to the extent that he is (or to the extent that there is something worth noticing as) typically "existentialist." (2) At the beginning of *Being and Time*, Heidegger expresses his awareness of the difficulties of his writing, and claims that its roughness and unfamiliarity have been necessitated by the radical novelty (or perhaps ancientness) of his point of view. So a modification of our characterization would remain fully faithful to his writing: there is no existing way of writing (writing philosophy) in which what he says can be told. (3) It is true that he insists on the possibility of existential *knowledge* in a way Kierkegaard would deny. He is not, that is, willing to leave science and knowledge as the (or one) fixed enemy of authentic human existence; nor, on the other hand, would he regard some given alternative to knowledge (for example, feeling or the irrational) as a fixed route to such existence. But, with respect to the former, this position requires him to discover a new mode of philosophical knowledge, which means that it is not obvious that he asserts exactly what Kierkegaard denies; and, with respect to the latter, it would be equally wrong to say of Nietzsche or Kierkegaard—as I take to be popularly supposed—that feeling or irrationality are their hoped-for alternatives to our intellectualized existences.

I have said that these philosophies were not merely mutually incomprehensible but mutually distrustful. Perhaps neither specifically blames the other for the catastrophes and dislocations of modern life, but each sees the other as symptomatic of the mentality which sustains catastrophe and blocks the only source of help. The one wishes to recover Reason from superstition; the other wishes to recover the self from Reason. Yet both are modern philosophies;

both are, by intention and in feeling, revolutionary departures from traditional philosophy. That is, perhaps, a characteristic of philosophy generally: every departure believes itself to be escaping from an empty, hateful past, and to be setting the mind at last on the right road. Yet it is striking that the terms "analytical" and "existential" were initially coined to purify philosophy of the identical fool's gold in its tradition—the tendency to issue in speculative systems. The discovery of analytical philosophy is that such systems make statements which are meaningless or useless; the discovery of existentialism is that such systems make life meaningless.

If history and thought do not march to Hegelian theses and antitheses, it is still true that what a philosopher finds wrong with philosophy is an intimate measure of what he or she thinks right, and important to say. The terms or categories in which a philosophy criticizes its competitors, and its culture, are an essential part of its positive achievement. But we should add immediately that what cannot be caught in those particular terms of criticism cannot be appreciated in that particular philosophy. The characteristic and specific differences of such terms of criticism are a principal theme of this essay, the principal way in which the various philosophical positions are distinguished. While this emphasis will not be expected to correct the mad divergence between analytical philosophy and existentialism, it may suggest a way of tracing it more accurately—and even of seeing why its correction would be desirable. Such an exercise will, in any case, be necessary if we are to learn the philosophical-cultural history which has fed the divergence, and it is this knowledge, unattempted, so far as I am aware, that would guide any serious attempt to transcend it.

II

However familiar the announcement, or sense, of revolution in thought, the fact that in hardly more than half a century, and within the line of analytical philosophy alone, we have had to absorb at least three such revolutions constitutes something of a record. The first grows out of the development of the new logic, mathematical logic, in the nineteenth century, associated most importantly with the name of Gottlob Frege. For its application to philosophy the most famous spokesmen were the young Bertrand Russell and his student Ludwig Wittgenstein. The commanding and continuously fruitful insight of their view was expressed by the dictum that the real form of a proposition is its logical form, or contrariwise, that the obvious linguistic form of a proposition masks or distorts its real form, and that this masking or distortion, unrecognized, has produced many of the deepest problems of philosophy since Plato. For example, philosophers have recurrently puzzled themselves over the possibility of asserting that something does not exist; for to assert the nonexistence of any given thing you have to name it, and if you can name it then mustn't it exist? If it doesn't exist, then the name can mean nothing at all, because the only thing a name can mean is the thing it refers to.

Even if you do not feel the paradox in saying that a name may be the name of nothing, and are convinced, indeed, that it is false, you may have trouble explaining why it is false, and why it should have seemed obviously and necessarily true to so many philosophers, and what a name is if it need not refer to anything. What Russell, following Frege, demonstrated can be put in something like the following way: In such a statement as "The deepest bell in the campanile is flat" it would seem that the isolated descriptive phrase, "The deepest bell in the campanile," in its ordinary grammatical dress, meant something, namely, that particular bell; and that if it did not mean that bell, it meant nothing. But such an idea would have the consequence that one could not know whether that phrase meant anything until he had discovered whether the thing it named or denoted did, in fact, exist. And that is intolerable. The phrase obviously does mean something, not only before we know whether what it names exists, but whether what it names exists or not. Indeed, we could not discover whether what it purports to name does or does not exist unless we knew, before determining that fact, what the name means, and so knew what to look for as its bearer. The solution of this puzzle took the form of saying that although the descriptive phrase means nothing in isolation, it does mean something in the context of the whole sentence. Yet if it means (refers to) nothing in isolation, then how does it suddenly start referring to something in the context of the whole sentence? The answer is: It doesn't refer to, name, or denote anything at all. When the whole sentence is put into logical form, it turns into a compound form which may be read as follows: Something is the deepest bell in the campanile; everything satisfying that description is flat; if anything satisfies that description it is identical with the first thing—or: nothing else is the deepest bell. In this splayed form, what emerges is that the brunt of reference falls wholly upon logical terms such as "everything" and "something" in conjunction with the variable pronoun "it," the whole complex being bound together by the cross reference of pronouns and the logical relations of conjunction and implication ("if-then") and identity. Such terms and relations seem to be fundamental to all language, and their meaning obviously does not depend on there being any particular thing in the world.[1]

This procedure is known as Russell's Theory of Descriptions, and from its promulgation in the first decades of this century, it became the accepted example of what a philosophical analysis should be. My account cannot convey the sense of the power this theory was felt to have, promising as it did a mode of solving the outstanding philosophical problems about naming, meaning, identity, existence, etc., not to mention problems in the understanding of mathematics. I hope, however, that it may serve these purposes: first, to convey a sense of one way in which the term "analysis" has been used by analytical philosophers, as referring to the procedure of translating statements from ordinary language into their corresponding form in logic; second, to suggest one way in which problems of philosophy came to seem problems of language (and of logic); and third, to elicit one particular criticism of past philosophy, that its problems have come from misunderstanding the logic of our language.

This wedding of logic and philosophy was given one definitive sanctification and perhaps its most famous, in Wittgenstein's first

---

[1]In this account I have followed W. V. O. Quine's presentation in "On What There Is." This paper is reprinted in his *From a Logical Point of View* (Cambridge, Mass., 1953), which includes the relevant bibliography, in particular, references to the classical papers of Frege and Russell.

book, the *Tractatus Logico-Philosophicus*, written just before and during the First World War, and published in 1922. Within a few years, it became a major inspiration of a group of philosophers and scientists in Vienna who had been meeting to discuss various philosophical problems they shared. This group called themselves the Vienna Circle, and the point of view they espoused became known as "Logical Positivism." In 1929 this group declared itself in a public manifesto setting forth what they called a "scientific conception of the world," and reviewing problems in the philosophy of mathematics and science which they were concerned to solve.

Of the complex of motives and hopes this view contained, two or three are immediately relevant to our purpose. The new logic was to serve not so much to analyze and solve traditional philosophical problems and to unmask the logical disorder of the natural languages as to construct formal systems in which the structure of science would be logically displayed, to show the way in which concepts feed from a base of empirical observation. According to this view, science, physical science in particular, contains or will contain everything we can know about the world, and it is work enough for an ambitious philosophy to show the structure and sources of that knowledge. Indeed, such purpose is its only intellectually defensible ambition (apart from expanding the subject of pure logic itself), for, with notable exceptions, the traditional problems of philosophy, it can be seen, are not extremely difficult and understandably obscure, but meaningless. One needs only to subject these problems to the test of the famous Verifiability Theory of Meaning, to ask, of any statement or question which is not purely logical, what observations of the world would show it true or false; if you find that no observation could confirm its truth or falsity, then the statement or question is demonstrably without meaning. On the basis of this test most metaphysical, ethical, aesthetic, and religious questions turn out to be meaningless. They have no answers because they are not significant questions; they are pseudo questions. Such radical dismissal of subjects is no doubt somewhat indiscriminate, nor did it help much that the view went on to describe such statements as "merely" without cognitive or scientific meaning, while acknowledging that they may have some kind of emotive or poetic meaning, because that disposition still seemed to say nonscientific statements lacked something, had something wrong or suspicious about them. No doubt something *is* wrong or suspicious about many of them, and if the dismissal of these subjects as not philosophically respectable was indiscriminate, that failure of discrimination was fully matched in the attacks launched against positivism by those who felt attacked in it, the violence of which seems fair evidence that, for all the difficulty the positivists continued to have in formulating their criterion of meaning to the satisfaction of all concerned, it had caught a guilty conscience napping.[2]

The latest phase of analytical philosophy is the most difficult for me to characterize in these brutally few strokes. It is most familiarly known, I believe, as ordinary language philosophy; but when confronted with that phrase I feel as I suppose any philosopher or writer does when he sees his commitments collapsed into a rubric. I feel like denying it and leaving the room. But what is unfair for one is unfair for another, so let it stand.

The relevant components are these: In the background there is Russell's contemporary and colleague at Cambridge University, G. E. Moore. Neither a logician nor a scientist, Moore had only good sense to go on in his studies, and he found himself asking, faced with a traditional metaphysical thesis, "What on earth can anyone mean by saying *that*?" On earth is precisely where he tried to find the answer, bringing the question all the way down to the ground. If a philosopher were to say, "There are no material things," Moore would consider it enough to show that he *knew* this to be false by saying, "Here's one human hand and here's another; so there are at least two material things"; or if the philosopher said, "Time is unreal," Moore would be ready with, "If you mean that no event ever follows or precedes another event, you are certainly wrong; for *after*

[2]A. J. Ayer's *Language, Truth and Logic* remains the best-known, and the best, popularization of the positivist position. He has edited a convenient and useful selection of the original positivist writings (*Positivism*, New York, 1959), which weakens any excuse for confining one's knowledge of the view to his early book.

lunch I went for a walk, and after that I took a bath, and after that I had tea."

Such responses will hardly explain why Moore was, for many years, so influential a figure in English philosophy.[3] It does, however, underline one significant fact: philosophical theses or conclusions often contradict our common beliefs about the world, denying, for example, that we can see physical objects or that we know that other persons have the same feelings and thoughts we do, or that we can know any statement about the world to be certainly true; or they may suggest as possible something we fully believe to be false, for example, that we may now be dreaming or hallucinating our present experiences. Philosophers have always recognized a tension between philosophy and common sense, and some have considered the testing and the overthrow, if necessary, of common belief to be one of their virtues. What Moore's work began to suggest is that in the conflict with common belief, philosophy is wrong; that instead of philosophy's results overthrowing common belief, an appeal to those beliefs and the language in which they are expressed (ordinary language, the language in which philosophy itself is mostly expressed) shows that the philosopher cannot literally or fully have meant what he said. What on earth can he mean?

After the Second World War, the large force of philosophers who had been on leave from Oxford University regrouped, and within a few years were undertaking major campaigns within the English-speaking philosophical world. Under the new direction of Gilbert Ryle and J. L. Austin, many of them vowed, so to speak, that they would never again be led down the philosophical path. As with most vows, it faded and became clouded over, but while it lasted in its pure form it created its own kind of exhilaration. Instead of rehearsing yet

---

[3]The exemplifications I gave of Moore's address to philosophy are taken, or adapted, from Norman Malcolm's "Moore and Ordinary Language." This paper is reprinted in a small collection of essays entitled *Ordinary Language* (Englewood Cliffs, N.J., 1964), which contains a serviceable bibliography of its topic. No explanation of Moore's influence would be complete which failed to describe the force and originality of his personality. The most extended account I know of is given in J. M. Keynes's *Two Memoirs* (London, 1949).

again what the hero of Beckett's *Endgame* calls "the old questions, the old answers," these philosophers took ordinary questions, with new examples, sensible examples, and gave ordinary, sensible answers to them. The surprising result was that their results were surprising. In their work, the term "ordinary" in "ordinary language philosophy" meant simply that the words and problems and examples discussed would not be chosen from the philosophical repertory. If we have learned anything in the past couple of millennia, they were in effect saying, it is that this repertory is not adequate to its reputation. If we are to ask the old questions, like "What is knowledge?", then let us not begin by asking, in the old way, how we know, for example, that the external world exists, or that another world exists, or that there is a table or a sheet of paper in front of me. No person in his right mind, or at least in his ordinary frame of mind, asks such questions. And if to philosophize means merely to go out of one's mind, then let us fully admit that fact, and either make serious efforts to give the subject up, or radically to transform it, or else not be surprised that philosophy is treated with distant suspicion.

In avoiding philosophical theory—which, like any fault, is easier to see in others—Oxford philosophy came most immediately into conflict with its competitors within the analytical temper of philosophy, namely with Russell's theory of descriptions and of logical translation, and with positivism's theory of nonlogical, nonscientific discourse. For example, the Oxford group accepted positivism's sense that scientific or descriptive statements are different from ethical and aesthetic and religious utterances. (I say "positivism's sense"; but the mere fact *that* there is a difference had been noticed as early as Plato's *Euthyphro*, and it became a dominant theme of moral philosophy from the time of Hume's *Treatise* and Kant's *Critique of Practical Reason*.) But the positivist went on, as though *explaining* the difference, to say that scientific statements have cognitive meaning and that nonscientific statements do not. The Oxford philosophers rejected these critical or theoretical terms, as they rejected all the theoretical terms they recognized as such, and asked: what meaning, or use, *do* ethical statements, for example, have? Why compare them—and why unfavorably?—with scientific statements? Perhaps, seen in their own light, they lack nothing, but, as it were, have a logic of their own.

The feature of ordinary language philosophy which seems to me of the greatest significance is the *pervasiveness* of its conflict with accepted philosophical opinion; and here I mean not just the completeness of its distrust, something it shares with positivism, but the possibility it provides of detailed and intimate assessment of philosophical assertion. Modern philosophy has often been said to begin in doubt and skepticism, but few philosophers have been able to press their doubts very far, particularly not about their own assumptions, however radical their conclusions may have been. (Nietzsche is the most obvious exception in Continental philosophy.) The philosophy of ordinary language seems to me designed to nudge assumptions into the light of day, not because it demonstrably makes no assumptions of its own, but because there is no point at which it must, or even may, stop philosophizing. This perhaps explains why philosophizing of this sort issues in such various criticisms of other philosophy, and why such criticisms as it has so far offered can seem dishearteningly easy and trivial. The moral I draw, however, is not that the philosophy is easy and trivial, but that its criticisms are themselves to be subjected to the same methods which have produced them.

One example must suffice for a taste of one sort of procedure typified, and apotheosized, in Austin's work, generally regarded as the purest example of Oxford analysis. He notes that in ordinary English we ask questions of the form "Why do you believe so-and-so?" and "How do you know so-and-so?" but almost never, it seems, questions of the form "Why do you know so-and-so?" and "How do you believe so-and-so?"[4] From such simple facts as these, advancing through dozens of facts of equally humble extraction, what appears to emerge is that perhaps belief and knowledge are not related in the way philosophers have commonly supposed. The most famous historical image of this relation is that of Plato's "divided line" in the

[4]These questions occur in Austin's "Other Minds," reprinted in his *Philosophical Papers* (Oxford, 1961) and in *Logic and Language* (Oxford, 1953, 2nd series), a collection of papers edited by A. Flew.

Republic: we begin in complacency and ignorance and move up gradually to more firmly founded beliefs; then, under further pressure to examine our beliefs, move further in the same direction until we arrive at real knowledge. But Austin's little contrast, supported by further strands and knots of little contrasts and comparisons, suggests that belief and knowledge are not to be thought of in this way. They lead him to emphasize these facts: I cannot be more certain than I am of some beliefs, so that when I say I know, what I am expressing is not some further unattainable range of belief—belief secured absolutely, as it were, against all future contingency—but a different stance I take toward that certainty. In saying I know, I commit myself differently. I assume authority in new ways, authorize you explicitly to take my word, and stake my reputation or my mind more starkly. And if I refuse ever to take such steps, I am not being *cautious*, but irresponsible or obsessional.

What are we to say, then, of the philosophical image of the relation of belief and knowledge? That it is out of its mind? That philosophers have played tricks on us, and perhaps been in collusion to deceive us? That they have misused the ordinary words of their language (for theirs is no different from ours)? That they have changed the meanings of their words, or used them perfunctorily, inattentively, more or less randomly and without seriousness? These are all terms of criticism used, or implied, by such a philosopher as Austin. The trouble is that they are either unbelievable descriptions of traditional philosophizing, or else they undermine the assumptions of Austin's own philosophizing. Take the suggestion that philosophers have not meant what they say quite seriously. They have, however, been speaking from within their own language and it is not obvious that they have (except when they *obviously* have) meant their words in any unordinary technical sense. How *can* they not have been serious, or spoken randomly? And if they can and have, then any of us may and do speak in these ways at any time. But in that case, such discoveries as Austin has seemed to make would either be impossible or utterly inconsequential, which in turn suggests that just to the extent Austin's discoveries are significant, traditional philosophy becomes more significant, or significant and problematical in a new way. We really do mean what we say, even though we may not always appreciate its implications, and may fail of meaning in particular ways. And the same is true for philosophers. Yet we are in conflict with them—or, if we are philosophers, then we are in conflict with ourselves as normal men and women. The situation might perhaps be explained if one could show that there is something about the very act of philosophizing which produces unseriousness or randomness or unnoticed and self-defeating drift in our words. But nothing in Austin's work, or in Oxford philosophy generally, shows that anything of the kind is in fact the case.

This conflict between philosophy and everyday language is also at the heart of the later philosophizing of Wittgenstein, where he does indeed begin to take apart the act of philosophizing itself. With his first book, the *Tractatus*, he claimed to have provided definitive solutions to the problems of philosophy; accordingly, he withdrew from the subject to become, among other things, a school teacher in his native Austria. Some ten years later, in the early thirties, he came to feel that these solutions were no longer satisfactory, and he returned to philosophy, and to England, to begin the work of writing and private lecturing which was soon rumored to be the major new influence in English philosophy, but which was made publicly available only with the appearance of his *Philosophical Investigations* in 1953, some two years after his death.

In that book he says, "What we do is to bring words back to their everyday uses." Presumably, then, he felt that in philosophy words were unhinged from their contexts; it now became a problem for him *how* this could happen and why it happened, what there is about philosophy that makes it happen and how language can allow it to happen. None of the criticisms of the tradition produced by Moore or the Oxford philosophers or the positivists seemed to him to be right, to do justice to the pain, the pervasiveness, even the mystery of that conflict. He could not, for example, be content to say that in this conflict philosophy had been playing tricks or spoken with lack of seriousness, if for no other reason than because he had had the experience of producing his first book, and he knew that such criticisms were not true of it. If he was to philosophize again, then the experience of that first book must be as continuous a matter of investigation for him as the new insights he had come to. Here we see dramatized a major difference between the superficially, and sometimes deeply, similar thoughts of Austin and Wittgenstein. Austin is helped to dismiss philosophical results which conflict with his own because the philosophers he takes to task mostly appear not to claim to be original; it may be true of them, at least at the moment he catches them, that they are inattentive in some obvious way, or lack philosophical seriousness. On the other hand, the thinkers Wittgenstein confronts in his *Investigations* are Plato, St. Augustine, Frege, William James, and the early Russell, thinkers whom, whatever their faults, it will be somewhat harder to convict of lacking philosophical seriousness. Not that either Austin or Wittgenstein spends much of his time confronting other philosophers directly. Austin always concentrates on proceeding with his accumulation of surprises, and on showing us the obvious, but unnoticed, ways, and connections of ways, in our uses of words. Moreover, he shares with Sir Francis Bacon the sense that past philosophy is often a matter of empty, childish prattling, and that to dote on the greatness of the past merely stands in the way of present productive work. Wittgenstein's writing, on the other hand, is writing in continuous confrontation of philosophy, not of other *philosophers* (the names I cited appear in his book only once or twice each), but of that dimension of the mind which insists on philosophizing no matter how often the arguments of philosophy have been refuted. Part I of the *Investigations* (which is some four-fifths of the book, and just over 170 pages) consists of 690 numbered sections, most of which are miniature dialogues between himself—or that part of himself which maintains a firm grip on the world all men share—and nameless interlocutors who manifest over and over, from every direction and in all moods, those temptations or dissatisfactions or compulsions which drive ordinary men away from the everyday world and out to philosophy. The force of this mode of composition depends upon whether the interlocutors voice questions and comments which come from conviction, which are made with passion and attention, and which, as one reads, seem always something one wants oneself to say, or feels the power of. If they do, then their voices cannot, in any *obvious* way, be criticized or dismissed. If these voices were to be described in one word, the one that for me best captures the experiences they suggest is the existentialist's term "inauthentic," that new term of philosophical criticism directed against our lives. I have said that for the Oxford philosopher, "ordinary language" and "ordinary contexts" mean not much more than "nonphilosophical language" and "nonphilosophical contexts." In Wittgenstein's work, "ordinary" or "every-day" contexts and examples are, I suggest, meant to carry the force of "authentic" examples authentically responded to in language.

III

Anyone who has looked into Wittgenstein's *Investigations* will appreciate the difficulties of saying briefly what the book is about and of conveying its particular tone and force. I want now to follow up my suggestion of its relation to existentialism and try the experiment of comparing it with Kierkegaard's writing, in particular the writing in his *Concluding Unscientific Postscript*.

Both Wittgenstein and Kierkegaard see their worlds as laboring under illusion. Both see their function as authors to be the uncovering or diagnosing of this illusion, and freeing us from it. In both, the cure requires that we be brought (back) to our human existence.

For Kierkegaard the illusion is that such a thing as Christendom exists, that one can be a Christian simply by being born in a Christian state, of Christian parents, and by being given a Christian name and nomenclature. Moreover, it is an illusion to suppose that there are any Christians, for no one, or almost no one—including himself—is now capable of the resignation and faith required to follow Christ. For Wittgenstein the illusion is perfection or generality or completeness. One of its forms is the idea that the intelligibility of our language rests upon a foundation of logic, or is secured by essences or rules. It is as though he had asked himself, ten years after his *Tractatus* was written, "How can logic show us the real form of language?" and had to answer, "It can't." That does not mean it is not often possible, and sometimes useful, to put utterances from a natural language into logical form. But from this possibility nothing follows of the sort that philosophers, including the young Wittgenstein, had thought followed. For example, it does not follow that one *must* put statements in logical form in order to see their function and, as it were, understand their intelligibility. And it would in particular not provide, as philosophers have supposed, a more exact set of statements, because the notion of "more exact" depends on the particular goal one has in mind: logic cannot provide it, once for all, for all goals. And if one says that logic provides an analysis of ordinary statements, then one must not go on to suppose that ordinary language needs analysis (or at least, that kind of analysis), nor that there is some final and complete analysis toward which ordinary language longs, nor that the analyzed form tells you more, in general, than the unanalyzed form. In some ways, for certain purposes, it tells you less. (In these important respects Wittgenstein is profoundly opposed to the conception of philosophy as analysis.)

Kierkegaard's diagnosis of our illusion, our illness, in the *Concluding Unscientific Postscript*, is that we have lost the capacity for subjectivity, for inwardness, and therewith the capacity for Christianity. We live in an Objective Age, an Age of Knowledge, and we have stopped *living* our lives in favor of knowing them. Wittgenstein's diagnosis is that we have, in part because of our illusions about language, fixed or forced ideas of the way things must be, and will not *look and see* how they are. Kierkegaard finds us trying to escape our existence and our history; Wittgenstein finds us wishing to escape the limits of human forms of language and forms of life. In Kierkegaard's descriptions, we live in the universal rather than in our particularity; in Wittgenstein's we crave generality instead of accepting the concrete.

In both, the cure is for us to return to our everyday existence. It will be obvious that this emphasis on diagnosis and cure continues the early image of the philosopher as the physician of the soul, and it also aligns these writers with the characteristic effort of modern thought to *unmask* its audience, its world, an effort as true of Marx and Nietzsche and Freud as it is of Kierkegaard and Wittgenstein. And the effort to unmask requires a few masks or tricks of its own.

Traditional forms of criticism, of logical refutation preeminently, are unavailing. Our new problems do not arise through inconsistency or falsehood; they are worse than false, and they are all too consistent. The problem is not whether the workers are paid enough, but why one has the right to *pay* them at all. The problem is not whether one has been baptized, but what it means to *become* baptized. The problem is not why man suffers, but why man interprets his suffering as punishment. The problem is not whether the life of pleasure is higher or lower than the life of knowledge, but why one cannot feel pleasure and why one desires to *know*. The problem is not whether universals or essences are *before* things or only *in* things, but why one has the idea that there are universals or essences.

Nothing is more characteristic of the writing in the *Philosophical Investigations* and in the *Unscientific Postscript* than its shunning of normal modes of argument and the insistence on the language and life of ordinary mortals. But this itself is not a new turn in philosophical writing. Here is a passage from a recent discussion of the so-called Revival of Learning in the Renaissance:

> In its simplest terms, this revolution consisted in a shift within the spectrum of the three primary liberal arts that were the nurture of all scholars, a shift from dialectic as the key discipline toward grammar and rhetoric. . . . The study of words and of style, the analysis of how a language is put together and what it may be made to do, the examination of an author in relation to his audience and the whole purpose of his work—these became increasingly the preoccupations of scholars. The Revival of Learning thus meant a shift of interest from philosophy [i.e., from philosophy in the style of Abelard and Aquinas] to philology, from logic to literature, from abstract truth to concrete, personal fact.[5]

That description, it seems clear to me, fits Wittgenstein's procedures and his motives as well as it fits existentialism and a familiar part of contemporary theology. When to this one adds Kierkegaard's and Wittgenstein's recurrent and obviously pointed use of humor,

[5] E. Harris Harbison, *The Christian Scholar in the Age of the Reformation* (New York, 1956), pp. 34–35.

paradox, aphorism, irony, parable, and dialogue, the memory and effect of these writers take on an hallucinatory similarity.

Readers of both of them have often found the cure they offer worse than the disease. Kierkegaard calls for the end of Christendom. He imagines, in his journal, that someone will object: If all men became Christians, if all men became celibate, ascetic, martyrs to the truth, and suffered the full fact of aloneness, the world would come to an end. To which he answers: "What a pity." No doubt that was itself meant ironically. And Wittgenstein asks, at one point: "Where does our investigation get its importance from, since it seems only to destroy everything interesting, that is, all that is great and important?" And he answers: "What we are destroying is nothing but houses of cards. . . . " But that seems little consolation for the loss of philosophy.

And in both writers the cure seems no cure. All we are given is the obvious, and then silence. Kierkegaard has some sport with the man who feels the need to make profound discoveries before he can find his salvation and know his true responsibilities. Kierkegaard's suggestion is that the only discovery that man needs is that he needs no new discovery. And Wittgenstein says, "If one tried to advance *theses* in philosophy, it would never be possible to question them, because everyone would agree to them." Yet they both claim that obviousness and silence provide *answers*, and moreover that nothing else does, that is, not to *their* questions.

Before I go further, I feel I should speak for a sense of impatience which has every right to break out. "One thing you've said is certainly true, namely, that the similarity between Kierkegaard and Wittgenstein is hallucinatory. They are simply different, so why try to deny it? Kierkegaard is important because he describes our lives and depicts salvation, whereas Wittgenstein speaks about words, and if about our lives, then about the commonest portions of our everyday life. It would be more honest simply to say that the term philosophy can refer either to a body of propositions supposed to comprise knowledge of some sort, or else to a mode of life, and that analytical philosophy is an example of the former and existentialism an example of the latter. Moreover, Kierkegaard writes in defense of

Christianity, saying over and over that his one thought is that Christianity is inwardness, that truth is subjectivity, that the enemy of truth is objectivity, scientific knowledge, and that since we have chosen the latter we have lost our souls and are damned.[6] Wittgenstein has nothing to say about such matters, and moreover thinks there is nothing wrong with science. He merely says that it is *not* philosophy, that philosophy's problems are not solved by science. Such a position may be an advance over positivism's servility to science, but it is still nowhere near making us servants of God."

It would not be profitable, or pleasant, to argue the question of the relative importance of our writers. Though it should be remembered that when Wittgenstein says "philosophy leaves everything as it is," he seems to think that is in itself an important thing to say—as though men, and not, perhaps, just philosophers, were always in danger of trying to make philosophy change things. And does one want it to? One does not want it, for example, to become merely another ideology—in the words of George Orwell, another of "the smelly little orthodoxies which are now contending for our souls." If philosophy could keep ideologies from changing the world out from under our lives, could help to let us grow into our future, knowing it as we go, that would be change enough, and important enough. And I would add that Kierkegaard said he was *un*important, or mattered at most accidentally to our lives. One may think this just more of his humor and irony; but I think that if he was in dead earnest about anything, he was about that.

Again, is it true to say that "philosophy is *either* a body of knowledge *or* a mode of life"? At the beginning of philosophy, in Plato and Aristotle, the knowledge it provided, going beyond "scientific" knowledge, was supposed to make one good, give one joy. With Christianity, such knowledge was found irrelevant for true, eternal happiness; the truth one needs is as easy, and at least as difficult, for a wise man as for a fool. Christendom has always been ambivalent

[6] I do not wish to be taken as suggesting that Nietzsche and Kierkegaard were unequivocal in their rejection of scientific knowledge. Sometimes they suggest that, in its place, it is unobjectionable. One trouble about it would then be that it just will not stay in its place. But their views about science remain, for me at least, as unclear as they are important.

about the merit of learning, until today we no longer know whether knowledge is itself saving or damning—perhaps imagining each in turn. But further, it is one of Kierkegaard's and Nietzsche's best discoveries—or rediscoveries—that knowledge itself exacts a mode of life. Kierkegaard's "objective thinker" is a well-known comic figure—like the Devil—though not everyone may appreciate his humor. And Nietzsche, in characterizing what he calls the "ascetic ideal," asks, or reasks in a new way: "Why do men wish to know? What does their concentration on, their faith in knowledge, do to them?" As the ideal of the knower becomes heightened in Christian spirituality, he will be the overthrow of that Christianity. Because he will press his knowledge until he knows his own motives to knowledge, knows that they are ones of passionate destructiveness, of fear and power over others disguised as self-control, of hatred and possessiveness disguised as disinterestedness. And he will go on to know that the same is true of the motives as a Christian. Perhaps then he will become capable of the knowledge that will be joyful.

It is true that Wittgenstein does not entertain such questions. And yet it is not clear what the effect will be of saying to philosophy: answers must be satisfying, and the old philosophical answers are not satisfying; *more* knowledge will not solve your problems. For that can lead one to ask: What will solve them, what will be satisfying? And now we are back to the question of silence which we broke off a moment ago.

At one point in the *Investigations*, Wittgenstein says, "Let us ask ourselves: why do we feel a grammatical joke to be *deep*?" And he adds parenthetically, "That is what the depth of philosophy is." One example of what he may have meant by a grammatical joke is perhaps the following: A child I was taking for a walk saw a younger child stumble and fall, and she asked me, "Why did the baby fall?" I answered, "He just lost his balance." The child immediately replied, "Where did he lose it?" and began looking around in puzzlement. (That is the sort of question that the child, a year or so later, will herself find enormously funny, and she will ask it just *for* the fun.) How are we to answer the child's question? We may feel: the baby didn't lose something in the way the child thinks, or: "lose" means something different when I say, "he lost his balance," from what it means when I say, "he lost his blanket." And we may feel that the child is not ready for certain explanations. That is doubtless right enough, but we may then imagine that *we* do possess the explanations, but for some reason cannot in fact hand them over to a child. But do we know how the baby "lost something" differently from the way the child thinks? How shall we say what the difference is? And do we know *our* meaning of "lost something" which is different from the meaning the child attaches to those words? How do we explain that meaning to ourselves? That we may not be able to provide ourselves with such explanations does not show that we do not really know what we mean; what it shows is that "knowing what we mean" is not always, though it sometimes is, a matter of having *explanations* for our meaning. Sometimes we know a thing, but cannot express our knowledge in explanations; sometimes we do not know a thing, but what we lack cannot be supplied by explanations. (We may, for example, need to come to *see* everything differently.) Our lack of explanation to ourselves also suggests that our difference from the child is not a difference in the explanations we can or cannot give. The child will eventually learn what we mean by the phrase "lost his balance," or perhaps we should say, she will learn how we use it; that will happen when she also learns how we use forms like "lost his way" and "lost his chance" and "lost his turn" and "lost his sense of humor." Wittgenstein says, "To imagine a form of language is to imagine a form of life." And we could, accordingly, say that the child is not ready to learn certain forms because she as yet lacks the forms of life in which those forms of language have a use, have a natural function. The extent to which we understand one another or ourselves is the same as the extent to which we share or understand forms of life, share and know, for example, what it is to take turns, or take chances, or know that some things we have lost we cannot look for but can nevertheless sometimes find or recover; share the sense of what is fun and what loss feels like, and take comfort from the same things and take confidence or offense in similar ways. That we do more or less share such forms rests upon nothing deeper; nothing *insures* that we will, and there is no foundation, logical or philosophical, which explains the fact that we do, which provides the real forms of which our lives, and language, are distortions.

What has to be *accepted*, Wittgenstein says, is forms of life. This is not the same as saying that our lives as we lead them—in particular, for Wittgenstein, our lives of theory—must be accepted. What it says, or suggests, is that criticism of our lives is not to be prosecuted in philosophical theory, but continued in the confrontation of our lives with their own necessities. He also says that language, and life, rests on conventions. What he means is, I suppose, that they have no necessity beyond what human beings do. He does not mean, for example, that we might all convene and decide or vote on what our human forms of life shall be, choose what we shall find funny or whether we will continue finding loss and comfort where we do. If we call these arrangements conventional, we must then also call them natural. The thought was perhaps expressed by Pascal when he said of human beings, "Custom is our nature." It is from such an insight that Wittgenstein and Kierkegaard explicitly avoid explanations of our lives and concentrate on descriptions of them as they are, together with the alternatives which present themselves at given moments. Or perhaps we should say: for them a philosophical explanation takes the form of a description, unlike explanations in science.

In the *Tractatus* Wittgenstein says, "The solution of the problem of life is seen in the vanishing of the problem," and in the *Investigations* he says: " . . . the clarity that we are aiming at is indeed complete clarity. But this simply means that the philosophical problems should *completely* disappear." Yet he calls these problems *solved* (*Investigations*), and he says that when "there are . . . no questions left . . . this itself is the *answer*" (*Tractatus*). Putting these remarks together, the implication is that the problems of life and the problems of philosophy have the same form—Wittgenstein would say they have the same "grammar": they are solved only when they disappear; answers are arrived at only when there are no longer questions. In the *Investigations*, this turns out to be more of an answer than, in this simple form, it seems to be; for here such an answer more explicitly dictates and displays the ways philosophy is to proceed in investigating problems, ways leading to what he calls "perspicuous representation," which means, roughly, that instead of accumulating new facts, or capturing the essence of the world in definitions, or perfecting and completing our language, we need to arrange the facts we already know or can come to realize merely by *calling to mind* something we know. Philosophical conflict, say as expressed in skepticism, does not arise from one party knowing facts the other party does not know. Wittgenstein also says that perspicuous representations are "the way we look at things," and he then asks, "Is this a 'Weltanschauung'?" The answer to that question is, I take it, not No. Not, perhaps, Yes, because it is not a special, or competing, way of looking at things. But not No, because its mark of success is that the world seem—be—different.[7]

I think of Kierkegaard's description in *Fear and Trembling* of the man who can, as he puts it, "express the sublime in the pedestrian," something he takes as possible only through the possession of faith. I would certainly sympathize with the feeling that *this* connection between Wittgenstein and Kierkegaard is fanciful; and yet it seems to me to throw into relief the *kind* of writing in which they both engage. For not just any mode of composition will tell us something we cannot fail to know and yet remain enlightening; not just any way of arguing will try to prevent us from taking what is said as a thesis or a result. Theses and results are things that can be believed and accepted; but Kierkegaard and Wittgenstein do not want to be believed and accepted, and therewith, of course, dismissed. And not just any way of addressing an audience will leave them as they are, leave them alone, but transformed.

These are effects we have come to expect of art, and perhaps it is because of such effects that a literary theorist like Northrop Frye says even of the art of literature—not merely, with Malraux, of the visual arts—that it is silent. Wittgenstein says that his *Philosophical Investigations* is a work of "grammar," and Kierkegaard calls his *Postscript* a "Mimic-Pathetic-Dialectic Composition," and he first thought of entitling it simply, "Logical Problems." To understand these descriptions would be to understand the works in question.

[7]I have lifted this paragraph out of a paper of mine, "Aesthetics and Modern Philosophy," which is reprinted in *Must We Mean What We Say?*

Kierkegaard speaks in his early works little, if at all, *about* his literary or philosophical methods, but he tells more and more about his methods as his books tumble into the world, and perhaps by the time of the *Unscientific Postscript*, and surely in the posthumous *Point of View of My Work as an Author*, he says rather too much about them. His principal methodological claim in the *Postscript* is that he is forced to use what he calls "indirect communication"—and his "forced to" means something close to "logically forced to," as if he were to say that what he wishes to communicate cannot be communicated any other way. Direct communication would be appropriate for transmitting beliefs, or presenting scientific results, etc. It is inappropriate, indeed impossible, for something else. For what else? One understands the sort of thing Kierkegaard has in mind when he says, "This can be communicated in no other way." It points to the fact that makes art itself possible, or necessary, but its application to Kierkegaard's composition is not perfectly clear, and a bit of analysis may be in order.

What would it mean to say, "Poetry communicates indirectly" or "What poetry says can be communicated in no other way"? (The former statement seems more fundamental, since we could, it seems, also say of science that what it says can be communicated no other way.) Let us take, for example, a poem of Wallace Stevens's in which he says, "Death is the mother of beauty." Suppose someone feels he doesn't really understand that line and asks for its meaning. I may try to help by such remarks as these: What the line means is that without a knowledge of death, of real and final change and loss, there would be no knowledge of life, and no art; we have art that we may not perish from the truth; and art itself is a kind of death, but in the service of the only life there is. What does it mean to say that Stevens *means* what I say he means by that line? Have I not, if my reading is accurate, communicated his meaning?—though communicated it in another way, if you like. Perhaps one feels: Yes and No. That feeling itself suggests that it is not *obvious* that Stevens's line has communicated something which can be communicated in no other way. Perhaps one still wishes to say: You haven't communicated the *very* meaning of that line, not said it *exactly*. But that suggests that I got the line *wrong*, that what I said it meant wasn't exactly right. No doubt something is lost when the line is explained; but no doubt something is gained, if the explanation is right, especially if it is exactly right. But Kierkegaard says *everything* is lost in reverting to direct communication, so our example must not be the sort he had in mind. This is also suggested in asking *which* of these communications—Stevens's line or my reading of it—one wants to call "direct" and which "indirect." The answer seems to be: In a sense the original line is more direct, but in another sense the explanation of the line is more direct.

Then let us take a different example. At the beginning of his poem, Stevens imagines a lady who knows what it means to say that death is the mother of beauty, and he pictures her, late one Sunday morning, in the center of his mortal heaven; and he finds that her thoughts wander, that she feels a pang of regret and yearning for the old heaven, the old promise. Or rather, what he finds is that

> she feels the dark
> Encroachment of that old catastrophe,
> As a calm darkens among water-lights.

If someone fails to understand these lines, I *may* try to help; but I cannot do what I did with the former line. I may say that "old catastrophe" refers to the failed promise of redemption, but I cannot explain any special weight he attaches to any of the particular words, nor show complexities in the thought. I cannot *explain* the lines at all. I may try to *describe* some particular scene and mood and gesture which captures the particular touch those lines have for me, hoping to lead you to the line itself. Then again, I may be unwilling to say anything, wanting to leave them as touchstones of intimacy. In that case, I will perhaps say or feel: The thought can be expressed in no other way. And here I mean that absolutely—no "in a sense" about it. But just for this reason the question whether the lines communicate directly or indirectly loses all significance here—there simply is no alternative way of communicating it. So this again cannot be the sort of case Kierkegaard has in mind.

These examples bring out a conflict between the characterizations, "must be communicated indirectly" and "can be communicated no other way."[8] It is only when there is some alternative way of communicating a thought that it makes sense to say that the thought has been, in a given instance, communicated directly or indirectly. Where there flatly is *no* other way in which thought can be communicated, then the unique expression of it can be called neither direct nor indirect; the contrast no longer applies.

So what can Kierkegaard mean by saying *both* that his communication is indirect *and* that there is no alternative to it?[9] Does he really mean, or need, only one of these characterizations? What leads him to his joint characterization can, I think, be seen in this: the thoughts he wishes to express seem easily to be expressed in familiar words— the words, say, of the Sermon on the Mount; people are always using the words and supposing themselves to know what they mean. But Kierkegaard finds that they do not know, or will not know, what the words really mean. They lose, or cover, their meaning when they are spoken apart from the (Christian) forms of life which give them their meaning. Yet they are the same *words*, and no others will do for the thoughts to be expressed. It is because the words can be uttered and meant in conflicting ways that Kierkegaard maintains the contrast between direct and indirect communication; it is because only one way of saying them gives the real, the Christian meaning that he says only one form of communication is possible.

This, then, is a very particular literary problem, a problem concerning a very particular situation of language, not one, as in the first example from Stevens's poem, in which there are alternative vehicles for expressing a thought, one of which can be said to convey it directly, the other indirectly; nor, as in the second example, a situation in which there is no alternative vehicle of expression for the thought and therefore no way in which it can be conveyed differently (directly or indirectly). It is one in which, while there is only one vehicle

---

[8]This is the chief point at which a reading of the original of this paper by Rogers Albritton forced revision and expansion. I am grateful to him.
[9]This is not merely a verbal matter concerning the words direct and indirect. Literary critics say similar things about metaphors and their relation to the words which purport to paraphrase them. I have treated the problem at greater length in the aesthetics paper cited in note 7.

of expression, there are two thoughts it can express, and moreover the thoughts are incompatible, mutually defeating. (Which thought is expressed by the one vehicle depends, as it were, on the direction in which it is travelling, outward or inward.) Examples of such vehicles are these:

Truth is subjectivity
Truth is appropriation
Christianity is inwardness
Faith is greater than knowledge
The mark of faith is certainty
The mark of faith is uncertainty
Faith lies in the grasp of the ordinary
Christianity demands that you: Die to the world
           Become a witness to the truth
           Love thy neighbor and thine enemy
           Deny your mother and father

And so on, through the content of the Christian message. This message is of such a form that the words which contain its truth may be said in a way which defeats that very truth. And Kierkegaard sees modern man as fated to say them the wrong way.

If one way of saying and hearing and understanding such words is to be called direct and the other indirect, then it must still be made clear that the relation between these modes is not the same as in our case of paraphrasing the poem (first example), because there the paraphrase ("direct communication") is meant to, and in successful cases it does, open us to the poem ("indirect communication"), whereas here the direct expression blocks the indirect. In using such words directly the relation between what one says and what there is in those words to be heard and understood is ironic, and, depending on the context and the consequences, comic or tragic. If you take (say) Christ's parable of the sower and the seed as an unvarnished tale, it is utterly trivial, pointless; heard and understood, it teaches the reception of the word of salvation. He that hath ears to hear, let him hear. Kierkegaard, bent with knowing the distance between what Christendom says and what it understands, tries to unstop its ears, to awaken the Christian by producing for him the irony, the comedy, and the tragedy of his existence.[10] Above all the irony, which is the specific for words and deeds which have the opposite of their intended effect, which mask what they seem to reveal, or produce what they were meant to avoid.

For Wittgenstein, the distance between what is said and what is meant is not ironic. The category of irony reemerges with poignant relevance in comparing existentialism with the positivist phase of analytical philosophy. Both say that ethical and religious utterances must be subjective; both say that rhetoric prevents an utterance from being genuine; both say that it is not philosophy's business to exhort anyone to the moral life; both say that philosophy provides no objective or empirical knowledge; and both say that science provides objective knowledge of the world. And in each case one of them means the opposite of what the other means, or has opposite feelings about it and draws opposite conclusions.[11]

Wittgenstein's audience is not the Christian inoculated against Christianity; and his dialogues are rather the reverse of the Socratic. Socrates' interlocutors have not found their lives, because they have failed to examine them. Wittgenstein's have lost their lives through thinking too much, or in the wrong way. What he seems to uncover is not that someone's words mean the opposite of what he says or that someone fails to recognize the implications of what he says. What he finds, rather, is that someone means something very *specific*, only *different* from what he thought he meant, or else means nothing at all just when he thought his meaning was clearest and deepest. He finds that someone has become obsessed with "pictures" of the way he imagines the world or the mind must be; or supposes himself to

[10]The reason Jesus gives for speaking in parables ("That hearing they may hear, and not understand") seems different, seems opposite, not to say un-Christian ("Lest at any time they should be converted, and their sins should be forgiven them"). A consideration of these differences will doubtless have to give at least these facts an accounting: that the audience of the one is the new Christian, while that of the other is the lost Christian; and that the powers of the speakers differ as heaven and earth.
[11]This inner, competitive, relation between Existentialism and Positivism is taken up, without recourse to the concept of irony, in moments of two essays roughly contemporary with this one, both collected in *Must We Mean What We Say?*: in an essay on Beckett's *Endgame*, p. 120; and in one on Kierkegaard's *Authority and Revelation*, pp. 171–72.

be communicating a piece of information when in fact no one could fail to know what he says (hence no one could be informed by it). Such a person—any person at such a moment—is lost not in parable but in fact; he has lost not the depth of his words but their surface, their ordinariness—not their power to save but their power to record; he is out of touch not with his individual existence but with his common human nature. Which of these is the greater loss it is perhaps less important to decide than to discern the necessities of each.

Wittgenstein's general diagnosis, as has been said, is that these are the eventualities which come, in philosophizing, when one is led to speak as if beyond the limits of human language, as it were, looking back at it. Therefore, what he does is to bring words back to their everyday uses. That this is a difficult thing to get people to do says something about the difficulty of philosophizing—and about the difficulty of *not* philosophizing. That a call for the return to the everyday requires its own ironies, hints, jokes, parables, and silences, says something about what this return requires—not an itinerary through new information to the goal of theory, but through renewed looking and seeing to the point of knowing where you are.

If I do not say that Wittgenstein's *Investigations* is a secularization of Kierkegaard's *Postscript*, that is partly because other of Kierkegaard's own writings may also be called secularizations of his religious works, and partly because the idea of secularization is all but useless; not just because it is so unclear, but because it suggests at once less intimacy between these writers than details of comparison will reveal, and also more intimacy than the different weight and shape of details within each writer will tolerate. When Kierkegaard finds the modern philosopher (in particular Hegel) supposing that he can traverse the infinite distance to God by erecting a very high and long system, he remarks that "philosophy rests not upon a mistaken presupposition, but upon a comic presupposition." One could almost expect to find that particular criticism numbered separately in the *Investigations*. For when Wittgenstein finds philosophers attempting to explain the workings of the mind by appealing to physiological mechanisms about which they know nothing, rather than to the noticeable inner and outer contexts in which the mind takes the forms which puzzled them in the first place (and these are the forms which physiological mechanisms will have to explain), or when he finds a philosopher supposing that he is *pointing* to a sensation by *concentrating his attention* on it, or finds him citing "evidence" for the "hypothesis" that other people "have" feelings "similar" to "our own," or finds him attempting to locate the essence of a phenomenon (say of intention, or meaning, or belief, or language) by stripping away all the characteristics which could comprise its essence, he does not say of them that they are making *mistakes*—as though greater attention and care could have gained them success. The success of someone trying to press his camel through the eye of a needle will not come with his addressing greater attention and care to the enterprise.

I might summarize what I have been saying in somewhat the following way: Wittgenstein and Kierkegaard take seriously the fact that we begin our lives as children; what we need is to be shown a path, and helped to take steps; and as we grow, something is gained and something is lost. What helps at one stage does not help at another; what serves as an explanation at one stage is not serviceable— we could say, it is not intelligible—at another. In grown-up philosophy, the problems we have *remain* answerable only through growth, not through explanation or definitions. The idea of growth is meant to emphasize that we are no longer to expect answers and solutions in traditional terms—any more than we can accept philosophical questions and answers as *given*. What has happened is that the *fact* that something is an "outstanding philosophical problem" has itself become problematic. This is true of all phases of analytical philosophy, but it is equally true of existentialism. And grown-ups give themselves as many useless or fraudulent explanations as they give children. What we must hope for is not that at some stage we will possess all explanations, but that at some stage we will need none. And the task remains to discover what we need. Wittgenstein puts it this way: We impose a requirement (for example, of perfection, or certainty, or finality) which fails to satisfy our real need. Kierkegaard could also have said that, as he also suggests that we impose

such requirements upon ourselves for just that reason, to avoid seeing what our lives really depend on.

Before stopping, we owe it to ourselves to ask of what real use it
was to say that Kierkegaard and Wittgenstein find the world suffering from illusions, and write to free us of them. Kierkegaard speaks
of such an illusion only relatively late in his authorship, after he has
written *through*, so to speak, the stages on life's way. Each stage has
its own mode of communication, and an individual in one stage cannot use the explanations which serve in another. From what existential stage does Kierkegaard see the world as under an illusion? I suggest: from none at all. In such writing he has become exactly the
objective thinker, the Hegelian world-historical-monger he so de-
spises. His description rests, to use his precise phrase, on a comic
presupposition. The notion of illusion suggests that there is a reality
to be seen. But if what is meant is an illusion held by *that* individual
in *his* existence, then the reality with which it contrasts must be one
held by that individual in his existence. And *that* reality cannot, on
Kierkegaard's own teaching, be known or seen in the way his use of
"illusion" suggests.

We might say that no human existence can properly be described
as under an illusion; for illusions are inevitable, or they vanish, in
ways the human modes of existence do not. The notion of illusion
suggests that different existences in their different worlds (for example, the same person at different stages) can be compared in ways
they cannot be. Similarly, we should say of the child who looked for
the baby's lost balance, not that she *mis*understood what I said to
her, but that she understood it in the only way she could, in her stage.

Nevertheless, saying of Kierkegaard that he wrote to free the individual of illusion repays investigation. It is a more useful thing to
say than, for example, as one sometimes hears, that he is a Romantic,
or to say that he is an individualist, or to say that he writes as a Christian. The first, if true, would be tragic, since a romantic view of life
is, in Kierkegaard's view, the other principal way (the way other than
"objectivity") to miss the plain facts of a Christian existence. The
second would be ironic, because in the sense that *he* means "individ-

ual," there are no individuals any more than there are Christians. The last is unknowable, for whether a man is a Christian is a matter of his relationship to God, and that is an essential secret.

One of Wittgenstein's characterizations of his work has, I believe, been fairly widely quoted—that his aim is to show the fly the way out of the fly bottle. But he does not *announce* this as his aim—communicating a result or an intention. The context is a paragraph which, in its entirety, consists of the opening question, "What is your aim in philosophy?" and the closing answer, "To show the fly . . . etc." That response is made for that question. What kind of answer *can* that question have? I don't suggest that Wittgenstein does not *mean* the answer he gives, only that the answer is not to be taken as suggesting that he knows beforehand, and once for all, that all questions asked by philosophy are just so much buzzing, and that he can see them, before investigation, to be the product of illusion. What is the aim of philosophy? To respond to the particular question asked, and to get satisfying answers. And satisfaction is not had, and philosophy is not done, once for all.

◆

THE FACT
OF TELEVISION

◆

Again I am indebted to the editor of Dædalus, *Stephen Graubard,
this time for demanding that I say what I could about the phenomenon of television. The occasion was the convening of a study group for
which papers were prepared with a view, after discussion, to revising
and collecting them for publication as the Fall 1982 issue of* Daedalus,
*entitled "Print Culture and Video Culture." In addition to the bene-
fit derived from the reactions of the study group, the first version of
these remarks was read by William Rothman, who prepared a set of
comments that caused changes on every other page as I prepared a
second version. This was then read by Norton Batkin, Gus Blaisdell,
Jay Cantor, and Arnold Davidson, whose comments I used, as elsewhere, as I prepared the present, here reprinted, version.*

◇

Of course there are interesting facts *about* television, facts about its
technology, about the history of its programs, about the economic
structure of the networks that produce it. Most of these facts I do not
know, but I think I know what it would be like to learn them, and to
start to learn what they add up to. By speaking of the fact of television, I mean to call attention to something else, something I do not,
in the same way, think I know how to learn more about, something
like the sheer fact that television exists, and that this existence is at
once among the most obvious and the most mysterious facts of con-

temporary life. Its obviousness is that television has conquered, like the electric light, or the automobile, or the telephone. Its mystery is twofold: first, *how* it has conquered; and second, how we (we, for example, who write for and read *Dædalus*) have apparently remained largely uninterested in accounting for its conquering. (What it has conquered, I wish to leave, or to make, a question, part of the mystery. Has it conquered as a form of popular, or mass, entertainment? Popular as opposed to what? And what happened to the forms over which television triumphed?)

The twofold mystery comes to a twofold assumption, with which I begin, that there is something yet to be understood concerning both the interest in television and the refusal of interest in it. The latter half of the assumption is that the absence of critical or intellectual attention to television—both in kind and extent—is not satisfactorily understandable as a straightforward lack of interest, as if the medium were inherently boring. Individual intellectuals will, of course, straightforwardly find no interest there, as they may not in film. But the absence of interest in the medium seems to me more complete, or studied, than can be accounted for by the accidents of taste. That the absence is not accidental or straightforward is epitomized, I think, in the familiar disapproval evinced toward television in certain educated circles. Members of these circles would apparently prefer not to permit a TV set in the house; but if unable to hold to this pure line, they sternly limit the amount of time the children may watch, regardless of the content. If this line has in turn been breached, and the choice is between letting the kids watch at home or at a neighbor's house, they are apt to speak guiltily—or at any rate awkwardly—about their and their children's knowledge of its programs. As if in reaction, other intellectuals brazen out a preference for commercial over public television.

Such behavior suggests to my mind a fear of television for which I have heard no credible explanation. Sometimes people say, loosely I suppose, that television is addictive. And of course it would be a plausible explanation of both television's attraction and its repulsion if it were credible to attribute addictive powers to it, to believe quite literally that the tube is not only in the service of boobs, but that it turns otherwise useful citizens into boobs. (I will cite such a view toward the end of these remarks.) But I have no acquaintance with anyone who treats television in all seriousness as if it were the equivalent of, say, heroin. Even if marijuana presented a more analogous level of fear, adults worried about its effects would not make it available to their children, even on a strictly limited basis, unless perhaps they were already dealing with addiction. Nor does the disapproval of television seem to me very close to the disapproval of comic books by an earlier generation of parents, described so well by Robert Warshow in "Paul, the Horror Comics, and Dr. Wertham."[1] Like any concerned parent who wants to provide his or her children with the pleasures of cultivation, and who does not underestimate how exacting those pleasures are to command, Warshow was worried—having investigated and dismissed as groundless the then fashionable claim that comics incited their readers to violence—about the sheer time comics seem to steal from better things. But he decided that his son's absorption would pass and that less harm would be done by waiting it out than by prohibiting it. The difference I sense from the disapproval of television may be that Warshow was not himself tempted by a craving to absorb himself in comic books, so that he had first-hand evidence that the absorption would die naturally, whereas adults today may have no analogous evidence from their own experience of television, fearing their own addictiveness. Or is there some surmise about the *nature* of the pleasure television provides that sets off disapproval of it, perhaps like surmises that once caused the disapproval of novel-reading or, later, of movie-viewing? If this were the case, one might expect the disapproval to vanish when television comes of age, when its programs achieve an artistic maturity to match that of the great novels and movies. Is this a reasonable faith?

Certainly I have been among those who have felt that television cannot have come of age, that the medium *must* have more in it than what has so far been shown. True, I have felt, at the same time, that so much money and talent have been lavished on it, that *if* there is

[1] In *The Immediate Experience* (New York, 1964).

anything more in the medium, it could hardly have escaped discovery. From this thought, one of two conclusions may be drawn: that there is indeed nothing more to be discovered and that the medium is accordingly one of poverty and boredom (I once found myself in a discussion of these matters impatiently observing that television is no more a medium of art than the telephone, the telegraph, or the telescope); or, since this is not quite credible, that the poverty lies not in the medium's discoveries, but rather in our understanding of these discoveries, in our failure as yet to grasp what the medium is for, what constitutes its powers and its treasures.

Since I am inclined to the latter of these conclusions, to speculate on what might constitute a better route of understanding is what I conceive my task here to be (together with some speculation about what kind of issue "the understanding of a medium" is). This means that I accept the condition of both conclusions, namely that television *has* come of age, that *this*, these programs, more or less as they stand, in what can appear to be their poverty, is what there *is* to understand. For suppose we agree that television's first major accomplishments can be dated no later than 1953, the time of the coverage of the first Eisenhower Inauguration. In that case, it has had thirty years in which to show itself. If Griffith's major films around 1915 are taken to date the birth of film as a medium of art, then it took only ten more years to reach the masterpieces of Chaplin and Keaton; and over the next twenty years, America, to go no further, established a momentum in producing definitive movies—movies that are now among the permanent pleasures of art theaters, of museum programs, of film studies programs, and of late night television—that was essentially slowed (or so the story goes) only with the help of the rising television industry. One of our questions should be: Did television give back as good as it took away?

The acceptance of television as a mature medium of art further specifies what I mean in calling my subject here the fact of television. A further consequence of this characterization, or limitation of my subject, is that I am not undertaking to discuss the progress and results of experimental video artists. This is not meant to imply that I am uninterested in what might be called "the medium of video."

On the contrary, it would be a way of describing my motive here as an interest in what television, as it stands, reveals about this medium. I do not mean to assume that this description captures a topic of assured significance or fruitfulness. I do hope, rather, that it is one way of picking up the subject of this issue of *Dædalus*, concerning the supposed general influence of video on our culture at large, on a par with the influence of print. In developing my contribution, I will take my bearings from some thoughts I worked with in speculating about the medium of film in *The World Viewed*.[2] That book also addresses what I am calling the nature of the medium, by asking what the traditional masterpieces, or successes, among movies reveal it to be, not especially what experimental work finds it to be. It is a guiding thesis of that book that major films are those in which the medium is most richly or deeply revealed. (This remains controversial. A reviewer of my recently published *Pursuits of Happiness: The Hollywood Comedy of Remarriage*[3] found that book pretentious and sometimes preposterous, in part because he cannot believe that even the best of Hollywood films are as self-reflective, or intelligent, about their source in the medium of film—if, in a sense, less explicit—as is the work of "modernist self-referential artists" like Godard and Antonioni. Hollywood is a mythical locale, part of whose function is to cause people to imagine that they know it without having taken its works seriously, like America.)

An immediate difference presents itself between television and film. To say that masterpieces among movies reveal the medium of film is to say that this revelation is the business of individual works, and that these works have a status analogous to traditional works of art: they last beyond their immediate occasions; their rewards bear up under repeated viewings; they lend themselves to the same pitch of critical scrutiny as do any of the works we care about most seriously. This seems not to be true of individual works of television. What is memorable, treasurable, criticizable, is not primarily the individual work, but the program, the format, not this or that day of "I Love Lucy," but the program as such. I say this "seems" to me to

[2]Enlarged edition, Cambridge, Mass., 1979.
[3]Cambridge, 1981.

be so, and what I will have to say here depends on its being so. But my experience of television is much more limited than my experience of movies and of pretelevision radio, so my views about the treasuring of television's works may be especially unreliable. Still, I think that people who have been puzzled by the phenomenon of television as I have been—evidenced by being more grateful, if grudgingly so, to some of it, than familiar aesthetic concepts will explain—must commonly have had the thought, or intuition, that its value is a function of its rule of format. My speculations here are intended as something like experiments to test how far one would have to go to follow this intuition, with reasonable intellectual satisfaction, through the aesthetic range of the phenomenon we know as television.

I have begun by citing grounds on which to deny that the evanescence of the instance, of the individual work, in itself shows that television has not yet come of age aesthetically. (Even were it to prove true that certain television works yet to be made may become treasured instances, as *instances*, such as the annual running of *The Wizard of Oz*—which serves to prove my case, since this is not an object made by and for television—my topic here remains television as it stands in our lives now.) But movies also, at least some movies, maybe most, used to exist in something that resembles this condition of evanescence, viewable only in certain places at certain times, discussable solely as occasions for sociable exchange, almost never seen more than once, and then more or less forgotten. For many, perhaps still for most people, this is still the fate of film. (It is accordingly also true that some people, perhaps still most, would take it as true of movies that individual works do not bear up under repetition and criticism. That this is a possible way to take film, I was just asserting, and I was implying that it is also partial. I will give a name to this way of taking it presently.) But from the beginning of the art of film, there have been those who have known that there was more to movies, more to think about, to experience, in their ordinary instances, than met the habitual eye. In recent years, this thought is becoming increasingly common (though not at all as common, I believe, as certain people living on the East and West coasts and in certain other enclaves imagine); whereas, as I have indicated, my impression is that comparatively few people maintain an aesthetic interest in the products of network television. A writer like Leslie Fiedler asserts a brazen interest in network television, or perhaps it is a sterling interest. But he insists that the source of his interest lies precisely in television's not producing art, in its providing, so to speak, a relief from art. And then again, it seems to me that he has said the same thing about movies, all movies, anyway all American movies. And if someone did appear to take the different interest, my question would persist: What is it he or she is taking this interest in?

A further caution—as it were, a technological caution—also conditions the remarks to follow. If the increasing distribution of videocassettes and disks goes so far as to make the history of film as much a part of the present experience of film as the history of the other arts is part of their present—hence, in this dimension, brings film into the condition of art—it will make less respectable the assumption of the evanescence of the individual movie, its exhaustion under one viewing, or always casual viewings; or rather, it will make this assumption itself evanescent, evidently the product of historical conditions, not inevitable. At the same time, if the distribution of videocassette recorders and cable television increases, as appears to be happening, to the size of the distribution of television itself, or to a size capable of challenging it, this will make problematic whether television will continue to exist primarily as a medium of broadcasting. I am not so much interested in predicting that such developments will actually come to establish themselves as I am in making conceptual room for understanding the aesthetic possibilities of such developments.

To say that the primary object of aesthetic interest in television is not the individual piece, but the format, is to say that the format is its primary individual of aesthetic interest. This ontological recharacterization is meant to bring out that the relation between format and instance should be of essential aesthetic concern. There are two classical concepts in talking about movies that fit the requirements of the thing I am calling a format, as it were, an artistic *kind*: the concepts of the serial and of the genre. The units of a serial are familiarly called its episodes; I will call the units of a genre its members. A thesis it seems to be worth exploring is that television, for some reason, works aesthetically according to a serial-episode principle rather than according to a genre-member principle. What are these principles?

In traditional terms, they would not be apt to invoke what I mean by different principles of composition. What is traditionally called a genre film is a movie whose membership in a group of films is no more problematic than the exemplification of a serial in one of its episodes. You can, for example, roughly *see* that a movie is a Western, or gangster film, or horror film, or prison film, or "woman's film," or a screwball comedy. Call this way of thinking about genre, genre-as-cycle. In contrast, in *Pursuits of Happiness*, the way I found I wanted to speak of genre in defining what I call the Hollywood comedy of remarriage, I will call genre-as-medium.

Because I feel rather backed into the necessity of considering the notion of a genre, I feel especially in need of the reader's forbearance over the next half dozen or so paragraphs. It seems that the notion of a genre has lately been receiving renewed attention from literary theorists, but the recent pieces of writing I have started to look at on the subject (so far, I realize, too unsystematically) all begin with a sense of dissatisfaction with other writing on the subject, either with the way the notion has so far been defined, or with the confusion of uses to which it has been put, or both. I am not interested here in joining an argument but rather in sketching the paths of two (related) ideas of a genre; it is an interest in coming to terms with what seem to me to be certain natural confusions in approaching the notion of a genre. In *Pursuits of Happiness* I was letting the discussion of certain individual works, which, so far as I know, had never been put together as a group, lead me, or push me, into sketching a theory of genre, and I went no further with it than the concrete motivations in reading individual works seemed to me to demand. With that in mind, in the present essay I am beginning, on the contrary, with certain intuitions concerning what the general aesthetic powers of video turn upon, and I am hoping to get far enough in abstracting these powers from the similar, hence different, powers of film, to get in a position to test these intuitions in concrete cases. (I may, how-ever, just mention that two of the books I have been most helped by are Northrop Frye's *A Natural Perspective*[4] and Tzvetan Todorov's *The Fantastic*.[5])

Before going on to give my understanding of the contrasting no-tions of a genre, I should perhaps anticipate two objections to my terminology. First, if there is an established, conventional use of the word "genre," and if this fits what I am calling genre-as-cycle, why not keep the simple word and use some other simple word to name the further kind of kind I am thinking of, the kind I am calling genre-as-medium—why not just call the further kind a set or a group or a pride? Second, since film itself is thought of as a medium (for exam-ple, of art), why insist on using the same word to characterize a gath-ering of works *within* that medium? As to this second objection, this double range of the concept of a medium is deployed familiarly in the visual arts, in which painting is said to be a medium (of art, in contrast, say, to sculpture or to music—hardly, one would think, the same contrast), and in which gouache is also a medium (of painting, in contrast to water color or oil or tempera). I wish to preserve, and make more explicit—or curious—this double range in order to keep open to investigation the relation between work and medium that I call the revelation, or acknowledgment, of the one in the other. In my experience, to keep this open means, above all, resisting (by understanding) the temptation to think of a medium simply as a familiar material (for instance, sound, color, words), as if this were an unprejudicial observation rather than one of a number of ways of taking the material of a medium, and recognizing instead that only the art can define its media, only painting and composing and movie making can reveal what is required, or possible (what means, what exploits of material), for something to be a painting, a piece of mu-sic, a movie. As to the first objection—my use of "genre" in naming both of what I claim are different principles or procedures of com-position—my purpose is to release something true in both uses of the word (in both, there is a process of generating in question), and

[4]New York, 1965.
[5]Translated by Richard Howard (Ithaca, N.Y., 1975).

to leave open to investigation what the relation between these processes may be. The difference may be consequential. I think, for example, that it is easier to understand movies as some familiar kind of commodity or as entertainments if you take them as participating not in a genre-as-medium but in genres-as-cycles, or if you focus on those movies that *do* participate, without remainder, in genres so conceived. Movies thought of as members of genres-as-cycles is the name of the way of taking them that I earlier characterized as evanescent. The simplest examples of such cycles used to be signaled by titles such as *The Son of X, The Curse of X, X Meets Dracula*, and so on. Our sophistication today requires that we call such sequels *X II, X III*, and so on, like Super Bowls. It is part of Hollywood's deviousness that certain sequels may be better than their originals, as perhaps *The Bride of Frankenstein* is, or Fritz Lang's *The Return of Frank James*.

Still another word about terminology, before going on to consider the thesis that television works according to a serial-episode rather than a genre-member principle. In picking up the old movie term "serial" to mark the contrast in question, I am assuming that what used to be called serials on film bears some internal relation to what are called series on television. But what I am interested in considering here is the idea of serialization generally, wishing again to leave open what the relations are between serials and series (as I wish to leave open, hence to recall, the occurrence of serialization in classical novels, in photographs, in paintings, in music, in comic strips). One might find that the closest equivalent on television to the movie serial is the soap opera, since this shares the feature of more or less endless narration across episodes, linked by crises. But in going on now to consider a little my thesis about serialization in television, I am exploring my intuition that the repetitions and recurrences of soap operas bear a significant relation with those of series, in which the narrative comes to a classical ending each time, and indeed that these repetitions and recurrences are modes of a requirement that the medium of television exacts in all its formats. A program such as "Hill Street Blues" seems to be questioning the feature of a series that demands a classical ending for each instance, hence questioning the distinction between soap opera and series. Similarly, or oppositely, the projected sequence of movies instanced by *Star Wars* and *The Empire Strikes Back* seems to be questioning the distinction between a serial and a cycle by questioning the demand of a serial (a narrative that continues over an indefinite number of episodes) *not* to come to a classical ending before the final episode. This would bring the sequence closer in structure to literary forms such as (depending on individual taste) the King Arthur legends, the Shakespeare Henry plays (perhaps in a Lamb-like retelling), or Tolkien's *Lord of the Rings* trilogy.

A genre, as I use the notion in *Pursuits of Happiness*, and which I am here calling genre-as-medium, behaves according to two basic "laws" (or "principles"), one internal, the other external. Internally, a genre is constituted by members, about which it can be said that they share what you might picture as every feature in common. In practice, this means that, where a given member diverges, as it must, from the rest, it must "compensate" for this divergence. The genre undergoes continuous definition or redefinition as new members introduce new points of compensation. Externally, a genre is distinguished from other genres, in particular from what I call "adjacent" genres, when one feature shared by its members "negates" a feature shared by the members of another. Here, a feature of a genre will develop new lines of refinement. If genres form a system (which is part of the faith that for me keeps alive an interest in the concept), then in principle it would seem possible to be able to move by negation from one genre through adjacent genres, until all the genres of film are derived. Hitchcock's corpus provides convenient examples: his *North by Northwest* shares an indefinitely long list of features with remarriage comedies, which implies, according to my work on the subject, that it is about the legitimizing of marriage. In this film, as in other adventures, by Hitchcock and by others, legitimacy is conferred by a pair's survival together of a nation-saving adventure.[6] But that film can further be understood as negating the feature of the remarriage genre according to which the woman has to undergo

[6]I spell this out in "North by Northwest," reprinted in this book.

something like death and revival. When this happens in Hitchcock, as in *Vertigo*, the Hitchcock film immediately preceding *North by Northwest*, it causes catastrophe. In *North by Northwest* it is the man who undergoes death and revival (and for a reason, I claim, having to do with the structure of the remarriage form). A dozen years earlier, in *Notorious*, Hitchcock compensates for the feature of the woman's death and revival (hence, maintaining the happiness of a remarriage ending) by emphasizing that her death and revival are not the condition of the man's loving her, but the effect of his failure to acknowledge her (as happens, seminally, according to my discussion of the genre, in *The Winter's Tale*).

The operations of compensation and negation are meant to specify the idea of a genre in *Pursuits of Happiness*, in contrast to what I take to be the structuralist idea of a genre as a form characterized by features, as an object is characterized by its properties, an idea that seems to me to underlie, for example, Todorov's work on the fantastic tale. I put it this way:

> An alternative idea . . . is that the members of a genre share the inheritance of certain conditions, procedures, and subjects and goals of composition, and that in primary art each member of such a genre represents a study of these conditions, something I think of as bearing the responsibility of the inheritance. There is, on this picture, nothing one is tempted to call *the* features of a genre which all its members have in common (p. 28).

Such operations as compensation and negation are not invoked either in genre-as-cycle or in serial-episode procedure. So I am saying that they are made by serialization as opposed to the generation in genre-as-medium. But in neither sense of genre are the members of a genre episodes of a continuing story or situation or setting. It is not the same narrative matter for Frankenstein to get a bride as for Rhoda (in a popular television series of a few years ago bearing her name) to get a husband. The former is a drama on its own; the latter serves a history, a before and after.

In speaking of a procedure of serialization, I wish to capture what seems to me right in the intuition of what are called narrative "formulas." When theorists of structural or formal matters speak of "formulas" of composition, they are thinking, I believe, of genre-as-cycle or of serial-episode construction, in which each instance is a perfect exemplification of the format, as each solution of an equation, or each step in a mathematical series, is a perfect instance of the formula that "generates" it. The instances do not compete with one another for depth of participation, nor comment upon one another for mutual revelation; and whether an instance "belongs" to the formula is as settled by the formula as is the identity of the instance. (Such remarks are really recipes—most untested—for what a formula would look like; hence, for what would count as "generation" in this context. I am taking it that no item of plot need be common to all the episodes of, say, "Rhoda" so that the formula that does the generating is sufficiently specified by designating the continuing characters and their relations with one another (characters and relations whose recurrent traits are themselves specifiable in definite ways). This is the situation in the situation comedy. A certain description of the situation would constitute the formula of the comedy. Then the substitution of the unknown new element to initiate the generation, the element of difference, can be any event that alters the situation comically—Rhoda develops a rash; her sister is being followed by the office lothario; her mother's first boyfriend has just showed up; and so on. A minimum amount of talent is all it takes to write out the results of the generation competently—which of course does not necessarily mean salably; a much higher order is required to invent the characters and relations, and cast them, in such a way as to allow new generations readily and consistently to be funny.) Whereas in genre-as-medium none of this is so. In what I call the genre of remarriage comedy, the presence or absence of even the title of the genre does not insure that an instance does or does not belong to the genre. Belonging has to be won, earned, as by an argument of the members with one another; as adjacency of genre must be proved, something irrelevant to the existence of multiple series, which, further, raise no issue of the definition and refinement a genre undergoes. ("Belonging has to be won, as by an argument. . . . " Here is an allegory of the relation of the principal pair in such comedies. In their adventures of conversation, the pair are forever taking each other by surprise, forever interesting each other anew. To dream up these surprises and interests demands an exercise of talent that differs not only, or primarily, in its degree of energy from the energies I imagine in connection with developing a series, but differs in its order of deployment: here, the initiating idea is next to nothing compared with the details of the working out, which is what one would expect where the rule of format is, so to speak, overthrown. Here, what you might call the formula, or what in *Pursuits of Happiness* I call the myth, is itself under investigation, or generation, by the instances.)

What difference does any of this make? I expect no simple or direct answer to the question of the difference between generation and serialization. Perhaps they name incompatible ways of looking at human activities generally, or texts. It might be thought, for example, that a series and its formulas specify the construction of the popular arts, whereas genre-as-medium and its arguments specify the construction of the higher arts. John G. Cawelti's *Adventure, Mystery, and Romance: Formula Stories as Art and Popular Culture*[7] perhaps suggests this. Charles Rosen's *The Classical Style*[8] states a related distinction within high art, between the great and the mediocre, or between the original and the academic. Vladimir Propp's classical analysis of the fairy tale virtually declares that you would not expect a sophisticated work of art to obey formulas in that way.[9] But this merely transfers the question: What is "that way"?

One wants to answer by saying something like, "Mechanically or automatically (or formulaically?)." But maybe this is specific to fairy tales, not to all forms you might call popular. Are black-figure and red-figure vase paintings less formulaic? And are they less than high art? American quilts of the nineteenth century are surely not less formulaic, yet the effect of certain of them is breathtaking, not unlike the directness of certain nonobjective paintings. Like those paintings (I think of certain works of Rothko, Louis, Noland, Olitski,

[7]Chicago, 1976.
[8]New York, 1971.
[9]*Morphologie du conte*, trans. Marguerite Derrida (Paris, 1970).

Stella), these examples exist essentially as items of a series. It would follow that the concept of existence in a series, of being composed according to a serial-episode principle, does not distinguish popular from high art, only if, for instance, one accepts such painting as high art, something not everyone does. And it would follow only if the concept of a series in painting (or quilts) captures the same thought as the concept of a serial in film and a series in television. So far as the thought is one of establishing a formulaic relation between instances, the relation between paintings in a series certainly seems at least as strong (as, so to speak, mechanical) as the relation of episodes to one another. In fact, the relation between the paintings seems *too* strong to yield works of art: here, the instances seem purely generated, or determined, by a format with finite features, each of which can be specified and varied to yield new items. (I think here of Stella's Z-forms, or Noland's Chevrons or Ribbons, or Louis's Unfurleds.) The relation between members is exhaustively constituted, one may say, by their mutual differences, as if to illustrate a linguist's vision, or that of the more advanced of today's textualists, according to which language, and meaning, and hence whatever replaces or precedes art, is constituted not by signs (inherently) possessing or containing meaning, but by the weave of the relation of difference among them (say their synthesis of distinctive features). But at the same time, the idea of the series can be taken to dispute the linguistic or textualist appeal to difference, since this appeal generally accompanies, even grounds, a claim that the sensuous properties of the signs themselves are arbitrary. What painting in series argues is rather the absolute *non*arbitrariness of format, because the artistic discovery is precisely that *this* synthesis of features generates instances, each of which maintains itself as a proposal of beauty. The achievement may be felt as something like an empirical discovery of the a priori—not unlike a certain aspiration of philosophy. (The implications of the fact of series for modern painting's disputing of received ideas of craft and style and medium, and its proposal of surprising consequences for thinking about the relation of painting and photography, is the subject of a pivotal chapter, "Excursus: Some Modern Painting," in *The World Viewed*.)

Another home of the idea of the formulaic is jazz, whose improvisations over most of its history are explicitly made possible by shared formulas, say of riff and progression. But the role of the formulaic in improvisation is familiar in other arenas of performance—in other regions of music (say, in improvising cadenzas), in other recitations (say, the singing of epics), and in other theater (say, commedia dell'arte). When people say they miss television as it was when it was produced live, what they may be missing is the sense of the improvisatory. And it may be that the diminished role of improvisation on television is an instance of a familiar process in certain phases of the history of performance, during which the scope of improvisation is progressively diminished in favor, let us say, of the literary; in which, for example, it is no longer open to the performer to fill in the continuo part or to work out his or her own cadenza, for these are instead written out, fixed. Yet room remains for the improvisatory in television's formats, which I will specify after saying something about what those formats are, or are of.

I note here that the idea of improvisation has internal, and opposite, associations with the idea of serialization. In movie serials and in soap operas, the sense of suspense turns on the necessity for improvisation, of manner as well as of plot—humanity as expressed by the power and the readiness to improvise, as much as by the power and the readiness to endure. The issue is how the hero and heroine can survive *this*, this unprecedented precipice; how the authors can get themselves out. The issue has its comic equivalents, emotional and intellectual. It may be this connection of serialization with improvisation that links serialization with the idea or the fact of the popular. Contrariwise, serialization in music and in painting are as if made to reduce improvisation to a minimum, as if to prove that necessities can be found that are as beautiful in their consequences as contingencies can prove to be.

The point of going into the distinction of two modes of composition was to get at television's way of revealing its medium; it represents an effort to get at something one can see as the aesthetic interest of television. That there is such an interest invited by it, related to, but different from, an interest in what we call its economy, its sociology, and its psychology, and that this interest is still insufficiently understood—which contributes to an insufficiently developed critical tradition concerning television—is the way I am taking the issue of this issue of *Dædalus*. It is the point from which any contribution I may make to it is apt to proceed. If it proves sensible to locate television's aesthetic interest in a serial-episode mode of composition, as contrasted with a genre-member mode, then an investigation of the fact of television ought to contribute to understanding why there should be two principles of aesthetic composition.

What I have said they are principles of is the revelation (I habitually call this the acknowledgment) of an artistic medium. I specify this revelation in *The World Viewed*, by way of articulating what I call there "the material basis" of film. While I propose to continue here to be guided by such an idea, I do not mean just to assume that this idea makes good sense. I claim at most merely that what I am saying here makes sense *if* the procedures of *The World Viewed* make sense. This is far from certain, but there is more evidence of their working out there than anything I can provide here.

About halfway through *The World Viewed*, I give a provisional, summary characterization of the material basis of movies, apart from which there would be nothing to call a movie, just as without color on a delimited two-dimensional support there would be nothing to call a painting; I call the basis *a succession of automatic world projections*.[10] To capture my intuition of the comparable material basis of the (aesthetic) medium of television, I begin by recurring to the one remark about television that crops up in *The World Viewed*. The moment is one at which I am at pains to distinguish the fact of movies in relation to the fact of theater, on the blatant ground that in a theater the actors appear in person and in a film they do not. I quote a response André Bazin gives to this blatant ground,[11] one in which he downplays the difference in question, denying that "the screen is incapable of putting us 'in the presence of' the actor": Bazin wishes

[10]P. 72; this is taken further and modified to characterize cartoons in "More of The World Viewed," pp. 167ff.
[11]*What Is Cinema?* trans. Hugh Gray (Berkeley, 1967), p. 97.

to say that it relays the actors' presence to us as by mirrors. My response is to note that Bazin's idea here really fits the fact of live television, in which what we are presented with is happening simultaneously with its presentation. This remains reasonably blatant, anyway unsurprising. What surprised me was to find myself going on to object: "But in live television what is present to us while it is happening is not the world, but an event standing out from the world. Its point is not to reveal, but to cover (as with a gun), to keep something on view" (p. 26).

Taking this tip, I will characterize the material basis of television as *a current of simultaneous event reception*. This is how I am conceiving of the aesthetic fact of television that I propose to begin portraying. Why the ideas of *a current* and of *simultaneity* fit here in place of the ideas of *succession* and of *the automatic*, and why that of *event* than of *world*, and why *reception* than *projection*, are not matters decidable in advance of the investigation of each of these concepts. The mode of perception that I claim is called upon by film's material basis is what I call viewing. The mode of perception I wish to think about in connection with television's material basis is that of *monitoring*. The cause for this choice, initially, seems to be that, in characterizing television's material basis, I have not included transmission as essential to it; this would be because I am not regarding broadcasting as essential to the work of television. In that case, the mysterious sets, or visual fields, in our houses, for our private lives, are to be seen not as receivers, but as monitors. My claim about the aesthetic medium of television can now be put this way: its successful formats are to be understood as revelations (acknowledgments) of the conditions of monitoring, and by means of a serial-episode procedure of composition, which is to say, by means of an aesthetic procedure in which the basis of a medium is acknowledged primarily by the format rather than primarily by its instantiations.

What are the formats, or serializations, of television? I mean to be referring to things perfectly, grossly obvious: sitcoms, game shows, sports, cultural coverage (concerts, opera, ballet, etc.), talk shows, speeches and lectures, news, weather reports, movies, specials, and so on.

A notable feature of this list is the amount of talk that runs across the forms. This is an important reason, no doubt, for the frequent description of television as providing "company." But what does this talk signify, how does it in particular signify that one is not alone, or anyway, that being alone is not unbearable? Partly, of course, this is a function of the simultaneity of the medium—or of the fact that at any time it might be live and that there is no sensuous distinction between the live and the repeat, or the replay: the others are *there*, if not shut in this room, still caught at this time. One is receiving or monitoring them, like callers; and receiving or monitoring, unlike screening and projection, does not come between their presence to the camera and their presentness to us.

I recognize that even in the present sketch of a way to approach matters, this appeal to the idea of "no sensuous distinction" between the live and the repeat, or the replay or the delayed, and the connection of this distinction with a difference in modes of presence and presentness, is going too fast over consequential issues. It doesn't even include the fact that television can work in film as well as in tape. William Rothman has suggested to me that since television can equally adopt a movie mode or a video mode, we might recognize one dimension of television's "company" in the understanding of the act of switching from one mode to another as the thing that is always live, that is, effected simultaneously with our watching. This points to the feature of the current (suggesting the contemporary as well as indicating the continuous) in my articulation of this aesthetic medium's physical basis. It is internal to television formats to be made so as to participate in this continuity, which means that they are formed to admit discontinuities both within themselves and between one and another, and between these and commercials, station breaks, news breaks, emergency signal tests, color charts, program announcements, and so on, which means formed to allow these breaks, hence these recurrences, to be legible. So that switching (and I mean here not primarily switching within a narrative but switching from, say, a narrative to one or another breaks, for a station or for a sponsor, and back again) is as indicative of life as—in ways to be specified— monitoring is.

(I think in this context of the as yet undefined aesthetic position of commercials. Foreigners to commercial television often find them merely amusing or annoying interruptions (or of course, in addition, marks of a corrupt civilization); native explainers will sometimes affect to find them more interesting than the so-called programs they interrupt. Surely, ordinary people, anyway people without either of these axes to grind, can feel either way on occasion. Nor do I doubt, in all soberness, that *some* commercials just are more interesting than *some* programs. What the effort, or claim, to favor commercials over programs suggests to me is that the aesthetic position of commercials, what you might call their possibility—what makes them aesthetically possible rather than merely intolerable—is not their inherent aesthetic interest (one would not sit still, with mild interest, for periodic minute-length transmissions of, say, a passage of Garbo's face or of a Chaplin routine: these glimpses of the masterful would be *pointless*), but the fact that they are readable, not as interruptions, but as *interludes*. Of course they can be handled all but intolerably, like late-night used car ads, or offers of recordings "not sold in any store." But even in these cases, the point of tolerability is the requirement of live switching—life, moreover, that is acknowledged by the habitual invitation at these peculiar late hours to "come on down" or to order by writing or by "calling now." Where there's life, there's hope.)

The fact of television's company is expressed not simply by the amount of talk, but by the massive repetitiveness of its formats for talk. Here I am thinking not merely of the shows explicitly *of* talk, with their repetitious sets and hosts and guests. Broadcasts of sports events are embedded in talk (as sports events are), and I can see the point even of game shows as providing occasions or covers for talk. Of course these shows are reasonably exciting, visually and aurally, with their obligatory jumping and screaming; and even, some of them, mildly educational. But is this excitement and education sufficient to account for the willingness to tune them in endlessly, for the pleasure taken endlessly in them? Nor am I satisfied to cite the reputed attractions, or fantasies, of striking it rich—anymore than, in thinking about the attractions of Hollywood thirties comedies, was I satisfied to account for their popularity by the widespread idea that they were fairy tales for the depression. I am struck by the plain fact that on each of the game shows I have watched, new sets of contestants are introduced to us. What strikes me is not that we are interested in identifying with these ordinary people, but simply that we are introduced to them. The hardest part of conversation, or the scariest part, that of improvising the conventional phrases of meeting someone and *starting* to talk, is all there is time for on these formats; and it is repeated endlessly, and without the scary anticipation of consequences in presenting the self that meetings in reality exact. The one who can get us perennially acquainted, who faces the initiation time and again, who has the power to create the familiar out of strangeness—the host of the show—is heavily rewarded for his abilities; not, indeed, by becoming a star, but by becoming a personality, even a celebrity, famous for nothing but being visible and surviving new encounters.

The appearance just now, or reappearance, of the idea of improvisation indicates the principal room I said was left for the improvisatory in television's persistent formats, its dimension of talk. I would not wish exactly to say that improvisation is localized there, since the dimension of talk is itself all but universally present; but each format for talk will have its own requirements or opportunities for improvisation. The most elaborate of these are, naturally, presented by talk shows themselves, with their monologues, and hence the interruptions and accidents that expert monologues invite, and with their more or less extended interviews. Here, the fact that nothing of consequence is said matters little compared with the fact that something is spoken, that the momentarily famous and the permanently successful are seen, like us, to have to find words for their lives. The gift of the host is to know how, and how far, to put the guests recurrently at ease and on the spot, and to make dramas of overcoming the one with the other, and both with his or her capacity at any time to top what has been said. This is not the same as turning every event into a comic routine, as Jonathan Winters and Robin Williams have the talent and imagination to do. They are too anarchic to entertain guests, or too relentlessly absorbed by their inventions, as if inhabited by them, to invite and prepare for conversation. Johnny Carson is so good at taking conversation near, but not over, the abyss of embarrassment, he has made so good an alliance, not to say conspiracy, with the camera, that he can instruct his audiences' responses with a glance in our direction (i.e., in the direction of the camera)—a power the comedian shares with the lion tamer. Again, it is rather beside the point that the so-called color commentaries for sports events are not particularly colorful, since the point of the role is rather the unpreparedness of response itself. So hungry are we for the unrehearsed, the unscripted, that the persons at news desks feel obliged to please us by exchanging pleasantries with each other (sometimes abbreviated to one of them pleasantly speaking the other's name) as transitions between stories, something that may itself, of course, be scripted—a possibility that epitomizes what it is that causes our hunger here. This provides a primitive version of the complex emotion in having an actor step outside his or her character as part of her or his performance—as, for example, in Bergman's *The Story of Anna*, or Godard's *Two or Three Things I Know about Her*, or as dramatized in the more recent *The French Lieutenant's Woman*. Since the practice of exchanging pleasantries reveals that the delivery of news is a form of acting (it may, I suppose, have been meant to conceal the fact)—hence, that for all television can bring out, the news itself is as likely as not to be fictional, if only because theatricalized—there must be something else television brings out that is as important to us as the distinction between fact and fiction, some matter of life and death. This would be its demonstration that, whether fact or fiction, our news is still something that can humanly be responded to, in particular, responded to by the human power of improvisation. But what news may be so terrible that we will accept such mediocre evidence of this power as reassuring? I will at the end give an answer to this question.

A more immediate question is this. If I am right in taking improvisation to be as apt a sign of human life as we have to go on, and a sign that survives the change from live to taped production, why is it that people who miss the live on television do not recognize where the quality of the live is preserved? It may be that they miss the life primarily of television's old dramatic productions. But it is not television's obligation to provide its audience with the experience of live theater—beyond going out into the world to bring us worthwhile actual performances (live or on tape). Why is the live not seen where it can still be found, and first of all in the improvisations of talk, of exchange? Is this region too tawdry for those who have pictures of something higher? I do not deny a certain paradoxicality in finding life in what is reputedly the dullest, deadest feature of television, namely the omnipresent "talking head." Then the question for us should be: Where did this feature get its deadly reputation?

The remaining category of the material basis of television, after current and simultaneity and reception, the category of the event, is equally to the point here, but to bring out its significance, it will help to look first at the formats that are not made primarily for talk—for example, sports and cultural coverage. These make up the bulk of the television fare ingested by many of my acquaintances (and, except for movies, by me). The characteristic feature of these programs is that they are presented as events, that is to say, as something unique, as occasions, something out of the ordinary. But if the event is something the television screen likes to monitor, so, it appears, is the opposite, the *uneventful*, the repeated, the repetitive, the utterly familiar. The familiar repetitions of the shows of talk—centrally including here situation comedies—are accordingly company because of their embodiment of the uneventful, the ordinary.

To find comfort or company in the endlessly uneventful has its purest realization, and emblem, in the literal use of television sets as monitors against the suspicious, for example, against unwanted entry. The bank of monitors at which a door guard glances from time to time—one fixed, say, on each of the empty corridors leading from the otherwise unattended points of entry to the building—emblematizes the mode of perception I am taking as the aesthetic access to television.

The multiplicity of monitors, each linked to a more or less fixed camera, encodes the denial of succession as integral to the basis of the medium. In covering a sports event, a network's cameras are, similarly, placed ahead of time. That their views are transmitted to us one at a time for home consumption is merely an accident of economy; in principle, we could all watch a replica of the bank of monitors the producer sees. In that case, we might speak of television's material basis by putting simultaneity into the plural. When there is a switch of the camera whose image is fed into our sole receiver, we might think of this not as a switch of comment from one camera or angle to another camera or angle, but as a switch of attention from one monitor to another monitor. Succession is replaced by switching, which means that the move from one image to another is motivated not, as on film, by requirements of meaning, but by requirements of opportunity and anticipation—as if the meaning is dictated by the event itself. As in monitoring the heart, or the rapid eye movements during periods of dreaming—say, monitoring signs of life—most of what appears is a graph of the normal, or the establishment of some reference or base line, a line, so to speak, of the uneventful, from which events stand out with perfectly anticipatable significance. If classical narrative can be pictured as the progress from the establishing of one stable situation, through an event of difference, to the reestablishing of a stable situation related to the original one, serial procedure can be thought of as the establishing of a stable condition punctuated by repeated crises or events that are not developments of the situation requiring a single resolution, but intrusions or emergencies—of humor, or adventure, or talent, or misery—each of which runs a natural course and thereupon rejoins the realm of the uneventful; which is perhaps to say, serial procedure is undialectical.

As I do not wish to claim that generation and serialization exhaust the field of narration, so I do not wish to claim that they are exclusive. So in saying that television organizes its formats in ways that explore the experience and the concept of the event, and hence of the experience and the concept of the uneventful, I am not saying that film lacks an analogous exploration, only that each medium will work out its stabilities in its own way. The ways will be as close as monitoring is to viewing, and to define such a closeness, and distance, is the sort of task my remarks here are meant to interest us in doing. For example, film and video may occupy themselves with nature, but if the distinction I have pointed to between viewing and monitoring is a valid one, then our experience of nature, its role in this stretch of our lives, should split itself over the different presentations. In *The World Viewed* I suggest a sense in which

> the film frame generally . . . has the opposite significance of the frame in painting. Following Bazin's suggestion that the screen works as much by what it excludes as by what it includes, that it functions less to frame than to mask (which led me to speak of a photograph as of a segment of the world as a whole), I interpreted the frame of a film as forming its content not the way borders or outlines form, but rather the way looms and molds form (p. 200).

In such a light, I was led to say, "we are told that people seeing the first moving pictures were amazed to see the motion, as if by the novelty. But what movies did at first they can do at last: spare our attention wholly for *that* thing *now*, in the frame of nature, the world moving in the branch. . . . It is not novelty that has worn off, but our interest in our experience" (ibid.). Now, sparing our attention and expending it wholly, which goes into what I mean by viewing, is not a characterization of monitoring, which is rather preparing our attention to be called upon by certain eventualities. The world is not in the monitored branch, whose movement is now either an event (if, say, you are watching for a sign of wind) or a mark of the uneventful (a sign that the change has not yet come). The intimacy of such a difference prompts me to emphasize that by monitoring and viewing, I mean to be calling attention to aspects of human perception generally, so that film and video will not be expected to capture one of these aspects to the exclusion of the other, but rather to stress one at the expense of the other—as each may be stressing different aspects of art; video of its relation to communication, film of its relation to seduction.

My use of the concept of the uneventful is produced by my understanding of the *Annales* historians' interest in getting beyond the events and the dramas of history to the permanencies, or anyway to the longer spans, of common life.[12] This is worth making explicit as a way of emphasizing that the concepts in which I have been speaking of the phenomena of television and movies are as much in need of investigation as are the phenomena themselves. Everything seems to me so doubtful, or intangible, in this area. I would like to have useful words in which to consider why the opera and the ballet I have seen on television in recent years have seemed to me so good, whereas films I recall of opera and of ballet have seemed to me boring. Is it that television can respect the theatricality or the foreign conventionality of those media without trying, as film greedily would, to reinterpret them? And is this well thought of as television's ability to respect the independence of the theatrical event? I did like Bergman's *Magic Flute*, but I also felt that the piece looked like a television production. The question is this easy to beg. And does the idea of respecting the event go into the reason puppets and muppets are at home on television in a way they are not in movies?

Here an answer suggests itself to a question my assumption of the primacy of format might at any time raise: Isn't the television "special" an exception to the rule of this primacy, since, by definition, a special occurs uniquely? The answer is not merely that uniqueness proposes a television format (like farewells, awards, roasts) that any number of stars and celebrities can occupy, and occupy again and again, so long as not regularly, that is, serially. The answer has also to specify what the format is that can occur outside a series. Take the fact that the entertainment special, designed to showcase a star or celebrity, familiarly takes the form of a variety show. The fittingness of the variety show format for television I can now attribute to the fact that a variety show just is a *sequence of events*, where events are interpreted as autonomous acts or routines constituted by incidents of excitement that are understandable as essentially repeatable, in another show and in another town. The concept of event here captures the sense of the variety and the discreteness—that is, the integrity—of the items of such shows, as it does in naming the items of track and field meets, and of bouts on a fight card.

[12]See "The Ordinary as the Uneventful" in this book, and, for example, the essays of Fernand Braudel cited there in note 1.

The broadcasts of cultural events may also seem another set of exceptions to the rule of format, other instances of unique occurrences. But what is unique here, and what is above all memorable, is the performance itself, say of Balanchine's ballet on Stravinsky's *Agon*, the performance at which the pair of dancers of the difficult canon passage got off to a false start and had to begin again. Beyond the performance, the television presentation itself may be of interest, perhaps because of its novel camera installations, which make for a greater fidelity to the details of the performance, or because it was the first to use subtitles in a particular way. But these features of the presentation form an essentially repeatable format, usable and refinable in future broadcasts of ballet performances. If, however, the television presentation becomes so integral to the performance, the performance itself having been designed to incorporate the possibilities of presentation into its own integrity, that the ideas of "repeating" the format or of refining such things as camera "installations" no longer make clear sense, then the television format would have been led to the condition of genre-as-medium. I have seen too little in the way of such works to have any useful response to them. They must in any case be part of the realm of experimental video art, which, as said, I am here leaving out of account.

I note that the variety format also fit the requirements of radio in its network days. It is, I think, commonly said that in its beginning, television "took over" many programs, or ideas for programs, from radio. Empirically or legally, no one could deny this, but ontologically, so to speak, or aesthetically, it should be wondered why radio was so ready a source for television. The better thought may be that television took its formats from many of the same places radio had taken them, for example, from vaudeville, and that the reason they could share these sources is that both are forms of broadcasting and monitoring, that is, currents of simultaneous event reception. Since one of these currents is made for the ear and the other also for the eye, it may be wondered what ratio of these senses is called upon by various events. Why, for example, is the weather given its own little dramatic slot on news programs, whereas the performance of the stock market is simply announced? Does this have to do with the weather's providing more visual interest than the market, or with its natural involvement in drama, or with its perennial role as a topic of conversation between strangers, or with its being an allegory of our gathering frame of mind, or simply with the fact of interest in predicting it (as if retaining some control over the future)? If the interest in predicting it were exhausted by its practical bearing on our plans for the days ahead, announcing it would serve as well as dramatizing it or making a little lecture about it. Prediction is of interest with respect to the stock market only, on the whole, to those who have a specialized connection with it, those, for example, who play it, for whom not just a day's outcome, but a day's events of fluctuation or stability, matter.

Of more fateful interest concerning the format of news is its invitation of the television item I have perhaps most notably omitted in my more or less informal itemizing of formats, namely, that of the event shaped expressly for the possibilities of television coverage itself, something that came upon most viewers' consciousnesses most memorably with the civil rights and antiwar demonstrations of the sixties, and subsequently with the staging of terrorist actions. In citing the theatricality of scripted news recitation, and in emphasizing television's tropism toward the event, I am indicating what the possibilities of the medium are that shaped events seek to attract; but the fact of television no more explains the occurrence of such events than it explains the effects of weather on our consciousness. For what would have to be explained, as my reference to the *Annales* historians is intended to register, is exactly our continued attraction by events, our will to understand our lives, or to take interest in them, from their dramas rather than from their stabilities, from the incident and the accident rather than from the resident, from their themes rather than from their structures—to theatricalize ourselves. But this is something that Thoreau, for one, held against the interest in reading newspapers a century and a half ago, an interest he described as amounting virtually to an addiction.

The *Annales* historians' idea of the long time span oddly applies to the altogether extraordinary spans of narrative time commanded by serialization. The ultimate span is that commanded by successful soap operas, in which the following of its yarns can go on off and on for years. I said a while ago that serial procedure is undialectical. Here I might add that the span of soap operas can allow them to escape history, or rather to require modification of the concept of history, of history as drama, history as related to the yarns of traditional novels. The lapse of fictional time in a soap world can be immeasurably shorter (or slower) than that of the span of time over which one may watch them. (Forty or so years ago my mother frequently tuned the radio to a fifteen-minute serial called "Helen Trent," as she and I were getting ready to go off, respectively, to work and to school. The idea of the serial was announced each morning by asking whether a woman can find romance after thirty-five, or maybe it was forty. I can imagine that this serial still persists. But if so, Helen Trent must still be something like thirty-five or forty years old.) However dire their events, they are of the interminable everyday, passages and abysses of the routine, which may help explain the ease with which members of their audience take their characters (so it seems) as "real." Without attempting to account for the specialized features of the stories and audiences that make soap operas possible, I call attention to the fact that the most prestigious, even sensational efforts originating on television in recent years have been serials— either the snobby sort the BBC has patented ("Upstairs/Downstairs," "The Forsythe Saga," "Tinker, Tailor," "Brideshead Revisited"), or the antisnobby American sort ("Roots," "Dallas"). Here I am merely assuming, without argument, that eleven weekly hour-length episodes of, say, "Brideshead Revisited" command an order of time incommensurate with film time. It is equivalent in its effect neither to something on film that would last eleven hours, nor to something that would last eleven weeks (whatever such things would be), nor, I think, to eleven films of an hour each. Not only does an hour signify something in television time that has no bearing on film time, but it is internal to the establishment of its formats that television obeys the rhythm, perhaps even celebrates the articulations, the recurrences, of the order of the week, as does Genesis. The way in which it celebrates this, by further dividing and repeating the day in terms of minutes and seconds, would be a function of television's establishment in industrialized societies, with their regimentation of time.

It may be thought that one of the formats I listed earlier itself proves that one should make much less of the differences between film and video than I am inclined to make, or rather proves the emptiness of the differences: I mean the perfectly common format of running movies on television. Of course, no one would claim that the experience of a movie is just the same run on television as projected on a screen, and everyone will have some informal theory or other about what the difference consists in—that the television image is smaller, that the room is not otherwise dark, that there is no proper audience, hence that the image is inherently less gripping, and so on. But how much difference do such differences make? It seems to me that subtleties here can be bypassed or postponed, because a difference, sufficient to give us to think, between the medium of film and that of video is that, in running a film on television, the television set is (interpretable as) a moviola; though unlike a moviola, a monitor may be thought of as a device for checking a film without projecting it. A way to begin characterizing the difference, accordingly, is that the experience of a film on television is as of something over whose running you have in principle a *control*; you are not *subjected* to it, as you are by film itself or television itself.

But to go further with this line of difference would require a theory of the moviola, or editing viewer; I mean a theory of the relation between the experience of this way of screening a film and that of its full or public screening. The moviola may be thought of as providing a reproduction of the original, or as effecting a reduction of it. In the latter case, we need to think, for example, that a piano reduction of a symphonic score is not merely a reduction of physical scale; perhaps it should be thought of as an extreme case of reorchestration. Equally, a piece for piano can be transcribed for orchestra, and so on. Are there analogous intermediate and reciprocal operations lending comprehensibility, or perspicuousness, to the relation between small and large screens? (Naturally, it may seem that the relation between small and large screens, being merely mechanical, should be clearer than the relation between transcriptions and their originals. My point is that as a matter of fact, of the fact of experience, this is not so.) In the former case, that of reproduction, we need a theory of the reproduction, which can cover everything from a black-and-white half-page photograph in an art book of a fresco a hundred times its size, to a duplicate cast of a statue.

It is a contrary of the long time span that applies to individual episodes, whose events are, however dramatic, transient. So the aesthetics of serial-episode construction comes to a suggestion that what is under construction is an argument between time as repetition and time as transience. Without considering that this is a way of characterizing the thinking of Nietzsche's *Zarathustra*, and following that, of Heidegger's *What Is Called Thinking?*, I surmise that something had better be said, in conclusion, about what these speculations seem to add up to.

I go back to the fear or repulsion or anxiety that I have found television to inspire in what I called educated circles, and I ask whether the considerations we have been assembling provide a realistic level of explanation for this fact of television. To indicate the depth of the level required, I mention a book recommended to me by several sources as I was casting about for touchstones in starting notes for my present remarks, *Four Arguments for the Elimination of Television* by Jerry Mander.[13] The book wishes to convince its readers that television, like "tobacco, saccharin, some food dyes, certain uses of polychlorinated biphenyls, aerosols, fluoroscopes and X rays to name a few" may cause cancer and for that reason alone ought to be banned. And there are plenty of other reasons: it is addictive, and "qualifies more as an instrument of brainwashing, sleep induction and/or hypnosis than anything that stimulates conscious learning processes"; it is a form of sense deprivation, causing disorientation and confusion; it suppresses and replaces creative human imagery; it is an instrument of transmutation, turning people into their TV images; it contributes to hyperactivity; "it accelerates our alienation

[13]New York, 1978, pp. 348, 394.

from nature and therefore accelerates the destruction of nature." Is this a disturbance merely of style? Perhaps the most astonishing stretch of what I have been able to read of this book is its section in praise of Victor Tausk's description of the "Influencing Machine." Mander is convinced that television *is* the realization of the ultimate influencing machine. But the point of Tausk's extraordinary paper is that to think there are in reality such machines is symptomatic of schizophrenia.[14] I cannot tell whether Mander knows this, and whether, if he does, he is declaring that he is schizophrenic, and if he is, whether he is claiming that television has driven him so, even as it is so driving the rest of us, and perhaps claiming that it is a state in which the truth of our condition has become particularly lucid to him. Without telling these things, I am still prepared to regard this book, the very fact that numbers of reasonable people apparently take it seriously, as symptomatic of the depth of anxiety television can inspire.

The depth of it seems to me also expressed in the various more or less casual hypotheses one hears about, for example, the role of television in determining reactions to the Vietnam War. Some say it helped end this war, others (understandably) that it made the war seem unreal. One of the most haunting images I know from television is the footage of the Vietnamese priest immolating himself in protest against the war. Bergman considers this image in *Persona*, as if considering at once the refuge there is in madness and its silence, and the refuge there is in television. The maddened, speechless heroine stares at the burning priest both as if she has been given an image of her pain, even a kind of explanation of it, and as if she is the cause of such pain in the world, as of its infection by her.

But the role of television in explanations of catastrophe was in preparation before the war in Vietnam. Consider that the conquering of television began just after World War II, which means, for the purposes of the hypothesis I wish to offer here, after the discovery of concentration camps and of the atomic bomb; of, I take it, the discovery of the literal possibility that human life will destroy itself;

[14]An English translation of Tausk's paper, "On the Origin of the 'Influencing Machine' in Schizophrenia," originally published in 1919, is included in *The Psychoanalytic Reader*, ed. Robert Fliess (New York, 1948), pp. 31–64.

that is to say, that it is *willing* to destroy itself. (This, too, had been in sufficient preparation; it was realistically described by Nietzsche. In my taking this as a lesson of the Second World War, the lesson there seems no way for us to learn realistically, I detect the lingering effect, for all its excess, of a once well-known essay of Norman Mailer's, "The White Negro.") And the conquering continued with the decline of our cities and the increasing fear of walking out at night, producing the present world of shut-ins. Not to postpone saying it any longer, my hypothesis is that the fear of television—the fear large or pervasive enough to account for the fear of television—is the fear that what it monitors is the growing uninhabitability of the world, the irreversible pollution of the earth, a fear displaced from the world onto its monitor (as we convert the fear of what we see, and wish to see, into a fear of being seen). The loss of this inhabitability would mean, in Heidegger's view, the loss of our humanity, whether or not we remain alive. Of course children may not have contracted the fear; and the child in us is capable of repressing the fear, ambivalently. My hypothesis is meant to respond to the mind's demand of itself to take up the slack of mismatch between the fact of television and the fact of our indifference to its significance—as though this slack were itself an expression of the fact that a commodity has conquered, an appliance that is a monitor, and yet that what it monitors, apart from events whose existence preceded its own (cultural coverage, sports, movies), are so often settings of the shut-in, a reference line of normality or banality so insistent as to suggest that *what* is shut out, that suspicion whose entry we would at all costs guard against, must be as monstrous as, let me say, the death of the normal, of the familiar as such.

I am not unaware that the charge of psychosis may well now be shifted in my direction. If so, it should have been leveled at me at least a decade ago, when *The World Viewed* appeared, since the concluding paragraph of that book prepares such a hypothesis:

A world complete without me which is present to me is the world of my immortality. This is an importance of film—and a danger. It takes my life as my haunting of the world, either because I left it unloved or because I left unfinished business. So there is reason for me to want the camera to deny the coherence of the world, its coherence as past: to deny that the world is complete without me. But there is equal reason to want it affirmed that the world is coherent without me. That is essential to what I want of immortality: nature's survival of me. It will mean that the present judgment upon me is not yet the last.

The development I have introduced here lies in the thought that the medium of television makes intuitive the failure of nature's survival of me.

I suppose it is a tall order for the repetitions and transiences of television, the company of its talk and its events, to overcome the anxiety of the intuition the medium embodies. But if I am right, this is the order it more or less already fulfills, proving again the power of familiarity, for good and ill, in human affairs; call it our adaptability. That this anxiety has a fitting object, in the possible disappearance of nature, does not, for me, rule out a psychological etiology for it, say in guilt, toward that same object. And—who knows?—if the monitor picked up on better talk, and probed for intelligible connections and for beauty among its events, it might alleviate our paralysis, our pride in adaptation, our addiction to a solemn destiny, sufficiently to help us allow ourselves to do something intelligent about its cause.

Design by David Bullen
Typeset in Mergenthaler Imprint
by Wilsted & Taylor
Printed by Maple-Vail
on acid-free paper